Study Guide Chapters 1-17

Accounting, 23e or Financial Accounting, 11e

Carl S. Warren
Professor Emeritus of Accounting
University of Georgia, Athens

James M. Reeve
Professor Emeritus of Accounting
University of Tennessee, Knoxville

Jonathan E. Duchac
Professor of Accounting
Wake Forest University

SOUTH-WESTERN
CENGAGE Learning™

Australia • Brazil • Japan • Korea • Mexico • Singapore • Spain • United Kingdom • United States

SOUTH-WESTERN
CENGAGE Learning

For product information and technology assistance, contact us at **Cengage Learning Academic Resource Center, 1-800-423-0563**

For permission to use material from this text or product, submit all requests online at **www.cengage.com/permissions**
Further permissions questions can be emailed to **permissionrequest@cengage.com**

ISBN-13: 978-0-324-66427-0
ISBN-10: 0-324-66427-3

South-Western, Cengage Learning
2640 Eagan Woods Drive
Suite 220
Eagan, MN 55121

Cengage Learning is a leading provider of customized learning solutions with office locations around the globe, including Singapore, the United Kingdom, Australia, Mexico, Brazil, and Japan. Locate your local office at: **international.cengage.com/region**

Cengage Learning products are represented in Canada by Nelson Education, Ltd.

For your course and learning solutions, visit **academic.cengage.com**

Purchase any of our products at your local college store or at our preferred online store **www.ichapters.com**

Printed in the United States of America
2 3 4 5 6 7 11 10 09

CONTENTS

CHAPTER

1 Introduction to Accounting and Business

QUIZ AND TEST HINTS

The following hints may be helpful to you in preparing for a quiz or a test over the material covered in Chapter 1.

1. Terminology is important in this chapter. Review the "Key Terms" section at the end of the chapter and be sure you understand each term. Do the Matching and Fill-in-the-Blank exercises included in this Study Guide. Expect multiple-choice, true/false, or matching questions to include the terms introduced throughout the chapter. For example, you should be able to distinguish between the different types of businesses and between financial and managerial accounting. Pay special attention to the terms beginning on page 2 through the end of the chapter. These terms will be used frequently throughout the remainder of the text.
2. Know the accounting equation: Assets = Liabilities + Owner's Equity. Be able to compute one amount when given the other two. For example, if assets equal $100,000 and liabilities equal $60,000, owner's equity must equal $40,000. Be able to determine the effect of change in the basic elements on one another. For example, if assets increase by $10,000 and liabilities decrease by $5,000, owner's equity must increase by $15,000.
3. Be able to record business transactions within the framework of the accounting equation. Use the illustration on pages 11–14 as a basis for review and study. Pay particular attention to items that are increased and decreased by transactions a through h. Note the introduction of new terms such as account payable, account receivable, revenue, and expense. These new terms are highlighted in color in the text.
4. Be able to describe each of the financial statements listed on page 16. You may be required to prepare a short income statement, statement of owner's equity, and balance sheet. You will probably not be required to prepare a statement of cash flows.
5. Review the summary data for NetSolutions on page 14. Trace the numbers into the statements shown in Exhibit 6 on page 18. Know the format of each statement such as the number of columns and placement of dollar signs. Some of the numbers in Exhibit 6 appear on more than one statement. Sometimes a quiz or a test question will provide partially completed statements, and you will be required to complete the statements. Recognizing amounts that appear

on more than one statement will aid you in answering this type of question. Also, reviewing the Interrelationship Among Financial Statements section on page 21 will aid you in preparing for this type of question.

6. Review the GPS graphic at the beginning of the chapter and the "At A Glance" section at the end of the chapter. Read and review each of the Key Points and related Learning Outcomes. For each Learning Outcome that has an Example Exercise, locate the Example Exercise in the chapter and be sure that you understand the solution and can work a similar item on a test. If you have any questions about an Example Exercise, read the section of the chapter immediately preceding the Example Exercise.

7. If your instructor covers the Financial Analysis and Interpretation item at the end of the chapter, you should know how to compute and interpret changes in the ratio of liabilities to owner's equity.

MATCHING

Instructions: Match each of the statements below with its proper term. Some terms may not be used.

A. account form
B. account payable
C. account receivable
D. accounting
E. accounting equation
F. assets
G. balance sheet
H. business
I. business entity concept
J. business transaction
K. corporation
L. cost concept
M. ethics
N. expenses
O. financial accounting
P. Financial Accounting Standards Board (FASB)
Q. generally accepted accounting principle (GAAP)
R. income statement
S. International Accounting Standards Board (IASB)
T. liabilities
U. limited liability company
V. managerial accounting
W. manufacturing
X. matching concept
Y. merchandising
Z. net income
AA. net loss
BB. objectivity concept
CC. owner's equity
DD. partnership
EE. prepaid expenses
FF. proprietorship
GG. revenue
HH. service
II. statement of cash flows
JJ. statement of owner's equity
KK. unit of measure concept

____ **1.** An organization in which basic resources (inputs), such as materials and labor, are assembled and processed to provide goods or services (outputs) to customers.

____ **2.** A type of business that changes basic inputs into products that are sold to individual customers.

____ **3.** A type of business that purchases products from other businesses and sells them to customers.

____ **4.** A business owned by one individual.

____ **5.** A business owned by two or more individuals.

____ **6.** A business organized under state or federal statutes as a separate legal entity.

____ **7.** A business that combines attributes of a partnership and a corporation.

____ **8.** An information system that provides reports to stakeholders about the economic activities and condition of a business.

____ **9.** Moral principles that guide the conduct of individuals.

____ **10.** A specialized field of accounting concerned primarily with the recording and reporting of economic data and activities to stakeholders outside the business.

____ **11.** A specialized field of accounting that uses estimated data to aid management in running day-to-day operations and in planning future operations.

____ **12.** The authoritative body that has the primary responsibility for developing accounting principles in the United States.

____ **13.** The authoritative body that sets accounting principles for many countries outside the United States.

____ **14.** A concept of accounting that limits the economic data in the accounting system to data related directly to the activities of the business.

____ **15.** The resources owned by a business.

____ **16.** The rights of creditors that represent debts of the business.

____ **17.** The rights of the owners.

____ **18.** Assets = Liabilities + Owner's Equity

____ **19.** An economic event or condition that directly changes an entity's financial condition or directly affects its results of operations.

____ **20.** The liability created by a purchase on account.

____ **21.** Items such as supplies that will be used in the business in the future.

____ **22.** A claim against the customer.

____ **23.** The amounts used in the process of earning revenue.

____ **24.** The amount a business earns by selling goods or services to its customers.

____ **25.** A summary of the revenue and expenses *for a specific period of time,* such as a month or a year.

____ **26.** A summary of the changes in owner's equity that have occurred *during a specific period of time,* such as a month or a year.

____ **27.** A list of the assets, liabilities, and owner's equity *as of a specific date,* usually at the close of the last day of a month or a year.

____ **28.** A summary of the cash receipts and cash payments *for a specific period of time,* such as a month or a year.

____ **29.** A concept of accounting in which expenses are matched with the revenue generated during a period by those expenses.

____ **30.** The form of balance sheet that resembles the basic format of the accounting equation, with assets on the left side and the liabilities and owner's equity sections on the right side.

FILL IN THE BLANK—PART A

Instructions: Answer the following questions or complete the statements by writing the appropriate words or amounts in the answer blanks.

1. An organization in which basic resources (inputs), such as materials and labor, are assembled and processed to provide goods or services (outputs) to customers is a(n) ________________.
2. A business organized under state or federal statutes as a separate legal entity is a(n) ____________________.
3. An information system that provides reports to stakeholders about the economic activities and condition of a business is ____________________.
4. Moral principles that guide the conduct of individuals are called ______________.
5. A specialized field of accounting that uses estimated data to aid management in running day-to-day operations and in planning future operations is called ____________________ accounting.
6. A concept of accounting that requires that economic data be recorded in dollars is the __________ ______ __________________ concept.
7. The resources owned by a business are called ________________.
8. The rights of the owners are called ______________ ______________.
9. Assets = Liabilities + Owner's Equity is the ____________________ ____________________.
10. Carson offered for sale at $75,000 land that had been purchased for $45,000. If Zimmer paid Carson $70,000 for the land, the amount that Zimmer would record for the purchase of the land in the accounting records is ________________.
11. The liability created by a purchase on account is referred to as a(n) ________________ ________________.
12. If liabilities are $85,000 and owner's equity is $45,000, the amount of the assets is ________________.
13. If assets are $375,000 and owner's equity is $295,000, the amount of the liabilities is ________________.
14. The amount a business earns by selling goods or services to its customers is called ________________.
15. If operations for an accounting period resulted in cash sales of $60,000, sales on account of $150,000, and expenses paid in cash of $195,000, the net income or (net loss) for the period is ______________________.
16. A summary of the changes in the owner's equity that have occurred *during a specific period of time*, such as a month or a year, is the ________________ _____ ______________ ______________.

17. The owner's equity at the beginning of the period was $19,000; at the end of the period, assets were $98,000 and liabilities were $41,000. The owner made no additional investments or withdrawals during the period. The net income or (net loss) for the period is ____________________.

18. The form of balance sheet that resembles the basic format of the accounting equation, with assets on the left side and the liabilities and owner's equity sections on the right side, is called the ______________ form.

19. If total assets increased by $85,000 and liabilities decreased by $9,000 during the period, the amount and direction (increase or decrease) of the period's change in owner's equity was ____________________.

20. Cash reported on the end-of-the-year balance sheet also is reported on the ____________________.

FILL IN THE BLANK—PART B

Instructions: Answer the following questions or complete the statements by writing the appropriate words or amounts in the answer blanks.

1. A type of business that changes basic inputs into products that are sold to individual customers is a(n) ____________________ business.
2. A type of business that purchases products from other businesses and sells them to customers is a(n) ____________________ business.
3. A business owned by one individual is called a(n) ________________.
4. A specialized field of accounting primarily concerned with the recording and reporting of economic data and activities to users outside the business is called ________________ accounting.
5. The authoritative body that has the primary responsibility for developing accounting principles in the United States is the ________________ ________________ ________________ ________________.
6. A concept of accounting that limits the economic data in the accounting system to data related directly to the activities of the business is the ________________ ______________ concept.
7. The rights of creditors that represent debts of the business are called ______________.
8. An economic event or condition that directly changes an entity's financial condition or directly affects its results of operations is called a(n) ______________ ________________.
9. Items such as supplies that will be used in the business in the future are called ______________ ______________.

10. A claim against the customer is called a(n) ______________ ______________.

11. If owner's equity is $46,000 and liabilities are $34,000, the amount of assets is ______________.

12. If assets are $98,000 and liabilities are $32,500, the amount of owner's equity is ______________.

13. The amounts used in the process of earning revenue are ______________.

14. A summary of the revenue and expenses *for a specific period of time*, such as a month or a year, is called a(n) ______________ ______________.

15. If operations for an accounting period resulted in cash sales of $90,000, sales on account of $40,000, and expenses paid in cash of $135,000, the net income or (net loss) for the period is ______________.

16. A list of the assets, liabilities, and owner's equity *as of a specific date*, usually at the close of the last day of a month or a year, is called a(n) ______________ ______________.

17. If total assets increased by $21,500 and owner's equity increased by $8,000 during a period, the amount and direction (increase or decrease) of the period's change in total liabilities was ______________.

18. A summary of the cash receipts and cash payments *for a specific period of time*, such as a month or a year, is called a(n) ______________ ______ ______________ ______________.

19. The owner's equity at the beginning of the period was $46,000; at the end of the period, assets were $99,000 and liabilities were $22,000. If the owner made an additional investment of $10,000 and withdrew $8,000 during the period, the net income or (net loss) for the period is ______________.

20. The owner's capital at the end of the year reported on the statement of owner's equity is also reported on the ______________.

MULTIPLE CHOICE

Instructions: Circle the best answer for each of the following questions.

1. Accountants employed by a particular business firm or not-for-profit organization, perhaps as chief accountant, controller, or financial vice-president, are said to be engaged in:

a. general accounting

b. public accounting

c. independent accounting

d. private accounting

2. A type of business that changes basic inputs into products that are sold to individual customers.

a. service business

b. manufacturing business

c. merchandising business

d. proprietorship business

3. The accounting concept that requires economic data be recorded in dollars.

a. cost concept

b. objectivity concept

c. business entity concept

d. unit of measure concept

4. The amounts for recording properties and services purchased by a business are determined using the:

a. business entity concept

b. cost concept

c. matching principle

d. proprietorship principle

5. Another way of writing the accounting equation is:

a. Assets + Liabilities = Owner's Equity

b. Owner's Equity + Assets = Liabilities

c. Assets = Owner's Equity – Liabilities

d. Assets – Liabilities = Owner's Equity

6. If total liabilities increased by $20,000 during a period of time and owner's equity increased by $5,000 during the same period, the amount and direction (increase or decrease) of the period's change in total assets is:

a. $20,000 increase

b. $20,000 decrease

c. $25,000 decrease

d. $25,000 increase

7. A business paid $6,000 to a creditor in payment of an amount owed. The effect of the transaction on the accounting equation was:
   a. an increase in an asset and a decrease in another asset
   b. a decrease in an asset and an increase in a liability
   c. a decrease in an asset and a decrease in a liability
   d. an increase in an asset and an increase in owner's equity

8. The total assets and the total liabilities of a particular business enterprise at the beginning and at the end of the year are stated below. During the year, the owner had withdrawn $30,000 for personal use and had made an additional investment in the enterprise of $25,000.

	Assets	Liabilities
Beginning of year....................	$290,000	$190,000
End of year.............................	355,000	220,000

   The amount of net income for the year was:
   a. $5,000
   b. $25,000
   c. $30,000
   d. $40,000

9. If revenue was $70,000, expenses were $59,000, and the owner's withdrawals were $25,000, the amount of net income or net loss was:
   a. net income of $11,000
   b. net income of $36,000
   c. net loss of $59,000
   d. net income of $70,000

10. Which of the following is not one of the major sections of the statement of cash flows?
    a. cash flows from marketing activities
    b. cash flows from investing activities
    c. cash flows from financing activities
    d. cash flows from operating activities

TRUE/FALSE

Instructions: Indicate whether each of the following statements is true or false by placing a check mark in the appropriate column.

	Statement	True	False
1.	Accounting is often characterized as the "language of business."	____	____
2.	Accountants who render accounting services on a fee basis and staff accountants employed by them are said to be engaged in private accounting.	____	____
3.	The accounting equation can be expressed as Assets – Liabilities = Owner's Equity.	____	____
4.	The concept that expenses incurred in generating revenue should be matched against the revenue in determining net income or net loss is called the cost concept.	____	____
5.	The financing activities section of the statement of cash flows includes cash transactions that enter into the determination of net income.	____	____
6.	The debts of a business are called its accounts receivable.	____	____
7.	A partnership is owned by not less than four individuals.	____	____
8.	A business transaction is the occurrence of an event or of a condition that must be recorded.	____	____
9.	A summary of the changes in the owner's equity of a business entity that have occurred during a specific period of time, such as a month or a year, is called a statement of cash flows.	____	____
10.	A claim against a customer for sales made on credit is an account payable.	____	____

EXERCISE 1-1

Instructions: Some typical transactions of Clem's Laundry Service are presented below. For each transaction, indicate the increase (+), the decrease (–), or no change (0) in the assets (A), liabilities (L), and owner's equity (OE) by placing the appropriate sign(s) in the appropriate column(s). More than one sign may have to be placed in the A, L, or OE column for a given transaction.

	A	L	OE
1. Received cash from owner as an additional investment	____	____	____
2. Purchased supplies on account	____	____	____
3. Charged customers for services sold on account ...	____	____	____
4. Received cash from cash customers	____	____	____
5. Paid cash for rent on building	____	____	____
6. Collected an account receivable in full	____	____	____
7. Paid cash for supplies	____	____	____
8. Returned supplies purchased on account and not yet paid for	____	____	____
9. Paid cash to creditors on account	____	____	____
10. Paid cash to owner for personal use	____	____	____

PROBLEM 1-1

Instructions: The assets, liabilities, capital, drawing, revenue, and expenses of Ed Casey, who operates a small repair shop, are expressed in equation form below. Following the equation are ten transactions completed by Casey. On each of the numbered lines, show by addition or subtraction the effect of each of the transactions on the equation. On the lines labeled "Bal.," show the new equation resulting from the transaction.

	Trans.	Assets			= Liabilities	+ Owner's Equity					
		Cash	+ Supplies	+ Land	= Accts. Pay.	+ Ed Casey, Capital	– Ed Casey, Drawing	+ Fees Earned	– Rent Exp.	– Supplies Exp.	– Misc. Exp.
1. Casey started a repair shop and deposited $40,000 cash in the bank for use by the business.	**(1)**										
2. Casey purchased $2,000 of supplies on account.	**(2)**										
	Bal.										
3. Casey purchased land for a future building site for $14,000 cash.	**(3)**										
	Bal.										
4. Casey paid creditors $1,800 on account.	**(4)**										
	Bal.										
5. Casey withdrew $2,000 for personal use.	**(5)**										
	Bal.										
6. Casey paid $2,800 for building and equipment rent for the month.	**(6)**										
	Bal.										
7. During the month, $900 of miscellaneous expenses were incurred on account by the business.	**(7)**										
	Bal.										
8. During the month, Casey deposited another $10,000 of personal funds in the business bank account.	**(8)**										
	Bal.										
9. Casey received $6,000 for cash service calls.	**(9)**										
	Bal.										
10. Casey used $600 worth of supplies.	**(10)**										
	Bal.										

PROBLEM 1-2

The amounts of the assets and liabilities of Tom's Painting Service at December 31 of the current year, and the revenues and expenses for the year are as follows:

Cash	$10,050
Accounts receivable	8,950
Supplies	4,000
Accounts payable	4,450
Sales	27,450
Supplies expense	5,450
Advertising expense	4,825
Truck rental expense	1,525
Utilities expense	700
Miscellaneous expense	1,400

The capital of Tom Wallace, owner, was $4,000 at the beginning of the current year. During the year, Wallace withdrew $1,000 and made an additional investment of $2,000.

Instructions: Using the forms provided, prepare the following:

(1) An income statement for the year ended December 31, 20--.

(2) A statement of owner's equity for the year ended December 31, 20--.

(3) A balance sheet as of December 31, 20--.

(1)

Tom's Painting Service

Income Statement

For Year Ended December 31, 20--

(2)

Tom's Painting Service

Statement of Owner's Equity

For Year Ended December 31, 20--

(3)

Tom's Painting Service

Balance Sheet

December 31, 20--

CHAPTER

2 Analyzing Transactions

Quiz and Test Hints

The following hints may be helpful to you in preparing for a quiz or a test over the material covered in Chapter 2.

1. Terminology is important in this chapter. Review the "Key Terms" section at the end of the chapter and be sure you understand each term. Do the Matching and Fill-in-the-Blank exercises included in this Study Guide. Pay special attention to major account classifications discussed on page 53 of the text.
2. Memorize the "Rules of Debit and Credit" and the "Normal Balances of Accounts" that are summarized in Exhibit 3 on page 55. All instructors will ask questions to test your knowledge of these items.
3. Be able to prepare general journal entries for the types of transactions presented in this chapter. Review the illustration beginning on page 56, and be sure you understand each entry. Be especially careful not to confuse debits and credits. Remember that a credit is indented slightly to the right when preparing a general journal entry. A good review is to rework the Illustrative Problem.
4. You should be familiar with the process of posting accounts for working assigned problems. However, you will probably not be required to post accounts on an examination.
5. You may be required to prepare an unadjusted trial balance from a list of accounts with normal balances.
6. You might expect one or two questions on how to correct errors. These types of questions may require you to prepare a correcting journal entry. Review the section of the chapter and illustration containing this information.
7. Review the GPS graphic at the beginning of the chapter and the "At A Glance" section at the end of the chapter. Read and review each of the Key Points and related Learning Outcomes. For each Learning Outcome that has an Example Exercise, locate the Example Exercise in the chapter and be sure that you understand the solution and can work a similar item on a test. If you have any questions about an Example Exercise, read the section of the chapter immediately preceding the Example Exercise.

8. If your instructor covers the Financial Analysis and Interpretation item at the end of the chapter, you should know how to compute and interpret horizontal analysis.

Matching

Instructions: Match each of the statements below with its proper term. Some terms may not be used.

A. account
B. assets
C. balance of the account
D. chart of accounts
E. credit balance
F. credits
G. debit balance
H. debits
I. double-entry accounting
J. drawing
K. expenses
L. journal
M. journal entry
N. journalizing
O. ledger
P. liabilities
Q. owner's equity
R. posting
S. revenues
T. slide
U. T account
V. transposition
W. trial balance
X. two-column journal
Y. unearned revenue

_____ **1.** An accounting form that is used to record the increases and decreases in each financial statement item.

_____ **2.** A group of accounts for a business.

_____ **3.** A list of the accounts in the ledger.

_____ **4.** Resources that are owned by the business.

_____ **5.** Debts owed to outsiders (creditors).

_____ **6.** The owner's right to the assets of the business.

_____ **7.** Increases in owner's equity as a result of selling services or products to customers.

_____ **8.** Assets used up or services consumed in the process of generating revenues.

_____ **9.** The simplest form of an account.

_____ **10.** Amounts entered on the left side of an account.

_____ **11.** Amounts entered on the right side of an account.

_____ **12.** The amount of the difference between the debits and the credits that have been entered into an account.

_____ **13.** The initial record in which the effects of a transaction are recorded.

_____ **14.** The process of recording a transaction in the journal.

_____ **15.** The form of recording a transaction in a journal.

_____ **16.** A system of accounting for recording transactions, based on recording increases and decreases in accounts so that debits equal credits.

____ **17.** The account used to record amounts withdrawn by an owner of a proprietorship.

____ **18.** The process of transferring the debits and credits from the journal entries to the accounts.

____ **19.** An all-purpose journal.

____ **20.** The liability created by receiving revenue in advance.

____ **21.** A summary listing of the titles and balances of accounts in the ledger.

____ **22.** The normal balance of the cash account.

____ **23.** The normal balance of the fees earned account.

____ **24.** An error in which the order of the digits is changed, such as writing $542 as $452 or $524.

____ **25.** An error in which the entire number is moved one or more spaces to the right or the left, such as writing $542.00 as $54.20 or $5,420.00.

FILL IN THE BLANK—PART A

Instructions: Answer the following questions or complete the statements by writing the appropriate words or amounts in the answer blanks.

1. An accounting form that is used to record the increases and decreases in each financial statement item is the ________________.
2. A list of the accounts in the ledger is called the ____________ _______ ________________.
3. Increases in owner's equity as a result of selling services or products to customers are called ____________________.
4. The simplest form of an account is the __________________.
5. Amounts entered on the left side of an account are ____________.
6. An increase in Accounts Receivable is recorded by a ____________ entry in the account.
7. An increase in Ken Lindgren, Capital is recorded by a ____________ entry in the account.
8. A decrease in Accounts Payable is recorded by a ____________ entry in the account.
9. A decrease in Salaries Expense is recorded by a ____________ entry in the account.
10. Unearned Revenue is a(n) ________________ account.
11. A decrease in Cash is recorded by a ____________ entry in the account.

12. The normal balance of the supplies account is a ____________ balance.

13. The normal balance of Lisa Jones, Capital is a ____________ balance.

14. The initial record in which the effects of a transaction are recorded is the __________________.

15. The process of recording a transaction in the journal is called ______________________.

16. The ______________-____________ ____________________ is a system of accounting for recording transactions, based on recording increases and decreases in accounts so that debits equal credits.

17. The process of transferring the debits and credits from the journal entries to the accounts is called ________________.

18. An all-purpose journal is the ________-______________ ______________.

19. Fees earned on account would be recorded by debiting the __________ account.

20. An error in which the order of the digits is changed mistakenly, such as writing $542 as $452 or $524, is called a(n) _______________________.

Fill in the Blank—Part B

Instructions: Answer the following questions or complete the statements by writing the appropriate words or amounts in the answer blanks.

1. A group of accounts for a business is called a(n) _________________.

2. Resources that are owned by the business are called _________________.

3. Debts owed to outsiders (creditors) are _____________________ of the business.

4. The owner's right to the assets of the business is the _______________ ________________.

5. Assets used up or services consumed in the process of generating revenues are reported as _____________________.

6. Amounts entered on the right side of an account are ______________.

7. The amount of the difference between the debits and the credits that have been entered into an account is the ___________________ of the account.

8. The recording of a transaction in a journal is called __________________.

9. The _________________ account is used to record amounts withdrawn by an owner of a proprietorship.

10. _________________ _________________ is the liability created by receiving the revenue in advance.

11. A decrease in Notes Payable is recorded by a ____________ entry in the account.

12. An increase in J. B. Moore, Drawing, is recorded by a ______________ entry in the account.

13. A decrease in Accounts Receivable is recorded by a ______________ entry in the account.

14. Wages Payable is a(n) _________________ account.

15. Patent Rights is a(n) _________________ account.

16. The normal balance of the prepaid insurance account is a ____________ balance.

17. The normal balance of the fees earned account is a ____________ balance.

18. A summary listing the titles and balances of accounts in the general ledger is called a(n) ____________ _________________.

19. An error in which the entire number is mistakenly moved one or more spaces to the right or the left, such as writing $542.00 as $54.20 or $5,420.00, is called a(n) ______________.

20. A ______________ entry is made for errors that have been journalized and posted.

MULTIPLE CHOICE

Instructions: Circle the best answer for each of the following questions.

1. The receipt of cash from customers in payment of their accounts would be recorded by a:
   - **a.** debit to Cash and a credit to Accounts Payable
   - **b.** debit to Cash and a credit to Accounts Receivable
   - **c.** debit to Cash and a credit to Fees Earned
   - **d.** debit to Cash and a credit to Fees Expense
2. The first step in recording a transaction in a two-column journal is to:
   - **a.** list the account to be credited
   - **b.** list the amount to be credited
   - **c.** list the amount to be debited
   - **d.** list the account to be debited
3. The drawing account of a sole proprietorship is debited when:
   - **a.** the owner invests cash
   - **b.** the owner withdraws cash
   - **c.** a liability is paid
   - **d.** an expense is paid

4. The equality of debits and credits in the ledger should be verified at the end of each accounting period by preparing a(n):
   a. accounting statement
   b. balance report
   c. trial balance
   d. account verification report
5. Of the following errors, the one that will cause an inequality in the trial balance totals is:
   a. incorrectly computing an account balance
   b. failure to record a transaction
   c. recording the same transaction more than once
   d. posting a transaction to the wrong account
6. Credits to cash result in:
   a. an increase in owner's equity
   b. a decrease in assets
   c. an increase in liabilities
   d. an increase in revenue
7. Debits to expense accounts signify:
   a. increases in owner's capital
   b. decreases in owner's capital
   c. increases in assets
   d. decreases in liabilities
8. When rent is prepaid for several months in advance, the debit is to:
   a. an expense account
   b. a capital account
   c. a liability account
   d. an asset account
9. When an asset is purchased on account, the credit is to:
   a. a capital account
   b. a revenue account
   c. a liability account
   d. an expense account
10. When a payment is made to a supplier for goods previously purchased on account, the debit is to:
    a. an asset account
    b. a liability account
    c. a capital account
    d. an expense account

TRUE/FALSE

Instructions: Indicate whether each of the following statements is true or false by placing a check mark in the appropriate column.

	True	False
1. Amounts entered on the left side of an account, regardless of the account title, are called credits or charges to the account.	____	____
2. The difference between the total debits and the total credits posted to an account yields a figure called the balance of the account.	____	____
3. A credit balance in the supplies account could result only from an error.	____	____
4. The income statement accounts are listed first in the chart of accounts followed by the balance sheet accounts.	____	____
5. The residual claim against the assets of a business after the total liabilities are deducted is called owner's equity.	____	____
6. Every business transaction affects a minimum of one account.	____	____
7. The process of recording a transaction in a journal is called posting.	____	____
8. A group of accounts for a business entity is called a journal.	____	____
9. A listing of the accounts in a ledger is called a chart of accounts.	____	____
10. A recording error caused by the erroneous rearrangement of digits, such as writing \$627 as \$672, is called a slide.	____	____

EXERCISE 2-1

Eight transactions are recorded in the following T accounts:

Cash			
(1)	20,000	(5)	2,500
(7)	2,000	(8)	3,500

Machinery			
(2)	6,300		

Ann Moran, Drawing			
(8)	3,500		

Accounts Receivable			
(4)	5,000	(7)	2,000

Accounts Payable			
(5)	2,500	(2)	6,300
		(3)	820
		(6)	1,600

Service Revenue			
		(4)	5,000

Supplies			
(3)	820		

Ann Moran, Capital			
		(1)	20,000

Operating Expenses			
(6)	1,600		

Instructions: For each debit and each credit, indicate in the following form the type of account affected (asset, liability, owner's equity, revenue, or expense) and whether the account was increased (+) or decreased (–).

Transaction	Account Debited		Account Credited	
	Type	Effect	Type	Effect
(1)				
(2)				
(3)				
(4)				
(5)				
(6)				
(7)				
(8)				

Problem 2-1

During June of the current year, Joan Star started Star Service Company.

Instructions:

(1) Record the following transactions in the two-column journal given below.

June 1. Invested $5,000 in cash, equipment valued at $14,500, and a van worth $21,000.

16. Purchased additional equipment on account, $5,500.

28. Purchased supplies on account, $500.

30. Paid $2,100 to creditors on account.

(2) Post to the appropriate ledger accounts on the following pages.

(3) Prepare a trial balance of the ledger accounts of Star Service Company as of June 30 of the current year, using the form that follows the ledger accounts.

(1)

JOURNAL

PAGE

	DATE		DESCRIPTION	POST. REF.	DEBIT	CREDIT	
1							1
2							2
3							3
4							4
5							5
6							6
7							7
8							8
9							9
10							10
11							11
12							12
13							13
14							14
15							15
16							16
17							17
18							18
19							19
20							20
21							21
22							22
23							23

(2) **LEDGER ACCOUNTS**

ACCOUNT *Cash* ACCOUNT NO. *11*

DATE		ITEM	POST. REF.	DEBIT	CREDIT	BALANCE	
						DEBIT	CREDIT

ACCOUNT *Supplies* ACCOUNT NO. *12*

DATE		ITEM	POST. REF.	DEBIT	CREDIT	BALANCE	
						DEBIT	CREDIT

ACCOUNT *Equipment* ACCOUNT NO. *18*

DATE		ITEM	POST. REF.	DEBIT	CREDIT	BALANCE	
						DEBIT	CREDIT

ACCOUNT *Vehicles* ACCOUNT NO. *19*

DATE		ITEM	POST. REF.	DEBIT	CREDIT	BALANCE	
						DEBIT	CREDIT

ACCOUNT *Accounts Payable* ACCOUNT NO. *21*

DATE		ITEM	POST. REF.	DEBIT	CREDIT	BALANCE	
						DEBIT	CREDIT

ACCOUNT *Joan Star, Capital* ACCOUNT NO. *31*

DATE		ITEM	POST. REF.	DEBIT	CREDIT	BALANCE DEBIT	BALANCE CREDIT

(3)

PROBLEM 2-2

On January 2, 20--, Judy Turner, an attorney, opened a law office. The following transactions were completed during the month.

a. Invested $20,000 cash and $13,200 worth of office equipment in the business.
b. Paid a month's rent of $2,500.
c. Paid $1,000 for office supplies.
d. Collected legal fees of $19,600.
e. Paid secretary a salary of $1,100.
f. Purchased $200 worth of office supplies on account.
g. Bought an auto for business use. It cost $13,000. Turner paid $2,600 down and charged the balance.
h. Withdrew $5,000 from the firm for personal use.
i. Paid $800 for auto repairs and maintenance.
j. Received a $240 telephone bill.
k. Paid the $240 telephone bill.
l. Paid premiums of $1,700 on property insurance.
m. Paid $2,000 on accounts payable.
n. Paid $5,000 cash for books for the law library.
o. Paid $500 cash for janitor service.

Instructions:

(1) Record the transactions in the T accounts that follow.
(2) Prepare a trial balance, using the form on the following page.

Cash

Office Supplies

Office Equipment

Prepaid Insurance

Auto

Library

Accounts Payable

Judy Turner, Capital

Rent Expense

Auto Repairs & Maintenance Expense

Judy Turner, Drawing

Salary Expense

Janitor Expense

Legal Fees

Telephone Expense

(2)

PROBLEM 2-3

The following errors were made in journalizing and posting transactions:

a. A $1,000 premium paid for insurance was debited to Prepaid Rent and credited to Cash.

b. A $200 purchase of supplies on account was recorded as a debit to Supplies and a credit to Accounts Receivable.

c. A withdrawal of $1,500 by the owner was debited to Cash and credited to the drawing account.

Instructions: Prepare entries in the two-column journal provided below to correct these errors.

JOURNAL PAGE

	DATE		DESCRIPTION	POST. REF.	DEBIT	CREDIT	
1							1
2							2
3							3
4							4
5							5
6							6
7							7
8							8
9							9
10							10
11							11
12							12
13							13
14							14
15							15
16							16
17							17
18							18
19							19
20							20
21							21
22							22
23							23
24							24
25							25

CHAPTER

3 The Adjusting Process

QUIZ AND TEST HINTS

The following hints may be helpful to you in preparing for a quiz or a test over the material covered in Chapter 3.

1. Terminology is important in this chapter. Review the "Key Terms" section at the end of the chapter and be sure you understand each term. Do the Matching and Fill-in-the-Blank exercises included in this Study Guide.
2. The major focus of this chapter is the adjusting process. You should be able to prepare adjusting entries for each of the four types of adjustments: prepaid expenses, unearned revenues, accrued expenses, and accrued revenues. You should also be able to prepare the adjusting entry for depreciation. Review the illustrations in the chapter, especially Exhibit 6, and the adjusting entries required in the Illustrative Problem.
3. Some instructors may give you an unadjusted trial balance and adjusted trial balance and require you to figure out what the adjusting entries must have been. This would be similar to Exercises 3-26 and 3-27 and Problems 3-4A and 3-4B.
4. Review the GPS graphic at the beginning of the chapter and the "At A Glance" section at the end of the chapter. Read and review each of the Key Points and related Learning Outcomes. For each Learning Outcome that has an Example Exercise, locate the Example Exercise in the chapter and be sure that you understand the solution and can work a similar item on a test. If you have any questions about an Example Exercise, read the section of the chapter immediately preceding the Example Exercise.
5. If your instructor covers the Financial Analysis and Interpretation item at the end of the chapter, you should know how to compute and interpret vertical analysis.

Matching

Instructions: Match each of the statements below with its proper term. Some terms may not be used.

A.	accounting period concept	**L.**	contra account
B.	accrual basis	**M.**	depreciation
C.	accrued expenses	**N.**	depreciation expense
D.	accrued revenues	**O.**	final trial balance
E.	accumulated depreciation	**P.**	fixed assets
F.	adjusted trial balance	**Q.**	matching concept
G.	adjusting entries	**R.**	objectivity concept
H.	adjusting process	**S.**	post-closing trial balance
I.	book value of the asset	**T.**	prepaid expenses
J.	cash basis	**U.**	revenue recognition concept
K.	closing entries	**V.**	unearned revenues

____ **1.** The accounting concept that assumes that the economic life of the business can be divided into time periods.

____ **2.** Under this basis of accounting, revenues and expenses are reported in the income statement in the period in which cash is received or paid.

____ **3.** Under this basis of accounting, revenues are reported in the income statement in the period in which they are earned.

____ **4.** The accounting concept that supports reporting revenues when the services are provided to customers.

____ **5.** The accounting concept that supports reporting revenues and the related expenses in the same period.

____ **6.** An analysis and updating of the accounts when financial statements are prepared.

____ **7.** The journal entries that bring the accounts up to date at the end of the accounting period.

____ **8.** Items that have been initially recorded as assets but are expected to become expenses over time or through the normal operations of the business.

____ **9.** Items that have been initially recorded as liabilities but are expected to become revenues over time or through the normal operations of the business.

____ **10.** Expenses that have been incurred *but not recorded* in the accounts.

____ **11.** Revenues that have been earned *but not recorded* in the accounts.

____ **12.** Physical resources that are owned and used by a business and are permanent or have a long life.

____ **13.** The decrease in the ability of a fixed asset to provide useful services.

____ **14.** The portion of the cost of a fixed asset that Is recorded as an expense each year of its useful life.

____ **15.** The asset account credited when recording the depreciation of a fixed asset.

____ **16.** The difference between the cost of a fixed asset and its accumulated depreciation.

____ **17.** The trial balance prepared after all the adjusting entries have been posted.

____ **18.** An account offset against another account.

Fill in the Blank—Part A

Instructions: Answer the following questions or complete the statements by writing the appropriate words or amounts in the answer blanks.

1. The ____________________ ______________ concept assumes that the economic life of the business can be divided into time periods.
2. Under the ______________ basis of accounting, revenues and expenses are reported in the income statement in the period in which cash is received or paid.
3. The _________________ ____________________ concept supports reporting revenues when the services are provided to customers.
4. _________________ journal entries bring the accounts up to date at the end of the accounting period.
5. Items that have been initially recorded as assets but are expected to become expenses over time or through the normal operations of the business are called _________________ _________________.
6. Expenses that have been incurred *but have not been recorded* in the accounts are called _________________ _________________.
7. The ____________________ _________________ account is debited for the amount of prepaid advertising expense expired during the period.
8. The ___________________ ___________________—_________________ account is credited for the amount of depreciation of equipment during the period.
9. The ____________________ ___________ account is debited for the amount of unearned fees that have been earned during the period.
10. The _____________ ____________________ account is credited for wages accrued at the end of the period.
11. If the adjusting entry to record depreciation expense on equipment is omitted, the net income for the period will be ____________________.

12. If the adjusting entry to record accrued fees earned at the end of the period is omitted, the owner's equity will be ____________________ on the balance sheet.

13. If the adjusting entry to record accrued wages expense at the end of the period is omitted, the liabilities will be ____________________ on the balance sheet.

14. If the balance of the supplies account on January 1 is $2,500, supplies purchased during the year were $10,000, and the supplies on hand at December 31 were $1,800, the amount for the appropriate adjusting entry at December 31 is ____________________.

15. The prepaid insurance account has a debit balance of $1,200 at the end of the year. If unexpired insurance at the end of the year is $800, the amount of prepaid insurance that should be reported on the end-of-year balance sheet is ____________________.

16. Physical resources that are owned and used by a business and are permanent or have a long life are called ______________ ______________.

17. The portion of the cost of a fixed asset that is recorded as an expense each year of its useful life is called ____________________.

18. The difference between the cost of a fixed asset and its accumulated depreciation is called the ______________ ______________ of the asset.

19. The net income reported on the income statement is $90,000. However, adjusting entries have not been made at the end of the period for insurance expense of $550 and accrued salaries of $750. The correct net income should have been ____________________.

20. The ____________________ trial balance is prepared after all the adjusting entries have been posted.

FILL IN THE BLANK—PART B

Instructions: Answer the following questions or complete the statements by writing the appropriate words or amounts in the answer blanks.

1. Under the ____________________ basis of accounting, revenues are reported in the income statement in the period in which they are earned.

2. The ____________________ concept supports the reporting of revenues and the related expenses in the same period.

3. An analysis and updating of the accounts when financial statements are prepared is called the ____________________ process.

4. Items that have been initially recorded as liabilities but are expected to become revenues over time or through the normal operations of the business are called ______________ ______________.

5. Revenues that have been earned *but have not been recorded* in the accounts are called ________________ ________________.

6. The decrease in the ability of a fixed asset to provide useful services is called ________________________.

7. The ________________________ ________________________ account is credited when recording depreciation of a fixed asset.

8. If the adjusting entry to record accrued interest revenue is omitted, the total assets will be ______________________ on the balance sheet.

9. If the adjusting entry to record the amount of prepaid insurance that has expired during the period is omitted, the owner's equity will be ______________________ on the balance sheet.

10. The ____________________ ____________________ account is debited for the amount of accrued interest expense at the end of the period.

11. The ____________________ ________________ account is credited for the amount of prepaid rent that has expired during the period.

12. The ________________________ __________________ account is debited for the amount of depreciation on equipment during the period.

13. The ___________ __________________ account is credited for the amount of accrued fees at the end of the period.

14. If the debit amount of an adjusting entry adjusts an income statement account, the credit amount of the adjusting entry must adjust a(n) ___________________ _______________ account.

15. If the debit amount of an adjusting entry adjusts a liability account, the credit amount of the adjusting entry must adjust a(n) __________________ account.

16. If the credit amount of an adjusting entry adjusts an asset account, the debit amount of the adjusting entry must adjust a(n) __________________ account.

17. If the adjusting entry to record the amount of prepaid insurance that has expired during the period is omitted, the net income for the period will be ____________________.

18. If the adjusting entry to record depreciation on equipment for the period is omitted, total assets will be ____________________ on the balance sheet.

19. If the balance of the supplies account on January 1 was $500, supplies purchased during the year were $1,750, and the supplies on hand at December 31 were $300, the amount for the appropriate adjusting entry at December 31 is __________________.

20. The prepaid insurance account has a debit balance of $3,600 at the beginning of the year. If unexpired insurance at the end of the year is $2,800, the amount of insurance expense that should be reported on the income statement is _________________.

MULTIPLE CHOICE

Instructions: Circle the best answer for each of the following questions.

1. Entries required at the end of an accounting period to bring the accounts up to date and to assure the proper matching of revenues and expenses are called:
   a. matching entries
   b. adjusting entries
   c. contra entries
   d. correcting entries

2. The amount of accrued but unpaid expenses at the end of the fiscal period is both an expense and a(n):
   a. liability
   b. asset
   c. deferral
   d. revenue

3. If the effect of the debit portion of an adjusting entry is to increase the balance of an expense account, which of the following describes the effect of the credit portion of the entry?
   a. decreases the balance of a contra asset account
   b. increases the balance of an asset account
   c. decreases the balance of an asset account
   d. increases the balance of an expense account

4. If the effect of the credit portion of an adjusting entry is to increase the balance of a liability account, which of the following describes the effect of the debit portion of the entry?
   a. increases the balance of a contra asset account
   b. increases the balance of an asset account
   c. decreases the balance of an asset account
   d. increases the balance of an expense account

5. The balance in the prepaid rent account before adjustment at the end of the year is $12,000, which represents three months' rent paid on December 1. The adjusting entry required on December 31 is:
   a. debit Prepaid Rent, $4,000; credit Rent Expense, $4,000
   b. debit Rent Expense, $4,000; credit Prepaid Rent, $4,000
   c. debit Prepaid Rent, $8,000; credit Rent Expense, $8,000
   d. debit Rent Expense, $8,000; credit Prepaid Rent, $8,000

6. At the end of the preceding fiscal year, the usual adjusting entry for accrued salaries owed to employees was omitted. The error was not corrected, but the accrued salaries were included in the first salary payment in the current fiscal year. Which of the following statements is true?
   a. Salary Expense was overstated and net income was understated for the current year.
   b. Salaries Payable is understated at the end of the current fiscal year.
   c. Salary Expense was overstated and net income was understated for the preceding year.
   d. Salary Expense and Salaries Payable were overstated for the preceding year.
7. The decrease in usefulness of fixed assets as time passes is called:
   a. consumption
   b. deterioration
   c. depreciation
   d. contra asset
8. The difference between the fixed asset account and the related accumulated depreciation account is called the:
   a. book value of the asset
   b. fair market value of the asset
   c. net cost of the asset
   d. contra account balance of the asset
9. If a $250 adjustment for depreciation is not recorded, which of the following financial statement errors will occur?
   a. Expenses will be overstated.
   b. Net income will be understated.
   c. Assets will be understated.
   d. Owner's equity will be overstated.
10. The net income reported on the income statement is $50,000. However, adjusting entries have not been made at the end of the period for supplies expense of $500 and accrued salaries of $1,300. Net income, as corrected, is:
    a. $48,200
    b. $48,700
    c. $50,500
    d. $51,800

TRUE/FALSE

Instructions: Indicate whether each of the following statements is true or false by placing a check mark in the appropriate column.

	Statement	True	False
1.	Most businesses use the accrual basis of accounting.	____	____
2.	When the reduction in prepaid expenses is not properly recorded, this causes the asset accounts and expense accounts to be overstated.	____	____
3.	Accumulated depreciation accounts may be referred to as contra asset accounts..	____	____
4.	If the adjusting entry to record accrued wages at the end of the year is omitted, net income, owner's equity, and total assets will be overstated..	____	____
5.	If the debit portion of an adjusting entry debits an expense, the credit portion must credit either a contra asset, an asset, or a liability account.	____	____
6.	The adjusting entry to record depreciation of fixed assets consists of a debit to a depreciation expense account and a credit to an accumulated depreciation account...............	____	____
7.	When expenses, such as employee wages, are not paid for until after they have been performed, the accrued expense is recorded in the accounts by an adjusting entry at the end of the accounting period.......................................	____	____
8.	A deferral is an expense that has not been paid or a revenue that has not been received...	____	____
9.	Accrued expenses may be described on the balance sheet as accrued liabilities...	____	____
10.	The amount of accrued revenue is recorded by debiting a liability account and crediting a revenue account...............	____	____

EXERCISE 3-1

Don Taylor closes his books at the end of each year (December 31). On May 1 of the current year, Don insured the business assets for three years at a premium of $5,400.

Instructions:

(1) Using the T accounts below, enter the adjusting entry that should be made by Taylor as of December 31 to record the amount of insurance expired as of that date. The May 1 premium payment is recorded in the T accounts.

Cash		Prepaid Insurance		Insurance Expense	
	May 1 5,400	May 1 5,400			

(2) Taylor's balance sheet as of December 31 should show the asset value of the unexpired insurance as .... $ ________

(3) Taylor's income statement for the year ended December 31 should show insurance expense of .... $ ________

EXERCISE 3-2

Jan Olin closes her books at the end of each month. Olin has only one employee, who is paid at the rate of $50 per day. The employee is paid every Friday at the end of the day. Each workweek is composed of five days, starting on Monday. Assume that the Fridays of this month (October) fall on the 7th, 14th, 21st, and 28th.

Instructions:

(1) Using the T accounts below, enter the four weekly wage payments for October. Then enter the adjusting entry that should be made by Olin as of October 31 to record the salary owed the employee but unpaid as of that date.

Cash		Salary Expense		Salaries Payable	

(2) Olin's income statement for October should show total salary expense of .... $ ________

(3) Olin's balance sheet as of October 31 should show a liability for salaries payable of .... $ ________

Exercise 3-3

Keller Co.'s unearned rent account has an unadjusted balance of $6,000 as of December 31 of the current year. This amount represents the rental of an apartment for a period of one year. The lease began on December 1 of the current year.

Instructions: Using the T accounts below, record the adjusting entry as of December 31 to recognize the rent income for the appropriate portion of the year. Then journalize the entry.

Unearned Rent	
	Dec. 1 6,000

Rent Revenue	

JOURNAL PAGE

	DATE		DESCRIPTION	POST. REF.	DEBIT	CREDIT	
1							1
2							2
3							3
4							4
5							5
6							6
7							7
8							8
9							9
10							10
11							11
12							12
13							13
14							14

EXERCISE 3-4

Garret Co. has accrued but uncollected interest of $320 as of December 31 on a note receivable.

Instructions: Using the T accounts below, record the adjusting entry for accrued interest income as of December 31. Then journalize the entry.

Interest Receivable		Interest Revenue	

JOURNAL PAGE

	DATE		DESCRIPTION	POST. REF.	DEBIT	CREDIT	
1							1
2							2
3							3
4							4
5							5
6							6
7							7
8							8
9							9
10							10
11							11
12							12
13							13
14							14

PROBLEM 3-1

An unadjusted trial balance for Bob's Service Company as of July 31, 20-- is shown below.

Bob's Service Company
Unadjusted Trial Balance
July 31, 20--

	Debit Balances	Credit Balances
Cash	9,218	
Accounts Receivable	7,277	
Supplies	2,750	
Prepaid Rent	8,712	
Tools & Equipment	21,829	
Accumulated Depreciation		1,535
Accounts Payable		7,117
Bob Jones, Capital		37,417
Bob Jones, Drawing	3,234	
Service Fees		28,699
Salary Expense	15,929	
Miscellaneous Expense	5,819	
	74,768	74,768

The data needed to determine end-of-month adjustments are as follows:

(a) Salaries accrued but not paid at the end of the month amount to $2,000.

(b) The $8,712 debit in the prepaid rent account is the payment of one year's rent on July 1.

(c) The supplies on hand as of July 31 cost $1,000.

(d) Depreciation of the tools and equipment for July is estimated at $400.

(e) Unrecorded fees for service rendered in July but collected in August amount to $2,100.

Instructions:

(1) Journalize the adjusting entries. Add additional accounts as needed.

(2) Determine the balances of the accounts affected by the adjusting entries and prepare an adjusted trial balance.

(1)

JOURNAL

PAGE

DATE		DESCRIPTION	POST. REF.	DEBIT	CREDIT

(2)

CHAPTER

4 Completing the Accounting Cycle

Quiz and Test Hints

The following hints may be helpful to you in preparing for a quiz or a test over the material covered in Chapter 4.

1. Terminology is important in this chapter. Review the "Key Terms" section at the end of the chapter and be sure you understand each term. Do the Matching and Fill-in-the-Blank exercises included in this Study Guide.
2. The flow of accounting information from the unadjusted trial balance into the adjusted trial balance and financial statements is an important part of this chapter. This flow of accounting information is summarized in the end-of-period spreadsheet (work sheet) shown in Exhibit 1, which you should review. Your instructor may or may not assign the end-of-chapter appendix on how to prepare the end-of-period spreadsheet (work sheet). If your instructor assigns this appendix, you may be provided with a partially completed spreadsheet on a test and be asked to complete it.
3. Be thoroughly familiar with the financial statements presented in Exhibit 2 in the text. Know the financial statement captions and how the statements tie together. In a test situation, you may be provided with partially completed financial statements that you would be asked to complete.
4. You should be able to prepare the closing entries in general journal form. You may have to prepare these entries from an end-of-period spreadsheet (work sheet), adjusted trial balance, income statement, statement of owner's equity, or ledger.
5. The accounting cycle is an essential part of accounting. Expect multiple-choice or other types of short answer questions related to the accounting cycle. Review the accounting cycle, which is summarized in Exhibit 8.
6. A comprehensive illustration of the accounting cycle is provided on pages 157–168. Many instructors give a test after Chapter 4 to make sure you understand each step in the accounting cycle. You should carefully review this illustration, which summarizes each of the ten steps in the accounting cycle.

7. Review the GPS graphic at the beginning of the chapter and the "At A Glance" section at the end of the chapter. Read and review each of the Key Points and related Learning Outcomes. For each Learning Outcome that has an Example Exercise, locate the Example Exercise in the chapter and be sure that you understand the solution and can work a similar item on a test. If you have any questions about an Example Exercise, read the section of the chapter immediately preceding the Example Exercise.

8. If your instructor covers the Financial Analysis and Interpretation item at the end of the chapter, you should know how to compute and interpret working capital.

9. Your instructor may or may not have discussed the material in the end-of-text appendix (Appendix B) on reversing entries. If your instructor covered the appendix, you should know what adjusting entries normally require reversing entries, and be able to prepare reversing entries.

MATCHING

Instructions: Match each of the statements below with its proper term. Some terms may not be used.

A. accounting cycle
B. adjusted trial balance
C. adjusting entries
D. closing entries
E. closing spreadsheet (work sheet)
F. current assets
G. current liabilities
H. end-of-period spreadsheet (work sheet)
I. fiscal year
J. Income Summary
K. long-term liabilities
L. natural business year
M. note receivable
N. owner's equity
O. permanent assets
P. post-closing trial balance
Q. property, plant, and equipment
R. real accounts
S. temporary accounts

____ **1.** A spreadsheet (work sheet) that managers and accountants may use to see the impact of adjustments on the financial statements.

____ **2.** Cash and other assets that are expected to be converted to cash or sold or used up, usually within one year or less, through the normal operations of the business.

____ **3.** A customer's written promise to pay an amount and possibly interest at an agreed-upon rate.

____ **4.** Liabilities that will be due within a short time (usually one year or less) and that are to be paid out of current assets.

____ **5.** Liabilities that usually will not be due for more than one year.

____ **6.** An account to which the revenue and expense account balances are transferred at the end of a period.

____ **7.** The trial balance prepared after the closing entries have been posted.

____ **8.** The annual accounting period adopted by a business.

____ **9.** A fiscal year that ends when business activities have reached the lowest point in an annual operating cycle.

____ **10.** The process that begins with analyzing and journalizing transactions and ends with the post-closing trial balance.

____ **11.** The entries that transfer the balances of the revenue, expense, and drawing accounts to the owner's capital account.

____ **12.** The section of the balance sheet that includes equipment, machinery, buildings, and land.

____ **13.** Accounts that report amounts for only one period.

FILL IN THE BLANK—PART A

Instructions: Answer the following questions or complete the statements by writing the appropriate words or amounts in the answer blanks.

1. A(n) ____________ ______________ is a work sheet that managers and accountants may use to see the impact of adjustments on the financial statements.

2. A(n) ____________ ____________________ is a customer's written promise to pay an amount and possibly interest at an agreed rate.

3. Liabilities that will be due within a short time (usually one year or less) and that are to be paid out of current assets are called ________________ ____________________.

4. In the end-of-period spreadsheet (work sheet), the adjusted trial balance amount for office equipment is extended to the ____________________ ______________ Debit column.

5. In the end-of-period spreadsheet (work sheet), the adjusted trial balance amount for the owner's drawing account is extended to the ______________________ ______________ Debit column.

6. After all of the account balances have been extended to the Income Statement columns of the end-of-period spreadsheet (work sheet), the totals of the Debit and Credit columns are $89,900 and $99,500, respectively. The difference of $9,600 is the __________ _______________ for the period.

7. After all of the account balances have been extended to the Balance Sheet columns of the end-of-period spreadsheet (work sheet), the totals of the Debit and Credit columns are $94,300 and $110,500, respectively. The difference of $16,200 is the __________ _______________ for the period.

8. Revenue and expense account balances are transferred to the _______________ _______________ account at the end of a period.

9. The drawing account is closed at the end of the period by crediting it for its balance and debiting the _______________ _______________ account.

10. The fees earned account is closed at the end of the period by debiting it for its balance and crediting the _______________ _______________ account.

11. The income summary account (net income) is closed at the end of the period by debiting it for its balance and crediting the _______________ _______________ account.

12. The trial balance prepared after the closing entries have been posted is called the _________-_______________ trial balance.

13. The ____________________ _____________ begins with analyzing and journalizing transactions and ends with the post-closing trial balance.

14. The year that ends when business activities have reached the lowest point in the annual operating cycle is called the _______________ _______________ _______________.

FILL IN THE BLANK—PART B

Instructions: Answer the following questions or complete the statements by writing the appropriate words or amounts in the answer blanks.

1. Cash and other assets that are expected to be converted to cash or sold or used up within one year or less through the normal operations of the business are classified on the balance sheet as _________________ _________________.

2. The __________________, _______________, and _________________, section of the balance sheet includes equipment, machinery, buildings, and land.

3. Liabilities that will not be due for usually more than one year are classified on the balance sheet as __________-__________ __________________.

4. In the end-of-period spreadsheet (work sheet), the adjusted amount for depreciation expense is extended to the _______________ __________________ Debit column.

5. In the end-of-period spreadsheet (work sheet), the adjusted amount for the fees earned account is extended to the _______________ __________________ Credit column.

6. After all of the account balances have been extended to the Income Statement columns of the end-of-period spreadsheet (work sheet), the totals of the Debit and Credit columns are $120,000 and $115,000, respectively. The difference of $5,000 is the ___________ ______________ for the period.

7. After all of the account balances have been extended to the Balance Sheet columns of the end-of-period spreadsheet (work sheet), the totals of the Debit and Credit columns are $280,000 and $240,000, respectively. The difference of $40,000 is the ___________ _____________ for the period.

8. The _______________ _______________ transfer the balances of the revenue, expense, and drawing accounts to the owner's capital account.

9. Revenue and expense account balances are transferred to the _______________ ________________ account at the end of a period.

10. The drawing account is closed at the end of the period by crediting it and debiting the ________________ ________________ account.

11. The office salaries expense account is closed at the end of the period by crediting it and debiting the ________________ ________________ account.

12. The income summary account (net loss) is closed at the end of the period by crediting it and debiting the ________________ ________________ account.

13. The ________________ ________________ is the annual accounting period adopted by a business.

14. Companies with fiscal years often have highly ____________ __________.

MULTIPLE CHOICE

Instructions: Circle the best answer for each of the following questions.

1. Notes receivable are written claims against:
   - **a.** creditors
   - **b.** owner's equity
   - **c.** customers
   - **d.** assets
2. In an end-of-period spreadsheet (work sheet), the:
   - **a.** adjusted trial balance amounts are extended to the Income Statement and Balance Sheet columns
   - **b.** the Adjustment columns are totaled
   - **c.** adjustments are extended to the Adjusted Trial Balance columns
   - **d.** all the above
3. If in the end-of-period spreadsheet (work sheet) the Income Statement Credit column is greater than the Income Statement Debit column:
   - **a.** a net income exists
   - **b.** a net loss exists
   - **c.** an asset account is debited
   - **d.** a liability account is credited

4. After all of the account balances have been extended to the Balance Sheet columns of the end-of-period spreadsheet (work sheet), the totals of the Debit and Credit columns are $377,750 and $387,750, respectively. What is the amount of net income or net loss for the period?
   a. $10,000 net income
   b. $10,000 net loss
   c. $377,750 net income
   d. $387,750 net income
5. After all of the account balances have been extended to the Income Statement columns of the end-of-period spreadsheet (work sheet), the totals of the Debit and Credit columns are $62,300 and $67,600, respectively. What is the amount of the net income or net loss for the period?
   a. $5,300 net income
   b. $5,300 net loss
   c. $62,300 net income
   d. $67,600 net loss
6. Which of the following accounts should be closed to Income Summary at the end of the fiscal year?
   a. Lisa Murray, Drawing
   b. Accumulated Depreciation—Equipment
   c. Sales
   d. Accounts Payable
7. Which of the following accounts will be closed at the end of the fiscal year by debiting Lisa Murray, Capital?
   a. Salaries Expense
   b. Sales
   c. Lisa Murray, Drawing
   d. Accounts Receivable
8. Which of the following accounts will ordinarily appear in the post-closing trial balance?
   a. Salaries Expense
   b. Lisa Murray, Drawing
   c. Sales
   d. Lisa Murray, Capital
9. The maximum length of an accounting period is normally:
   a. 6 months
   b. 1 year
   c. 2 years
   d. 3 years

10. The complete sequence of accounting procedures for a fiscal period is frequently called the:

a. end-of-period spreadsheet (work sheet) process

b. opening and closing cycle

c. accounting cycle

d. fiscal cycle

TRUE/FALSE

Instructions: Indicate whether each of the following statements is true or false by placing a check mark in the appropriate column.

	True	False
1. The balance of Accumulated Depreciation—Equipment is extended to the Income Statement columns of the end-of-period spreadsheet (work sheet).	____	____
2. The difference between the Debit and Credit columns of the Income Statement section of the end-of-period spreadsheet (work sheet) is normally larger than the difference between the Debit and Credit columns of the Balance Sheet section.	____	____
3. The first item normally presented in the statement of owner's equity is the balance of the owner's capital account at the beginning of the period.	____	____
4. The balance that is transferred from the income summary account to the capital account is the net income or net loss for the period.	____	____
5. The balances of the accounts reported in the balance sheet are carried from year to year and are called temporary accounts.	____	____
6. An account titled Income Summary is normally used for transferring the revenue and expense account balances to the owner's capital account at the end of the period.	____	____
7. If the Income Statement Debit column is greater than the Income Statement Credit column of the end-of-period spreadsheet (work sheet), the difference is net income.	____	____
8. A type of work sheet frequently used by accountants prior to the preparation of financial statements is called a post-closing trial balance.	____	____
9. At the end of the period, the balances are removed from the temporary accounts and the net effect is recorded in the permanent account by means of closing entries.	____	____
10. The annual accounting period adopted by a business is known as its fiscal year.	____	____

EXERCISE 4-1

The account titles and Adjustments columns of the end-of-period spreadsheet (work sheet) for Sally's Small Engine Repair are listed below.

	A	D	E
1	Sally's Small Engine Repair		
2	End-of-Period Spreadsheet (Work Sheet)		
3	For Month Ended August 31, 20--		
4		Adjustments	
5		Debit	Credit
6	Cash		
7	Accounts Receivable	(e) 3,200	
8	Supplies		(c) 700
9	Prepaid Rent		(b) 560
10	Tools/Equipment		
11	Accumulated Depreciation		(d) 1,000
12	Accounts Payable		
13	Sally Sand, Capital		
14	Sally Sand, Drawing		
15	Repair Fees		(e) 3,200
16	Salary Expense	(a) 1,500	
17	Miscellaneous Expense		
18	Salaries Payable		(a) 1,500
19	Rent Expense	(b) 560	
20	Supplies Expense	(c) 700	
21	Depreciation Expense	(d) 1,000	

Instructions: Prepare journal entries for the adjustments indicated for Sally's Small Engine Repair.

JOURNAL PAGE

	DATE		DESCRIPTION	POST. REF.	DEBIT	CREDIT	
1							1
2							2
3							3
4							4
5							5
6							6
7							7
8							8
9							9
10							10
11							11
12							12
13							13
14							14
15							15
16							16
17							17
18							18
19							19
20							20

EXERCISE 4-2

Instructions: The journal, the income summary account, the service fees account, the salary expense account, and the supplies expense account of Tony Brown as of March 31, the first month of the current fiscal year, follow. In the journal, prepare the entries to close Brown's revenue and expense accounts into the income summary account. Then post to the ledger.

JOURNAL PAGE *7*

	DATE		DESCRIPTION	POST. REF.	DEBIT	CREDIT	
1							1
2							2
3							3
4							4
5							5
6							6
7							7
8							8
9							9
10							10
11							11
12							12
13							13
14							14
15							15

ACCOUNT *Income Summary* ACCOUNT NO. *45*

DATE		ITEM	POST. REF.	DEBIT	CREDIT	BALANCE	
						DEBIT	CREDIT

ACCOUNT Service Fees ACCOUNT NO. 50

DATE		ITEM	POST. REF.	DEBIT	CREDIT	BALANCE DEBIT	BALANCE CREDIT
20– Mar.	15		5		4,850.00		4,850.00
	31		6		14,375.00		19,225.00

ACCOUNT Salary Expense ACCOUNT NO. 58

DATE		ITEM	POST. REF.	DEBIT	CREDIT	BALANCE DEBIT	BALANCE CREDIT
20– Mar.	31		5	8,550.00		8,550.00	

ACCOUNT Supplies Expense ACCOUNT NO. 67

DATE		ITEM	POST. REF.	DEBIT	CREDIT	BALANCE DEBIT	BALANCE CREDIT
20– Mar.	15		5	2,430.00		2,430.00	
	25		6	1,720.00		4,150.00	
	31		6	1,280.00		5,430.00	

PROBLEM 4-1

An end-of-period spreadsheet (work sheet) of Castle Shop for the fiscal year ended April 30, 20--, appears on the following page.

Instructions:

Prepare (1) an income statement, (2) a statement of owner's equity, and (3) a balance sheet using the forms on the following pages.

Problem 4-1

	A	B	C	D	E	F	G	H	I	J	K
1			Castle Shop								
2			End-of-Period Spreadsheet (Work Sheet)								
3			For the Year Ended April 31, 20--								
4		Unadjusted				Adjusted		Income		Balance	
5		Trial Balance		Adjustments		Trial Balance		Statement		Sheet	
6	Account Title	Dr.	Cr.	Dr.	Cr.	Dr.	Cr.	Dr.	Cr.	Dr.	Cr.
7	Cash	10,056				10,056				10,056	
8	Accounts Receivable	7,938		(e) 3,000		10,938				10,938	
9	Supplies	3,000			(a) 1,200	1,800				1,800	
10	Prepaid Rent	9,504			(b) 792	8,712				8,712	
11	Tools & Equipment	23,814				23,814				23,814	
12	Accum. Depreciation		1,674		(c) 1,000		2,674				2,674
13	Accounts Payable		7,764				7,764				7,764
14	Wages Payable				(d) 2,000		2,000				2,000
15	Unearned Fees		2,000	(f) 500			1,500				1,500
16	Castle, Capital		38,818				38,818				38,818
17	Castle, Drawing	3,528				3,528				3,528	
18	Service Fees		31,308		(e) 3,000		34,808		34,808		
19					(f) 500						
20	Wages Expense	17,376		(d) 2,000		19,376		19,376			
21	Supplies Expense			(a) 1,200		1,200		1,200			
22	Depr. Expense			(c) 1,000		1,000		1,000			
23	Rent Expense			(b) 792		792		792			
24	Misc. Expense	6,348				6,348		6,348			
25		81,564	81,564	8,492	8,492	87,564	87,564	28,716	34,808	58,848	52,756
26	Net Income							6,092			6,092
27								34,808	34,808	58,848	58,848

(1)

Income Statement

(2)

Statement of Owner's Equity

(3)

Balance Sheet

Problem 4-2

Instructions:

(1) On the basis of the data in the Adjustments columns of the end-of-period spreadsheet (work sheet) in Problem 4-1, journalize the adjusting entries.

(2) On the basis of the data in the Income Statement and Balance Sheet columns of the work sheet in Problem 4-1, journalize the closing entries.

JOURNAL

PAGE

DATE		DESCRIPTION	POST. REF.	DEBIT	CREDIT

JOURNAL

PAGE

	DATE		DESCRIPTION	POST. REF.	DEBIT	CREDIT	
1							1
2							2
3							3
4							4
5							5
6							6
7							7
8							8
9							9
10							10
11							11
12							12
13							13
14							14
15							15
16							16
17							17
18							18
19							19
20							20
21							21
22							22
23							23
24							24
25							25
26							26
27							27
28							28
29							29
30							30
31							31
32							32
33							33
34							34
35							35
36							36

CHAPTER

5 Accounting Systems

Quiz and Test Hints

The following hints may be helpful to you in preparing for a quiz or a test over the material covered in Chapter 5.

1. You should be familiar with the terminology related to accounting systems. Review the "Key Terms" section at the end of the chapter and be sure you understand each term. Do the Matching and Fill-in-the-Blank exercises included in this Study Guide.
2. Chapter 5 focuses on the recording of transactions using subsidiary ledgers and special journals. Carefully review the content and format of the various special journals illustrated throughout the chapter.
3. The postings to the control accounts for accounts receivable and accounts payable come from the column totals of the sales and cash receipts journals (accounts receivable) and purchases and cash payment journals (accounts payable).
4. Your instructor may provide a list of transactions and ask you to identify the journal in which each transaction would be recorded. Remember, if a transaction does not fit into any of the special journals, it would be recorded in the general journal. In addition, any time the accounts receivable or accounts payable accounts are debited or credited, their related subsidiary ledgers must also be posted. The diagram on page 205 is helpful in indicating the types of transactions recorded in each special journal. In addition, the Illustrative Problem is typical of the problems that commonly appear on quizzes and tests.
5. Review the GPS graphic at the beginning of the chapter and the "At A Glance" section at the end of the chapter. Read and review each of the Key Points and related Learning Outcomes. For each Learning Outcome that has an Example Exercise, locate the Example Exercise in the chapter and be sure that you understand the solution and can work a similar item on a test. If you have any questions about an Example Exercise, read the section of the chapter immediately preceding the Example Exercise.
6. If your instructor covers the Financial Analysis and Interpretation item at the end of the chapter, you should know how to compute and interpret changes in a company's segment disclosures.

Matching

Instructions: Match each of the statements below with its proper term. Some terms may not be used.

A.	accounting system	**H.**	e-commerce
B.	accounts payable subsidiary ledger	**I.**	general journal
C.	accounts receivable subsidiary ledger	**J.**	general ledger
D.	cash payments journal	**K.**	internal controls
E.	cash receipts journal	**L.**	purchases journal
F.	controlling account	**M.**	revenue journal
G.	customer relationship management (CRM)	**N.**	special journals
		O.	subsidiary ledger
		P.	supply chain management (SCM)

____ **1.** The journal in which all cash payments are recorded.

____ **2.** The journal in which all cash receipts are recorded.

____ **3.** The subsidiary ledger containing the individual accounts with customers (debtors).

____ **4.** Journals designed to be used for recording a single type of transaction.

____ **5.** The methods and procedures used by a business to collect, classify, summarize, and report financial data for use by management and external users.

____ **6.** The policies and procedures used to safeguard assets, ensure accurate business information, and ensure compliance with laws and regulations.

____ **7.** The subsidiary ledger containing the individual accounts with suppliers (creditors).

____ **8.** The journal in which all sales of services on account are recorded.

____ **9.** The account in the general ledger that summarizes the balances of the accounts in a subsidiary ledger.

____ **10.** The journal in which all items purchased on account are recorded.

____ **11.** The two-column form used for entries that do not "fit" in any of the special journals.

____ **12.** The primary ledger, when used in conjunction subsidiary ledgers, that contains all of the balance sheet and income statement accounts.

____ **13.** A ledger containing individual accounts with a common characteristic.

____ **14.** Internet applications to plan and coordinate suppliers.

____ **15.** Internet applications to plan and coordinate marketing and sales efforts.

FILL IN THE BLANK—PART A

Instructions: Answer the following questions or complete the statements by writing the appropriate words or amounts in the answer blanks.

1. All cash payments are recorded in the ____________ ________________ journal.
2. A journal that is designed to be used for recording a single type of transaction is called a ___________________ journal.
3. The policies and procedures used to safeguard assets, ensure accurate business information, and ensure compliance with laws and regulations are called _________________ _________________.
4. The purchase of supplies on account would be recorded in the ___________________ journal.
5. The adjusting entry for depreciation expense would be recorded in the ___________________ journal.
6. The payment of a note payable at its due date would be recorded in the ______________ ___________________ journal.
7. The closing entries at the end of the period would be recorded in the ___________________ journal.
8. The total of the revenue journal is posted at the end of the month to the fees earned and _________________ _____________________ accounts.
9. The total of the credit column of the cash payments journal is posted at the end of the month to the ________________ account.
10. All sales of services on account are recorded in the ___________________ journal.
11. The primary ledger, when used in conjunction with subsidiary ledgers, that contains all of the balance sheet and income statement accounts is called the ___________________ ledger.
12. ________________ ________________ ________________________ is an Internet-based computer application used to help plan and coordinate suppliers.

FILL IN THE BLANK—PART B

Instructions: Answer the following questions or complete the statements by writing the appropriate words or amounts in the answer blanks.

1. All cash receipts are recorded in the __________ ______________ journal.
2. The subsidiary ledger containing the individual accounts with customers is called the ________________ ____________________ subsidiary ledger.
3. The methods and procedures used by a business to collect, classify, summarize, and report financial data for use by management and external users is called the ___________________ system.
4. The subsidiary ledger containing the individual accounts with creditors is called the ________________ ____________________ subsidiary ledger.
5. The purchase of supplies for cash would be recorded in the __________ ______________ journal.
6. The adjusting entry for accrued fees earned would be recorded in the ________________ journal.
7. The issuance of an invoice to a customer for services rendered on account would be recorded in the ________________ journal.
8. The receipt of cash in payment of an account from a customer would be recorded in the __________ ________________ journal.
9. The total of the revenue journal is posted at the end of the month to the accounts receivable and __________ ________________ accounts.
10. The total of the credit column of the purchases journal is posted at the end of the month to the ________________ ____________________ account.
11. The ________________ account in the general ledger summarizes the balances of the accounts in a subsidiary ledger.
12. All items purchased on account are recorded in the ________________ journal.
13. Entries that do not "fit" in any of the special journals are recorded in a two-column journal called the ________________ journal.
14. A ledger containing individual accounts with a common characteristic is called a ________________ ledger.
15. ________________ ________________ ____________________ is an Internet-based computer application used to help plan and coordinate marketing and sales efforts.

Multiple Choice

Instructions: Circle the best answer for each of the following questions.

1. The job of installing or changing an accounting system is made up of three phases: (1) analysis, (2) design, and (3):
   a. installation
   b. verification
   c. management
   d. implementation
2. The individual amounts in the "Accounts Payable Cr." column of the purchases journal are posted to the appropriate account in the:
   a. general ledger
   b. general journal
   c. accounts payable subsidiary ledger
   d. accounts payable journal
3. Which of the following transactions should be recorded in the revenue journal?
   a. the purchase of supplies on account
   b. the receipt of cash for services rendered
   c. the billing of fees earned on account
   d. the payment of an account payable
4. The controlling account in the general ledger that summarizes the individual accounts with creditors in a subsidiary ledger is titled:
   a. Accounts Payable
   b. Purchases
   c. Accounts Receivable
   d. Sales Returns and Allowances
5. Internal control policies and procedures provide reasonable assurance that:
   a. the company will not be sued
   b. a net income will be earned
   c. management is competent
   d. business information is accurate
6. The controlling account for the customer's ledger is:
   a. Cash
   b. Accounts Receivable
   c. Accounts Payable
   d. Fees Earned

7. When are the amounts entered in the "Accounts Receivable Cr." column of the revenue journal posted?
   a. at regular intervals
   b. at the end of each month
   c. whenever the accounts receivable control account is posted
   d. whenever adjusting entries are prepared and posted
8. Which of the following is not a special journal?
   a. revenue journal
   b. general journal
   c. cash receipts journal
   d. purchases journal
9. What does a computerized system perform automatically?
   a. records original transactions
   b. provides adjusting entries
   c. posts transactions to the ledger
   d. month-end postings to controlling accounts
10. Which of the following advanced applications of e-commerce is used to plan and coordinate marketing and sales efforts?
   a. supply chain management
   b. customer relationship management
   c. product life-cycle management
   d. revenue and collection cycle

TRUE/FALSE

Instructions: Indicate whether each of the following statements is true or false by placing a check mark in the appropriate column.

		True	False
1.	The goal of systems design is to identify information needs and how the system should provide the information.	____	____
2.	Transactions involving the payment of cash for any purpose usually are recorded in a purchases journal.	____	____
3.	When there are a large number of individual accounts with a common characteristic, it is common to place them in a separate ledger called a detail ledger.	____	____
4.	For each transaction recorded in the purchases journal, the credit is entered in the "Accounts Payable Cr." column.	____	____
5.	Acquisitions on account that are not provided for in special debit columns are recorded in the purchases journal in the final set of columns called "Misc."	____	____
6.	Debits to creditors' accounts for invoices paid are recorded in the "Accounts Payable Dr." column of the cash payments journal.	____	____
7.	At the end of each month, the total of the amount column of the revenue journal is posted as a debit to Cash and a credit to Fees Earned.	____	____
8.	Each amount in the "Other Accounts Cr." column of the cash receipts journal must be posted individually to an appropriate general ledger account.	____	____
9.	Accounting systems must be continually reviewed for possible revisions in order to keep pace with the changing information needs of businesses.	____	____
10.	Many special journals are modified in practice to adapt them to meet the specific needs of a business.	____	____
11.	The high cost of computer hardware and software makes computerized accounting systems unaffordable to small- and medium-size businesses.	____	____
12.	After all posting has been completed for the month, if the sum of balances in the accounts receivable subsidiary ledger does not agree with the balance of the accounts receivable account in the general ledger, the errors must be located and corrected.	____	____

	True	False
13. The primary ledger that contains all of the balance sheet and income statement accounts is called the general ledger.	____	____
14. If a business uses computers to process accounting data, the concepts and methods for a manual system are not relevant.	____	____
15. B2C e-commerce is used by businesses to conduct purchase and sales transactions with other businesses..........	____	____

Exercise 5-1

Wilco Co. is a computer consulting business. Wilco Co. maintains a cash receipts journal, cash payments journal, revenue journal, purchases journal, and general journal. Selected transactions of Wilco Co. for the month of February are listed below.

Instructions: Indicate the journal in which each of the transactions would be recorded.

		Transaction	Journal
Feb.	1.	Purchased supplies on account from Winkler's Wholesale...........	____________
	6.	Wilco Co. rendered services to Phil's Grocery Store for cash......	____________
	8.	Received credit from Winkler's Wholesale for supplies returned. .	____________
	11.	Issued check no. 1099 for payment of supplies purchased on February 1, less return on February 8, to Winkler's Wholesale...	____________
	18.	Billed Sally's Shop-N-Save for services rendered on account.....	____________
	28.	Received full payment on account from Tony's Grocery Store.	____________

EXERCISE 5-2

The following transactions were completed by Mezza Co. during October of the current year.

Oct. 3. Billed Blanders Co. for services rendered on account, Invoice No. 2883, $8,250.

4. Billed Montana Co. for services rendered on account, Invoice No. 2884, $5,000.

8. Issued to Blanders Co. a credit for $1,000 due to a misunderstanding of services performed.

13. Received cash from Blanders Co. in payment of Invoice No. 2883.

14. Received cash from Montana Co. in payment of Invoice No. 2884.

25. Received cash for office supplies returned to the manufacturer, $300.

31. Services rendered for cash in October, $39,600.

Instructions: Record the above transactions in the revenue journal, cash receipts journal, or general journal provided below and on the next page.

REVENUE JOURNAL

DATE		INVOICE NO.	ACCOUNT DEBITED	POST. REF.	ACCTS. REC. DR. FEES EARNED CR.

CASH RECEIPTS JOURNAL

DATE		ACCOUNT CREDITED	POST. REF.	OTHER ACCOUNTS CR.	ACCOUNTS REC. CR.	CASH DR.

JOURNAL

PAGE

	DATE		DESCRIPTION	POST. REF.	DEBIT	CREDIT	
1							1
2							2
3							3
4							4
5							5
6							6
7							7
8							8
9							9
10							10
11							11
12							12
13							13
14							14

EXERCISE 5-3

The following transactions related to purchases and cash payments were completed by Kent Company during March of the current year.

March 2. Purchased store supplies on account from Eastside Co., $1,250.

8. Purchased store supplies on account from Bench Co., $600.

9. Received credit from Eastside Co., $300 for supplies returned.

16. Issued Check No. 230 to Bench Co. in payment of the balance due.

20. Issued Check No. 231 for a cash purchase of office supplies, $250.

27. Issued Check No. 232 to Eastside Co. in payment of the balance due.

28. Purchased the following on account from James & Co.: store supplies, $800; office supplies, $100.

Instructions: Record the above transactions in the purchases journal, cash payments journal, or the general journal provided on the next page.

PURCHASES JOURNAL

DATE		ACCOUNT CREDITED	POST. REF.	ACCOUNTS PAY. CR.	STORE SUPPLIES DR.	OFFICE SUPPLIES DR.	OTHER ACCOUNTS DR.

CASH PAYMENTS JOURNAL

DATE		CK. NO.	ACCOUNT DEBITED	POST. REF.	OTHER ACCOUNTS DR.	ACCOUNTS PAY DR.	CASH CR.

JOURNAL

PAGE

	DATE		DESCRIPTION	POST. REF.	DEBIT	CREDIT	
1							1
2							2
3							3
4							4
5							5
6							6
7							7
8							8
9							9
10							10
11							11

PROBLEM 5-1

Kleco Co., an architectural services firm, completed the following transactions with customers on account during September of the current year.

Sept. 8. Invoice No. 210 to Robert Poon, $1,220.

12. Invoice No. 225 to Jeff Lucas, $750.

24. Invoice No. 260 to Pamela Stark, $860.

30. Invoice No. 290 to Steve Kocan, $2,500.

Instructions:

(1) Record the above transactions in the revenue journal below.

(2) Post the individual items from the revenue journal to the T accounts for customers. Indicate that each item has been posted by placing a check mark (✓) in the Post. Ref. column of the revenue journal.

(3) Post the total of the revenue journal to the T accounts for Accounts Receivable and Fees Earned. Indicate that the posting is completed by inserting the appropriate account numbers in the journal under the amount posted.

REVENUE JOURNAL

DATE		INVOICE NO.	ACCOUNT DEBITED	POST. REF.	ACCTS. REC. DR. FEES EARNED CR.

GENERAL LEDGER

Accounts Receivable	113

Fees Earned	411

ACCOUNTS RECEIVABLE LEDGER

Steve Kocan	

Jeff Lucas	

Robert Poon	

Pamela Stark	

(4) Determine that the sum of the balances of the individual accounts in the accounts receivable subsidiary ledger agrees with the balance of the accounts receivable controlling account in the general ledger by completing the following summary form.

Steve Kocan	$
Jeff Lucas	
Robert Poon	
Pamela Stark	
Total accounts receivable	$

Problem 5-2

Willbury's, a retail store, completed the following transactions with creditors on account during April of the current year.

April 14. Purchased store supplies on account from Mills Co., $300.
16. Purchased office supplies on account from Quick Co., $175.
22. Purchased store equipment on account from Mills Co., $5,250.
30. Purchased store supplies on account from Mills Co., $280.

Instructions:

(1) Record the above transactions in the purchases journal below.

(2) Post the individual items from the purchases journal to the T accounts in the general and accounts payable subsidiary ledgers. Indicate that each item has been posted by placing a check mark (✓) or an account number in the appropriate Post. Ref. column of the purchases journal.

(3) Post the totals of the purchases journal to the general ledger T accounts. Insert the appropriate account numbers in the journal under the amount posted.

PURCHASES JOURNAL

DATE		ACCOUNT CREDITED	POST. REF.	ACCOUNTS PAYABLE CR.	STORE SUPPLIES DR.	OFFICE SUPPLIES DR.	OTHER ACCOUNTS DR.		
							ACCOUNT	POST. REF.	AMOUNT

GENERAL LEDGER

Store Supplies 115	

Office Supplies 116	

Store Equipment 121	

Accounts Payable 211	

ACCOUNTS PAYABLE LEDGER

Mills Co.	

Quick Co.	

(4) Determine that the sum of the balances of the individual accounts in the accounts payable subsidiary ledger agrees with the balance of the accounts payable controlling account in the general ledger by completing the following summary form:

Mills Co. .... $______________

Quick Co. .... ______________

Total accounts payable .... $______________

PROBLEM 5-3

The "Totals" line and one other line of the purchases journal of Hamilton Co. for the month of October are shown below. Also shown are selected T accounts taken from Hamilton's general ledger.

Instructions:

(1) Verify the equality of the debits and the credits in Hamilton's purchases journal for October by completing the following schedule:

Debit Totals		**Credit Totals**	
Store Supplies	____________	Accounts Payable ..	____________
Office Supplies ...	____________		
Other Accounts ...	____________		
Total	____________	Total	____________

(2) Post all amounts that require posting to the T accounts provided. Show the appropriate posting references in the purchases journal.

PURCHASES JOURNAL

DATE		ACCOUNT CREDITED	POST. REF.	ACCOUNTS PAYABLE CR.	STORE SUPPLIES DR.	OFFICE SUPPLIES DR.	OTHER ACCOUNTS DR. ACCOUNT	POST. REF.	AMOUNT
	29	*Hartkemeyer Co.*	✓	*7,620*			*Store Equip.*		*7,620*
	31			*15,890*	*3,650*	*1,250*			*10,990*

GENERAL LEDGER

Store Supplies 115	

Office Supplies 116	

Store Equipment 121	

Accounts Payable 211	

CHAPTER

6 Accounting for Merchandising Businesses

QUIZ AND TEST HINTS

The following hints may be helpful to you in preparing for a quiz or a test over the material covered in Chapter 6.

1. This chapter introduces merchandising business terminology that you should know. Review the "Key Terms" section at the end of the chapter and be sure you understand each term. Do the Matching and Fill-in-the-Blank exercises included in this Study Guide.
2. A major portion of this chapter describes the preparation of financial statements for a merchandising business. Particular emphasis may be placed on determining the cost of merchandise sold and preparing the income statement. Practice preparing the financial statements for NetSolutions. Your instructor may provide partially completed financial statements, and you will be required to complete the statements.
3. Review the chart of accounts in Exhibit 6 for a merchandising business as a basis for distinguishing the types of accounts used by merchandising businesses.
4. You should be able to prepare general journal entries for the types of transactions illustrated in the chapter. Be sure you can compute purchases discounts and sales discounts. Review the chapter illustrations. The Illustrative Problem in the Chapter Review is an excellent review of the types of entries you might have to prepare.
5. The accounting for freight costs can be confusing, but you will probably be required to prepare one or more journal entries, or answer one or more multiple-choice questions, involving such costs. Review the chapter discussion and illustration related to such costs.
6. The illustration of the journal entries for both the buyer and seller of merchandise on page 272 of the chapter provides an excellent review. Often, instructors will require students to prepare journal entries based upon the same data for both the buyer and the seller.
7. You should be able to prepare the adjusting entry for inventory shrinkage.

8. You should be able to prepare the closing entries for a merchandising business. These entries are similar to those you prepared in earlier chapters.

9. If your instructor lectures on accounting systems for merchandisers using Appendix 1 to the chapter, you may expect some questions related to special journals for merchandising businesses. Oftentimes instructors will provide a list of merchandise transactions and ask which special journal each should be recorded in. Also, you should know which general ledger accounts are affected when the column totals of the special journals are posted at the end of the accounting period.

10. If your instructor lectures on the periodic inventory system using Appendix 2 at the end of the chapter, you may have to prepare journal entries and financial statements using this system.

11. Review the GPS graphic at the beginning of the chapter and the "At A Glance" section at the end of the chapter. Read and review each of the Key Points and related Learning Outcomes. For each Learning Outcome that has an Example Exercise, locate the Example Exercise in the chapter and be sure that you understand the solution and can work a similar item on a test. If you have any questions about an Example Exercise, read the section of the chapter immediately preceding the Example Exercise.

12. If your instructor covers the Financial Analysis and Interpretation item at the end of the chapter, you should know how to compute and interpret changes in the ratio of net sales to assets.

13. If your instructor lectures on preparing a merchandising end-of-period spreadsheet (work sheet) from Appendix C at the end of the text, you may expect some questions related to the end-of-period spreadsheet (work sheet). Oftentimes instructors provide a partially completed spreadsheet (work sheet) and require students to complete it. You may find it a helpful exercise to cover up portions of the illustrated spreadsheet (work sheet) in Appendix C and see if you know how to complete the covered sections.

MATCHING

Instructions: Match each of the statements below with its proper term. Some terms may not be used.

A. account form
B. administrative expenses (general expenses)
C. cost of merchandise sold
D. credit memorandum
E. debit memorandum
F. FOB (free on board) destination
G. FOB (free on board) shipping point
H. gross profit
I. income from operations (operating income)
J. inventory shrinkage
K. invoice
L. loss from operations
M. merchandise inventory
N. multiple-step income statement
O. other expense
P. other income
Q. periodic inventory system
R. perpetual inventory system
S. physical inventory
T. purchases return or allowance
U. purchases discounts
V. ratio of net sales to assets
W. report form
X. sales discounts
Y. sales return or allowance
Z. selling expenses
AA. single-step income statement
BB. trade discounts

____ **1.** The cost that is reported as an expense when merchandise is sold.

____ **2.** Sales minus the cost of merchandise sold.

____ **3.** Merchandise on hand (not sold) at the end of an accounting period.

____ **4.** The inventory system in which each purchase and sale of merchandise is recorded in an inventory account.

____ **5.** The inventory system in which the inventory records do not show the amount available for sale or sold during the period.

____ **6.** A detailed listing of the merchandise for sale at the end of an accounting period.

____ **7.** The bill that the seller sends to the buyer.

____ **8.** Discounts taken by the buyer for early payment of an invoice.

____ **9.** From the buyer's perspective, returned merchandise or an adjustment for defective merchandise.

____ **10.** A form used by a buyer to inform the seller of the amount the buyer proposes to debit to the account payable due the seller.

____ **11.** From the seller's perspective, discounts that a seller may offer the buyer for early payment.

____ **12.** From the seller's perspective, returned merchandise or an adjustment for defective merchandise.

____ **13.** A form used by a seller to inform the buyer of the amount the seller proposes to credit to the account receivable due from the buyer.

____ **14.** Discounts from the list prices in published catalogs or special discounts offered to certain classes of buyers.

____ **15.** Freight terms in which the buyer pays the freight costs from the shipping point to the final destination.

____ **16.** Freight terms in which the seller pays the freight costs from the shipping point to the final destination.

____ **17.** A form of income statement that contains several sections, subsections, and subtotals.

____ **18.** Expenses that are incurred directly in the selling of merchandise.

____ **19.** Expenses incurred in the administration or general operations of the business.

____ **20.** The excess of gross profit over total operating expenses.

____ **21.** The excess of operating expenses over gross profit.

____ **22.** Revenue from sources other than the primary operating activity of a business.

____ **23.** Expenses that cannot be traced directly to operations.

____ **24.** A form of income statement in which the total of all expenses is deducted from the total of all revenues.

____ **25.** The amount by which the merchandise for sale, as indicated by the balance of the merchandise inventory account, is larger than the total amount of merchandise counted during the physical inventory.

____ **26.** The form of balance sheet in which assets are reported on the left-hand side and the liabilities and owner's equity on the right-hand side.

____ **27.** The form of balance sheet in which assets, liabilities, and owner's equity are reported in a downward sequence.

____ **28.** Measures how effectively a business is using its assets to generate sales.

FILL IN THE BLANK—PART A

Instructions: Answer the following questions or complete the statements by writing the appropriate words or amounts in the answer blanks.

1. The cost that is reported as an expense when merchandise is sold is called ________ ______ ____________________ ________.
2. Revenue is normally reported on the income statement of a service enterprise as fees earned. In contrast, revenue for a merchandising business is normally reported as ____________.
3. Gross profit minus ________________ ________________ yields income from operations for a merchandising business.
4. ____________________ ________________ is merchandise on hand (not sold) at the end of an accounting period.

5. The ________________ inventory system does not show the amount available for sale or sold during the period.
6. Beginning merchandise inventory plus cost of merchandise purchased equals ________________________ ___________________ ________ __________.
7. A buyer refers to returned merchandise or an adjustment for defective merchandise as a(n) _________________ _____________ _____ ________________________.
8. A seller refers to discounts offered to the buyer for early payment as ___________ __________________.
9. A seller informs the buyer of the amount that they propose to credit to the buyer's account receivable by issuing a ____________ memorandum.
10. If the buyer pays the freight costs from the shipping point to the final destination, the freight terms are referred to as ________ __________________ ____________.
11. A sales invoice for $5,000, terms 1/10, n/30, FOB shipping point, is paid within the discount period. Freight costs of $75 are paid and added to the invoice. The amount of the discount is __________.
12. A return of $300 has been recorded against a purchase invoice of $3,300, terms 2/10, n/30. The invoice is paid within the discount period. The amount of the discount is __________.
13. Merchandise with a list price of $1,000 is sold with a trade discount of 30%, terms 2/10, n/30. The amount to be recorded in the sales account is __________.
14. The _________________-_________ form of income statement contains several sections, subsections, and subtotals.
15. Expenses incurred in the administration or general operations of the business are reported on the income statement as ____________________ expenses.
16. The excess of operating expenses over gross profit is _____________ _________ __________________.
17. Expenses that cannot be traced directly to operations are reported on the income statement as _______________ expenses.
18. The amount by which the merchandise for sale, as indicated by the balance of the merchandise inventory account, is larger than the total amount of merchandise counted during the physical inventory is referred to as __________________ __________________.
19. Balances of selected accounts at the end of the year, before adjustments, are as follows: Sales, $900,000; Sales Returns and Allowances, $50,000; Sales Discounts, $10,000; Cost of Merchandise Sold, $600,000; Selling Expenses, $80,000; Administrative Expenses, $25,500; Interest Revenue, $5,000; Interest Expense, $2,000. The gross profit is ______________.
20. The ________________ form of balance sheet reports assets, liabilities, and owner's equity in a downward sequence.

FILL IN THE BLANK—PART B

Instructions: Answer the following questions or complete the statements by writing the appropriate words or amounts in the answer blanks.

1. Sales minus cost of merchandise sold is called __________ ____________.
2. Gross profit minus ____________________ ____________________ yields income from operations.
3. In the ____________________ inventory system each purchase and sale of merchandise is recorded in an inventory account when the transactions occur.
4. A(n) ____________________ ____________________ is a detailed listing of the merchandise for sale at the end of the accounting period.
5. A buyer refers to discounts taken for early payment of an invoice as ____________________ ____________________.
6. A buyer informs the seller of the amount the buyer proposes to debit to the seller's account payable by issuing a ______________ memorandum.
7. A seller refers to returned merchandise or an adjustment for defective merchandise as a(n) ____________ ____________ _____ ____________________.
8. Discounts from the list prices in published catalogs or special discounts offered to certain classes of buyers are called ___________ ____________________.
9. If the seller pays the freight costs from the shipping point to the final destination, the freight terms are referred to as __________ ____________________.
10. A sales invoice for $8,000, terms 2/10, n/30, FOB shipping point, is paid within the discount period. Freight costs of $125 are paid and added to the invoice. The amount of the discount is ______________.
11. A sales invoice for $15,000, terms 1/10, n/30, FOB shipping point, is paid within the discount period. Freight costs of $250 are paid and added to the invoice. The total amount paid by the buyer is ______________.
12. A return of $500 has been recorded against a purchase invoice of $3,800, terms 1/10, n/30. The invoice is paid within the discount period. The amount of the discount is ______________.
13. A buyer purchased merchandise for $10,000, terms 1/10, n/30, FOB destination. The seller pays freight costs of $500. If the buyer pays the invoice within the discount period, the amount paid by the buyer is ______________.
14. Merchandise with a list price of $12,000 is sold with a trade discount of 45%, terms 2/10, n/30. The amount to be recorded in the sales account is ______________.

15. Expenses that are incurred directly in the selling of merchandise are reported on the income statement as ________________ expenses.

16. The excess of gross profit over total operating expenses is ____________ _________ __________________.

17. Revenue from sources other than the primary operating activity of a business is reported on the income statement as ____________ ____________.

18. The ____________-____________ form of income statement deducts the total of all expenses from the total of all revenues.

19. Balances of selected accounts at the end of the year, before adjustments, are as follows: Sales, $750,000; Sales Returns and Allowances, $25,000; Sales Discounts, $10,000; Cost of Merchandise Sold, $500,000; Selling Expenses, $80,000; Administrative Expenses, $20,000; Interest Revenue, $5,000; Interest Expense, $2,000. The gross profit is ___________.

20. The ______________ form of balance sheet reports assets on the left-hand side and the liabilities and owner's equity on the right-hand side.

MULTIPLE CHOICE

Instructions: Circle the best answer for each of the following questions.

1. The basic differences between the financial statements of a merchandising business and a service business include reporting cost of merchandise sold on the income statement and the:
   - a. owner's equity section of the balance sheet
   - b. other income section of the income statement
   - c. inclusion of merchandise inventory on the balance sheet as a current asset
   - d. inclusion of an owner's equity statement

2. A buyer receives an invoice for $60 dated June 10. If the terms are 2/10, n/30, and the buyer pays the invoice within the discount period, what amount will the seller receive?
   - a. $60
   - b. $58.80
   - c. $48
   - d. $1.20

3. When a seller of merchandise allows a customer a reduction from the original price for defective goods, the seller usually issues to the customer a(n):
   - a. debit memorandum
   - b. credit memorandum
   - c. sales invoice
   - d. inventory slip

4. When the seller prepays the transportation costs and the terms of sale are FOB shipping point, the seller records the payment of the freight costs by debiting:
   a. Accounts Receivable
   b. Sales
   c. Freight In
   d. Accounts Payable
5. If the seller collects sales tax at the time of sale, the seller credits the tax to:
   a. Sales
   b. Accounts Receivable
   c. Sales Tax Payable
   d. Sales Tax Receivable
6. The account that appears in the chart of accounts for a merchandising business but not for a service business is:
   a. Accounts Receivable
   b. Advertising Expense
   c. Sales Returns and Allowances
   d. Accumulated Depreciation
7. The excess of net revenue from sales over the cost of merchandise sold is called:
   a. gross profit
   b. operating profit
   c. net profit from operations
   d. merchandising income
8. Income from operations is computed by subtracting from gross profit the:
   a. selling expenses
   b. general expenses
   c. total administrative expenses
   d. total operating expenses
9. After all adjusting entries are posted, the balances of all asset, liability, revenue, and expense accounts correspond exactly to the amounts in the:
   a. end-of-the-period spreadsheet (work sheet) trial balance
   b. general journal
   c. post-closing trial balance
   d. financial statements

10. In a multiple-step income statement of a merchandising business, which of the following would appear as "other income"?
    a. sales
    b. interest revenue
    c. sales discounts
    d. sales returns and allowances

TRUE/FALSE

Instructions: Indicate whether each of the following statements is true or false by placing a check mark in the appropriate column.

		True	False
1.	The two main systems for accounting for merchandise held for sale are called periodic and perpetual.	____	____
2.	In a perpetual inventory system, purchases of merchandise are recorded in the purchases account.	____	____
3.	In a periodic inventory system, no attempt is made to record the cost of merchandise sold at the date of the sale.	____	____
4.	A discount offered the purchaser of goods as a means of encouraging payment before the end of the credit period is known as a bank discount.	____	____
5.	Credit terms of "2/10, n/30" mean that the buyer may deduct 2% of the amount of the invoice if payment is made within 10 days of the invoice date.	____	____
6.	If the seller is to absorb the cost of delivering the goods, the terms are stated FOB (free on board) shipping point.	____	____
7.	The liability for the sales tax is incurred at the time the seller receives payment from the buyer.	____	____
8.	The purchases returns and allowances are credited to Merchandise Inventory.	____	____
9.	The chart of accounts for a merchandising business will differ from that of a service business.	____	____
10.	The accounting cycle for a merchandising business is significantly different from that of a service business.	____	____
11.	The physical inventory taken at the end of the period is normally larger than the amount of the balance of the merchandise inventory account.	____	____
12.	Any merchandise inventory shrinkage is normally debited to the merchandise inventory account.	____	____

	True	False
13. Expenses incurred directly and entirely in connection with the sale of merchandise are called administrative expenses.	____	____
14. Revenue from sources such as income from interest, rent, dividends, and gains resulting from the sale of fixed assets is classified as income from operations.	____	____
15. The single-step form of income statement has the advantage of being simple, and it emphasizes total revenues and total expenses as the factors that determine net income.	____	____
16. Gross profit is not calculated in the single-step form of income statement.	____	____
17. The excess of gross profit over total operating expenses is called income from operations.	____	____
18. The traditional balance sheet arrangement of assets on the left-hand side with the liabilities and owner's equity on the right-hand side is called the report form.	____	____
19. After the adjusting and closing entries have been recorded and posted, the general ledger accounts that appear on the balance sheet have no balances.	____	____
20. The closing entries are recorded in the journal immediately following the adjusting entries.	____	____

EXERCISE 6-1

The following information was taken from the records of Dawkins Co. for the year ended June 30, 2010.

Merchandise inventory, July 1, 2009	$130,000
Merchandise inventory, June 30, 2010	125,000
Purchases	600,000
Purchases returns and allowances	45,000
Purchases discounts	10,000
Sales	875,000
Freight in	7,500

Instructions: Prepare a partial income statement for Dawkins Co. through the reporting of gross profit.

EXERCISE 6-2

Instructions: Prepare entries for each of the following related transactions of Foley Co. in the journal given below.

(1) Purchased $5,000 of merchandise from Phillips Co. on account, terms 2/10, n/30.

(2) Paid Phillips Co. on account for purchases, less discount.

(3) Purchased $3,500 of merchandise from Farris Co. on account, terms FOB shipping point, n/30, with prepaid freight costs of $80 added to the invoice.

(4) Returned merchandise from Farris Co., $900.

(5) Paid Farris Co. on account for purchases, less return.

JOURNAL PAGE

DATE	DESCRIPTION	POST. REF.	DEBIT	CREDIT

EXERCISE 6-3

Instructions: Prepare entries for each of the following related transactions of Wilson Co. in the journal given below.

(1) Sold merchandise to customers using MasterCard, \$3,150. The cost of the merchandise sold was \$2,000.

(2) Sold merchandise for cash, \$2,850. The cost of the merchandise sold was \$1,380.

(3) Paid \$100 service fee on credit card sales.

(4) Sold merchandise on account to Rask Co., \$4,500, terms 2/10, n/30, FOB shipping point. Prepaid freight costs of \$150 at the customer's request. The cost of the merchandise sold was \$3,100.

(5) Received merchandise returned by Rask Co., \$400. The cost of the merchandise returned was \$275.

(6) Received cash on account from Rask Co. for sale and freight costs, less returns and discount.

JOURNAL PAGE

DATE		DESCRIPTION	POST. REF.	DEBIT	CREDIT

(continued)

JOURNAL

PAGE

	DATE		DESCRIPTION	POST. REF.	DEBIT	CREDIT	
1							1
2							2
3							3
4							4
5							5
6							6
7							7
8							8
9							9
10							10
11							11
12							12
13							13
14							14
15							15
16							16
17							17
18							18
19							19
20							20

EXERCISE 6-4

Baker Co. had the following purchases and sales transactions during the month of January.

Jan. 3. Purchased $25,000 of merchandise on account from Zeff Co., terms 2/10, n/30.

5. Returned merchandise purchased on account from Zeff Co. on January 3, $5,000.

12. Sold merchandise on account to Smith Co., $50,000, terms 1/10, n/30. The cost of the merchandise sold was $35,000.

13. Paid Zeff Co. for purchase on January 3, on account, less return and discount.

15. Received merchandise return on account from Smith Co., $8,000. The cost of the merchandise returned was $5,600.

22. Received payment in full on account from Smith Co., less return and discount.

Instructions: Prepare journal entries for the preceding transactions.

JOURNAL

PAGE

	DATE		DESCRIPTION	POST. REF.	DEBIT	CREDIT	
1							1
2							2
3							3
4							4
5							5
6							6
7							7
8							8
9							9
10							10
11							11
12							12
13							13
14							14
15							15
16							16
17							17
18							18
19							19
20							20
21							21
22							22
23							23
24							24
25							25
26							26
27							27
28							28
29							29
30							30
31							31
32							32
33							33
34							34
35							35
36							36

Exercise 6-5 (Periodic Inventory System) Appendix 2

Instructions: Prepare entries for each of the following related transactions of Foley Co. under the periodic inventory system in the journal given below.

(1) Purchased $5,000 of merchandise from Phillips Co. on account, terms 2/10, n/30.

(2) Paid Phillips Co. on account for purchases, less discount.

(3) Purchased $3,500 of merchandise from Farris Co. on account, terms FOB shipping point, n/30, with prepaid freight costs of $80 added to the invoice.

(4) Returned merchandise from Farris Co., $900.

(5) Paid Farris Co. on account for purchases, less return.

JOURNAL PAGE

	DATE		DESCRIPTION	POST. REF.	DEBIT	CREDIT	
1							1
2							2
3							3
4							4
5							5
6							6
7							7
8							8
9							9
10							10
11							11
12							12
13							13
14							14
15							15
16							16
17							17
18							18
19							19
20							20
21							21
22							22
23							23
24							24
25							25

EXERCISE 6-6 (PERIODIC INVENTORY SYSTEM) APPENDIX 2

Baker Co. had the following purchases and sales transactions during the month of January.

Jan. 3. Purchased $25,000 of merchandise on account from Zeff Co., terms 2/10, n/30.

5. Returned merchandise purchased on account from Zeff Co. on January 3, $5,000.

12. Sold merchandise on account to Smith Co., $50,000, terms 1/10, n/30. The cost of the merchandise sold was $35,000.

13. Paid Zeff Co. for purchase on January 3, on account, less return and discount.

15. Received merchandise return on account from Smith Co., $8,000. The cost of the merchandise returned was $5,600.

22. Received payment in full on account from Smith Co., less return and discount.

Instructions: Prepare journal entries for the preceding transactions under the periodic inventory system.

JOURNAL PAGE

	DATE		DESCRIPTION	POST. REF.	DEBIT	CREDIT	
1							1
2							2
3							3
4							4
5							5
6							6
7							7
8							8
9							9
10							10
11							11
12							12
13							13
14							14
15							15
16							16
17							17
18							18

PROBLEM 6-1

The following transactions were selected from among those completed by the Bowman Company during September of the current year:

Sept. 3. Purchased merchandise on account from Axel Co., list price $10,000, trade discount 15%, terms FOB destination, 1/10, n/30.

4. Purchased office supplies for cash, $800.

6. Sold merchandise on account to Hart Co., list price $5,000, trade discount 20%, terms 2/10, n/30. The cost of merchandise sold was $3,000.

7. Returned $2,000 of the merchandise purchased on September 3 from Axel Co.

10. Purchased merchandise for cash, $5,000.

12. Sold merchandise to customers using American Express, $5,500. The cost of merchandise sold was $3,200.

13. Paid Axel Co. on account for purchase of September 3, less return of September 7 and discount.

16. Received cash on account from sale of September 6 to Hart Co., less discount.

20. Paid $300 service fee for credit card sales of September 12.

24. Sold merchandise to Wilcox Co., $3,000, terms 1/10, n/30. The cost of merchandise sold was $1,750.

26. Sold merchandise for cash, $2,200. The cost of merchandise sold was $1,400.

30. Received merchandise returned by Wilcox Co. from sale on September 24, $1,000. The cost of the merchandise returned was $600.

Instructions: Journalize the transactions for the Bowman Co., using the journal forms provided below and on the following pages.

JOURNAL PAGE

	DATE		DESCRIPTION	POST. REF.	DEBIT	CREDIT	
1							1
2							2
3							3
4							4
5							5
6							6
7							7
8							8
9							9
10							10

JOURNAL

PAGE

	DATE		DESCRIPTION	POST. REF.	DEBIT	CREDIT	
1							1
2							2
3							3
4							4
5							5
6							6
7							7
8							8
9							9
10							10
11							11
12							12
13							13
14							14
15							15
16							16
17							17
18							18
19							19
20							20
21							21
22							22
23							23
24							24
25							25
26							26
27							27
28							28
29							29
30							30
31							31
32							32
33							33
34							34
35							35
36							36

JOURNAL PAGE

	DATE		DESCRIPTION	POST. REF.	DEBIT	CREDIT	
1							1
2							2
3							3
4							4
5							5
6							6
7							7
8							8
9							9
10							10
11							11

PROBLEM 6-2

The following accounts and their normal balances were taken from the general ledger of Miller Co. after the adjusting entries have been posted for the fiscal year ending March 31.

Cash	$ 49,620
Accounts Receivable	107,780
Merchandise Inventory	115,800
Office Supplies	1,250
Prepaid Insurance	8,740
Delivery Equipment	60,150
Accumulated Depreciation—Delivery Equipment	22,950
Accounts Payable	75,300
Salaries Payable	2,000
R. W. Miller, Capital	193,650
R. W. Miller, Drawing	30,000
Sales	1,016,700
Sales Returns and Allowances	13,010
Cost of Merchandise Sold	681,060
Sales Salaries Expense	78,250
Advertising Expense	13,090
Delivery Expense	42,100
Depreciation Expense—Delivery Equipment	9,050
Miscellaneous Selling Expense	13,950
Office Salaries Expense	55,800
Office Supplies Expense	9,100
Insurance Expense	16,000
Miscellaneous Administrative Expense	6,870
Interest Revenue	1,020

Instructions:

(a) Prepare a multiple-step income statement for Miller Co.

(b) Prepare a single-step income statement for Miller Co.

(c) Assume that the inventory shrinkage for Miller Co. for the period ending March 31 was $4,200. Prepare the adjusting entry to record the inventory shrinkage.

(a)

Multiple-Step Income Statement

(b)

Single-Step Income Statement

(c) **JOURNAL** PAGE

	DATE		DESCRIPTION	POST. REF.	DEBIT	CREDIT	
1							1
2							2
3							3
4							4
5							5
6							6

Problem 6-3

Using the information in Problem 6-2, prepare a statement of owner's equity for Miller Co.

PROBLEM 6-4

Using the information in Problem 6-2, prepare a balance sheet in report form for Miller Co. as of March 31, 20--.

Problem 6-5 (Periodic Inventory System)
Appendix 2

The following transactions were selected from among those completed by the Bowman Company during September of the current year:

Sept. 3. Purchased merchandise on account from Axel Co., list price $10,000, trade discount 15%, terms FOB destination, 1/10, n/30.

4. Purchased office supplies for cash, $800.

6. Sold merchandise on account to Hart Co., list price $5,000, trade discount 20%, terms 2/10, n/30. The cost of merchandise sold was $3,000.

7. Returned $2,000 of the merchandise purchased on September 3 from Axel Co.

10. Purchased merchandise for cash, $5,000.

12. Sold merchandise to customers using American Express, $5,500. The cost of merchandise sold was $3,200.

13. Paid Axel Co. on account for purchase of September 3, less return of September 7 and discount.

16. Received cash on account from sale of September 6 to Hart Co., less discount.

20. Paid $300 service fee for credit card sales of September 12.

24. Sold merchandise to Wilcox Co., $3,000, terms 1/10, n/30. The cost of merchandise sold was $1,750.

26. Sold merchandise for cash, $2,200. The cost of merchandise sold was $1,400.

30. Received merchandise returned by Wilcox Co. from sale on September 24, $1,000. The cost of the merchandise returned was $600.

Instructions: Journalize the transactions for the Bowman Co. under the periodic inventory system using the journal forms provided below.

JOURNAL PAGE

	DATE		DESCRIPTION	POST. REF.	DEBIT	CREDIT	
1							1
2							2
3							3
4							4
5							5
6							6
7							7
8							8
9							9
10							10

JOURNAL

PAGE

	DATE		DESCRIPTION	POST. REF.	DEBIT	CREDIT	
1							1
2							2
3							3
4							4
5							5
6							6
7							7
8							8
9							9
10							10
11							11
12							12
13							13
14							14
15							15
16							16
17							17
18							18
19							19
20							20
21							21
22							22
23							23
24							24
25							25
26							26
27							27
28							28
29							29
30							30
31							31
32							32
33							33
34							34
35							35
36							36

CHAPTER

7 Inventories

QUIZ AND TEST HINTS

The following hints may be helpful to you in preparing for a quiz or a test over the material covered in Chapter 7.

1. You should carefully review the new terminology introduced in this chapter. Review the "Key Terms" section at the end of the chapter and be sure you understand each term. Do the Matching and Fill-in-the-Blank exercises included in this Study Guide.
2. The chapter emphasizes determining the cost of inventory using the first-in, first-out (fifo), last-in, first-out (lifo), and average cost methods. Most instructors ask questions related to these cost flow assumptions using the perpetual and periodic inventory systems. The Illustrative Problem in the Chapter Review is an excellent study aid for this type of question.
3. The retail method and gross profit method of estimating inventory are also popular subjects for quiz and test questions with instructors. Be prepared to work each method.
4. The effect of inventory errors on the financial statements is a complex topic. If your instructor covers this topic, study the chapter illustrations carefully.
5. If your instructor covers the retail and gross profit methods of estimating inventory using the end of chapter appendix, be prepared to work each method. These are popular subjects for quiz and test questions, and several items have been included in this Study Guide to prepare you for these topics.
6. Review the GPS graphic at the beginning of the chapter and the "At A Glance" section at the end of the chapter. Read and review each of the Key Points and related Learning Outcomes. For each Learning Outcome that has an Example Exercise, locate the Example Exercise in the chapter and be sure that you understand the solution and can work a similar item on a test. If you have any questions about an Example Exercise, read the section of the chapter immediately preceding the Example Exercise.
7. If your instructor covers the Financial Analysis and Interpretation item at the end of the chapter, you should know how to compute and interpret changes in the inventory turnover ratio.

MATCHING

Instructions: Match each of the statements below with its proper term. Some terms may not be used.

A. average cost method
B. first-in, first-out (fifo) method
C. gross profit method
D. inventory turnover
E. last-in, first-out (lifo) method
F. lower-of-cost-or-market (LCM) method
G. net realizable value
H. number of days' sales in inventory
I. physical inventory
J. retail inventory method

____ **1.** A detailed listing of merchandise on hand.

____ **2.** A method of inventory costing that is based on the assumption that the costs of merchandise sold should be charged against revenue in the order in which the costs were incurred.

____ **3.** A method of inventory costing that is based on the assumption that the most recent merchandise inventory costs should be charged against revenue.

____ **4.** The method of inventory costing that is based on the assumption that costs should be charged against revenue by using the weighted average unit cost of the items sold.

____ **5.** A method of valuing inventory that reports the inventory at the lower of its cost or current market value (replacement cost).

____ **6.** The estimated selling price of an item of inventory less any direct costs of disposal, such as sales commissions.

____ **7.** A method of estimating inventory cost that is based on the relationship of the cost of merchandise available for sale to the retail price of the same merchandise.

____ **8.** A method of estimating inventory cost that is based on the relationship of gross profit to sales.

____ **9.** A ratio that measures the relationship between the volume of goods (merchandise) sold and the amount of inventory carried during the period.

____ **10.** A measure of the length of time it takes to acquire, sell, and replace the inventory.

FILL IN THE BLANK—PART A

Instructions: Answer the following questions or complete the statements by writing the appropriate words or amounts in the answer blanks.

1. A detailed listing of merchandise on hand is called a(n) ________________ ____________________.
2. The _________-______, _________-______ method of costing inventory is based on the assumption that the most recent merchandise inventory costs should be charged against revenue.
3. On June 1, there was beginning inventory of 5 units at $100 per unit. During June, the following three purchases were made: June 7, 10 units at $110 per unit; June 17, 15 units at $115 per unit; and June 23, 8 units at $116 per unit. If 12 units are on hand on June 30, the total cost of the ending inventory using the periodic system and the last-in, first-out cost flow is ______________.
4. During a period of consistently falling prices, the __________ (fifo or lifo) method will result in reporting the greater amount of gross profit.
5. The ___________-_____-________-_____-____________ method reports inventory at the lower of its cost or current market value (replacement cost).
6. During July, merchandise available for sale at cost and retail is $240,000 and $400,000, respectively. If $25,000 of merchandise at retail is on hand on July 31, the estimated cost of the merchandise on hand on July 31 is ______________.
7. At the end of the year, the physical inventory is overstated. As a result, the cost of merchandise sold will be ____________________.
8. At the end of the year, the physical inventory is understated. As a result, the owner's capital reported on the balance sheet will be ____________________.
9. The _________ ______________ method estimates inventory cost based on the relationship of gross profit to sales.
10. The _________________ _________________ ratio measures the relationship between the volume of goods (merchandise) sold and the amount of inventory carried during the period.

FILL IN THE BLANK—PART B

Instructions: Answer the following questions or complete the statements by writing the appropriate words or amounts in the answer blanks.

1. The __________-_______, __________-______ method of costing inventory is based on the assumption that the costs of merchandise sold should be charged against revenue in the order in which the costs were incurred.
2. The ________________ ____________ method costs inventory based upon the assumption that costs should be charged against revenue in accordance with the weighted average unit costs of the items sold.
3. On June 1, there was beginning inventory of 5 units at $100 per unit. During June, the following three purchases were made: June 7, 10 units at $110 per unit; June 17, 15 units at $115 per unit; and June 23, 8 units at $116 per unit. If 12 units are on hand on June 30, the total cost of the ending inventory using the periodic system and the first-in, first-out method is ______________.
4. The estimated selling price of an item of inventory less any direct costs of disposal, such as sales commissions, is called __________ ____________________ ______________.
5. If the cost of an item of inventory is $50, the current replacement cost is $45, and the selling price is $80, the amount included in inventory according to the lower-of-cost-or-market concept is ______________.
6. At the end of the year, the physical inventory is overstated. As a result, net income will be ____________________.
7. At the end of the year, the physical inventory is understated. As a result, gross profit will be ____________________.
8. The ______________ ____________________ method estimates inventory cost based on the relationship of the cost of merchandise available for sale to the retail price of the same merchandise.
9. During November, the cost of merchandise available for sale was $750,000. Sales of $900,000 were made during November at an average gross profit of 30% of sales. Using the gross profit method, the estimated cost of the inventory on hand on November 30 is ______________.
10. The __________________ ________ ____________ ____________ ______ ________________________ is a measure of the length of time it takes to acquire, sell, and replace the inventory.

MULTIPLE CHOICE

Instructions: Circle the best answer for each of the following questions.

1. The following units of a particular item were purchased and sold during the period:

Beginning inventory	10 units at $5
First purchase	15 units at $6
Sale	10 units
Second purchase	10 units at $7
Sale	8 units
Third purchase	15 units at $8
Sale	17 units

What is the total cost of the 15 units on hand at the end of the period, as determined under the perpetual inventory system by the lifo costing method?

a. $80
b. $90
c. $100
d. $120

2. Assuming the data given in No. 1, determine the total cost of the 15 units on hand at the end of the period assuming a perpetual inventory system and the fifo costing method.

a. $80
b. $90
c. $100
d. $120

3. Assuming the data given in No. 1, determine the total cost of the 15 units on hand at the end of the period assuming a periodic inventory system and the lifo costing method.

a. $80
b. $90
c. $100
d. $120

4. Assuming the data given in No. 1, determine the total cost of the 15 units on hand at the end of the period assuming a periodic inventory system and the fifo costing method.

a. $80
b. $90
c. $99
d. $120

5. Assuming the data given in No. 1, determine the total cost of the 15 units on hand at the end of the period assuming a periodic inventory system and the average costing method.

a. $80

b. $90

c. $99

d. $120

6. During a period of rising prices, the inventory costing method that will result in the lowest amount of net income is:

a. fifo

b. lifo

c. average cost

d. perpetual

7. If the replacement price of an item of inventory is lower than its cost, the use of the lower of cost or market method:

a. is not permitted unless a perpetual inventory system is maintained

b. is recommended in order to maximize the reported net income

c. tends to overstate the gross profit

d. reduces gross profit for the period in which the decline occurred

8. When lifo is strictly applied to a perpetual inventory system, the unit cost prices assigned to the ending inventory will not necessarily be those associated with the earliest unit costs of the period if:

a. a physical inventory is taken at the end of the period

b. physical inventory records are maintained throughout the period in terms of quantities only

c. at any time during a period the number of units of a commodity sold exceeds the number previously purchased during the same period

d. moving average inventory cost is maintained

9. If merchandise inventory at the end of the period is understated:

a. gross profit will be overstated

b. owner's equity will be overstated

c. net income will be understated

d. cost of merchandise sold will be understated

10. If merchandise inventory at the end of period 1 is overstated and at the end of period 2 is correct:

a. gross profit in period 2 will be understated

b. assets at the end of period 2 will be overstated

c. owner's equity at the end of period 2 will be understated

d. cost of merchandise sold in period 2 will be understated

TRUE/FALSE

Instructions: Indicate whether each of the following statements is true or false by placing a check mark in the appropriate column.

		True	False
1.	The two principal systems of inventory accounting are periodic and physical.	____	____
2.	When terms of a sale are FOB destination, title usually does not pass to the buyer until the commodities are delivered.	____	____
3.	If merchandise inventory at the end of the period is overstated, owner's equity at the end of the period will be understated.	____	____
4.	During a period of rising prices, the inventory costing method that will result in the highest amount of net income is lifo.	____	____
5.	If the cost of units purchased and the prices at which they were sold remained stable, all three inventory methods would yield the same results.	____	____
6.	When the rate of inflation is high, the larger gross profits that result from using the fifo method are frequently called inventory profits.	____	____
7.	As used in the phrase "lower of cost or market," *market* means selling price.	____	____
8.	When the retail inventory method is used, inventory at retail is converted to cost on the basis of the ratio of cost to replacement cost of the merchandise available for sale.	____	____
9.	Merchandise inventory is usually presented on the balance sheet immediately following receivables.	____	____
10.	If merchandise inventory at the end of the period is understated, gross profit will be overstated.	____	____

EXERCISE 7-1

Instructions: Complete the following summary, which illustrates the application of the lower-of-cost-or-market rule to individual inventory items of Unks Co.

	Quantity	Unit Cost Price	Unit Market Price	Total Cost	Total Lower of Cost or Market
Commodity A	750	$5.00	$4.80	$	$
Commodity B	460	6.00	7.00		
Commodity C	200	7.25	6.00		
Commodity D	300	4.80	4.30		
Total				$	$

EXERCISE 7-2

At the fiscal year end of October 31, 2007, the merchandise inventory was understated by $5,000. The error was discovered in 2008.

Instructions: In the spaces provided below, indicate the effect of the error on the sales, cost of merchandise sold, gross profit, net income, merchandise inventory (October 31, 2007), current assets, total assets, liabilities, and owner's equity for the year ending October 31, 2007. For each item, indicate (1) whether it is understated, overstated, or correct; and (2) the dollar amount of the error, if any.

Sales
(1) ____________________
(2) ____________________

Cost of Merchandise Sold
(1) ____________________
(2) ____________________

Gross Profit
(1) ____________________
(2) ____________________

Net Income
(1) ____________________
(2) ____________________

Merchandise Inventory (October 31, 2007)
(1) ____________________
(2) ____________________

Current Assets
(1) ____________________
(2) ____________________

Total Assets
(1) ____________________
(2) ____________________

Liabilities
(1) ____________________
(2) ____________________

Owner's Equity
(1) ____________________
(2) ____________________

PROBLEM 7-1

Hawkins Co. is a small wholesaler of hiking shoes. The accounting records show the following purchases and sales of the Mountain model during the first year of business.

A physical count of the Mountain model at the end of the year reveals that 12 are still on hand.

Purchases			
Date	Units	Price	Total Cost
Jan. 10	10	$48	$ 480
Feb. 15	100	54	5,400
July 3	65	55	3,575
Nov. 1	35	58	2,030
Total	210		$11,485

Sales	
Date	Units
Feb. 10	8
Apr. 1	95
Aug. 10	65
Nov. 15	30
	198

Instructions:

(1) Determine the cost of the Mountain model inventory as of December 31 by means of first-in, first-out (fifo) with a perpetual inventory system.

INVENTORY (Fifo Perpetual)

Date Purchased	Units	Price	Total Cost

(2) Determine the cost of the Mountain Model inventory as of December 31 by means of last-in, first-out (lifo) with a perpetual inventory system.

INVENTORY (Lifo Perpetual)

Date Purchased	Units	Price	Total Cost

(3) Determine the cost of the Mountain model inventory as of December 31 by means of first-in, first-out (fifo) with a periodic inventory system.

INVENTORY (Fifo Periodic)

Date Purchased	Units	Price	Total Cost

(4) Determine the cost of the Mountain model inventory as of December 31 by means of last-in, first-out (lifo) with a periodic inventory system.

INVENTORY (Lifo Periodic)

Date Purchased	Units	Price	Total Cost

(5) Determine the cost of the Mountain model inventory as of December 31 by means of average cost with a periodic system. (Round unit cost to two decimal places.)

INVENTORY (Average Cost)

Average unit cost = $________________________________ = $___________

______ units in the inventory @ $__________ = $______________

PROBLEM 7-2

Bartle Co. began operating on January 1 of the current year. During the year, Bartle sold 28,000 units at an average price of $80 each, and made the following purchases:

Date of Purchase	Units	Unit Price	Total Cost
January 1	5,400	$50	$ 270,000
March 1	4,100	54	221,400
June 1	4,800	56	268,800
September 1	8,400	61	512,400
November 1	5,400	69	372,600
December 1	1,900	73	138,700
	30,000		$1,783,900

Instructions: Using the periodic inventory system, determine the ending inventory, the cost of merchandise sold, and the gross profit for Bartle, using each of the following methods of inventory costing: **(1)** fifo, **(2)** lifo, and **(3)** average cost. (Round unit cost to two decimal places.)

	(1) Fifo	(2) Lifo	(3) Average Cost
Sales	$	$	$
Purchases	$ 1,783,900	$ 1,783,900	$ 1,783,900
Less ending inventory	$	$	$
Cost of merchandise sold	$	$	$
Gross profit	$	$	$

PROBLEM 7-3

APPENDIX

Knish Co. operates a department store and takes a physical inventory at the end of each calendar year. However, Knish likes to have a balance sheet and an income statement available at the end of each month in order to study financial position and operating trends. Knish estimates inventory at the end of each month for accounting statement preparation purposes. The following information is available as of August 31 of the current year:

	Cost	Retail
Merchandise inventory, August 1	$118,500	$170,000
Purchases in August	307,125	481,400
Purchases returns and allowances—August	8,000	8,900
Sales in August		493,200
Sales returns and allowances—August		14,200

Instructions:

(1) Determine the estimated cost of the inventory on August 31, using the retail method.

	Cost	Retail
Merchandise inventory, August 1	$ ______	$ ______
Purchases in August (net)	______	______
Merchandise available for sale	$ ______	$ ______

Ratio of cost to retail:

$ ______ / $ ______ = ______ %

Sales in August (net)	______
Merchandise inventory, August 31, at retail	$ ______
Merchandise inventory, August 31, at estimated cost ($______ × ______%)	$ ______

(2) Determine the estimated cost of inventory on August 31, using the gross profit method. On the basis of past experience, Knish estimates a rate of gross profit of 30% of net sales.

Merchandise inventory, August 1	$ ______
Purchases in August (net)	______
Merchandise available for sale	$ ______
Sales in August (net)	$ ______
Less estimated gross profit ($______ × ______%)	______
Estimated cost of merchandise sold	$ ______
Estimated merchandise inventory, August 31	$ ______

CHAPTER

8 Sarbanes-Oxley, Internal Control, and Cash

QUIZ AND TEST HINTS

The following hints may be helpful to you in preparing for a quiz or a test over the material covered in Chapter 8.

1. You may expect some general terminology questions (usually true/false or multiple-choice) related to Sarbanes-Oxley, internal controls, and cash. Review the "Key Terms" section at the end of the chapter and be sure you understand each term. Do the Matching and Fill-in-the-Blank exercises included in this Study Guide.
2. You should be able to prepare a bank reconciliation of the type illustrated in the chapter. Instructors often include short bank reconciliations of the type shown in the Illustrative Problem of the text and in Problem 8-1 of this Study Guide. Attempt to work the Illustrative Problem and the Study Guide Problem 8-1 without looking at the solution.
3. Be able to identify in which section of the bank reconciliation different types of reconciling items would be included. The form of the reconciliation illustrated on page 368 may be a helpful study aid. Have a friend read off the reconciling items from the chapter illustration of the bank reconciliation on page 370, and identify whether the item would appear in the section of the reconciliation beginning with "Cash balance according to bank statement" or the section beginning with "Cash balance according to company's records."

   Note that sometimes instructors may refer to the "Cash balance according to bank statement" as the "Balance per bank" and "Cash balance according to company's records" as "Balance per books."
4. You should be able to prepare journal entries to establish and replenish cash funds, including cash change funds and petty cash. In replenishing such funds, the cash short and over account may need to be debited (short) or credited (over).
5. You should read over and be generally familiar with the presentation of cash on the balance sheet.

6. Review the GPS graphic at the beginning of the chapter and the "At A Glance" section at the end of the chapter. Read and review each of the Key Points and related Learning Outcomes. For each Learning Outcome that has an Example Exercise, locate the Example Exercise in the chapter and be sure that you understand the solution and can work a similar item on a test. If you have any questions about an Example Exercise, read the section of the chapter immediately preceding the Example Exercise.
7. If your instructor covers the Financial Analysis and Interpretation item at the end of the chapter, you should know how to compute and interpret changes in the ratio of cash to monthly cash expenses.

MATCHING

Instructions: Match each of the statements below with its proper term. Some terms may not be used.

- **A.** bank reconciliation
- **B.** bank statement
- **C.** cash
- **D.** cash equivalents
- **E.** cash receipts journal
- **F.** cash short and over account
- **G.** Clinton-Gore Act of 2002
- **H.** compensating balance
- **I.** doomsday ratio
- **J.** electronic funds transfer (EFT)
- **K.** elements of internal control
- **L.** employee fraud
- **M.** internal control
- **N.** notes receivable
- **O.** petty cash fund
- **P.** ratio of cash to monthly cash expenses
- **Q.** Sarbanes-Oxley Act of 2002
- **R.** voucher
- **S.** voucher system

____ **1.** A law passed by Congress in response to the financial frauds and scandals of the early 2000s.

____ **2.** Provides assurance that assets are safeguarded, business information is accurate, and employees comply with laws.

____ **3.** The control environment, risk assessment, control activities, information and communication, and monitoring.

____ **4.** An intentional act of deceiving an employer for personal gain.

____ **5.** Coins, currency (paper money), checks, money orders, and money on deposit that is available for unrestricted withdrawal from banks and other financial institutions.

____ **6.** A set of procedures for authorizing and recording liabilities and cash payments.

____ **7.** A special form for recording relevant data about a liability and the details of its payment.

____ **8.** A system in which computers rather than paper (money, checks, etc.) are used to effect cash transactions.

____ **9.** The analysis that details the items responsible for the difference between the cash balance reported in the bank statement and the balance of the cash account in the ledger.

____ **10.** A special cash fund to pay relatively small amounts.

____ **11.** Highly liquid investments that are usually reported with cash on the balance sheet.

____ **12.** A minimum balance that banks require companies to maintain in their bank accounts.

____ **13.** A ratio that is useful for assessing how long a company can continue to operate without additional financing or without generating positive cash flows from operations.

Fill in the Blank—Part A

Instructions: Answer the following questions or complete the statements by writing the appropriate words or amounts in the answer blanks.

1. Coins, currency (paper money), checks, money orders, and money on deposit that are available for unrestricted withdrawal from banks and other financial institutions are reported in the financial statements as ________________.
2. Most companies' invoices are designed so that customers return a portion of the invoice called a(n) ____________________ _______________.
3. A(n) __________________ system is a set of procedures for authorizing and recording liabilities and cash payments.
4. Vouchers are ordinarily filed in the unpaid voucher file in order of _________ date.
5. A(n) ____________________ _________ _______________ system uses computers rather than paper (money, checks, etc.) to effect cash transactions.
6. A(n) __________ ________________________ details the items responsible for the difference between the cash balance reported in the bank statement and the balance of the cash account in the ledger.
7. In a bank reconciliation, a bank debit memorandum for a customer's check returned because of insufficient funds is ___________________ ________ the cash balance according to the company's records.
8. In a bank reconciliation, checks outstanding are ____________________ ________ the cash balance according to the bank statement.
9. A company erroneously recorded a check issued for $180 as $810. On the bank reconciliation, the difference of $630 would be added to the cash balance according to the ____________________ __________________.
10. Minimum cash balances that banks require companies to maintain in their bank accounts are called _____________ balances.

Fill in the Blank—Part B

Instructions: Answer the following questions or complete the statements by writing the appropriate words or amounts in the answer blanks.

1. The control environment is an ____________________ of internal control.
2. At the beginning of a work shift, each cash register clerk is given a cash drawer that contains a predetermined amount of cash. The amount of cash in each drawer is called a(n) ________________ fund.

3. If Cash Short and Over has a credit balance at the end of the period, the balance would be reported on the income statement in the section entitled ______________ ________________.

4. A(n) ________________ is a special form for recording relevant data about a liability and the details of its payment.

5. A voucher for the purchase of goods is normally supported by the supplier's invoice, a purchase order, and a(n) __________________ ________________.

6. A(n) ____________ __________ fund is used to pay relatively small amounts.

7. In a bank reconciliation, a bank credit memorandum for a note receivable collected by the bank is ___________________ ________ the cash balance according to the company's records.

8. In a bank reconciliation, deposits in transit are ___________________ ________ the cash balance according to the bank statement.

9. In a bank reconciliation, a bank debit memorandum for service charges is ___________________ ________ the cash balance according to the company's records.

10. A company may invest excess cash in highly liquid investments called __________ _____________ to earn interest.

MULTIPLE CHOICE

Instructions: Circle the best answer for each of the following questions.

1. For good internal control over cash receipts, remittance advices should be separated from cash received by mail and sent directly to the:
   - **a.** treasurer
   - **b.** cashier's department
   - **c.** accounting department
   - **d.** voucher clerk

2. An important characteristic of the voucher system is the requirement that:
   - **a.** vouchers be prepared by the treasurer
   - **b.** vouchers be paid immediately after they are prepared
   - **c.** paid vouchers are filed by due date
   - **d.** a voucher be prepared for each major expenditure

3. In a bank reconciliation, an NSF (not-sufficient-funds) check is:
   - **a.** added to the balance according to the bank statement
   - **b.** deducted from the balance according to the bank statement
   - **c.** added to the balance according to the company's records
   - **d.** deducted from the balance according to the company's records

4. In a bank reconciliation, deposits not recorded by the bank are:
   a. added to the balance according to the bank statement
   b. deducted from the balance according to the bank statement
   c. added to the balance according to the company's records
   d. deducted from the balance according to the company's records
5. The amount of the outstanding checks is included on the bank reconciliation as:
   a. an addition to the balance per bank statement
   b. a deduction from the balance per bank statement
   c. an addition to the balance per company's records
   d. a deduction from the balance per company's records
6. Receipts from cash sales of $7,500 were recorded incorrectly as $5,700. What entry is required in the depositor's accounts?
   a. debit Cash; credit Accounts Receivable
   b. debit Cash; credit Sales
   c. debit Accounts Receivable; credit Cash
   d. debit Sales; credit Cash
7. Accompanying the bank statement was a credit memorandum for a short-term, non-interest-bearing note collected by the bank. What entry is required in the company's accounts?
   a. debit Cash; credit Miscellaneous Income
   b. debit Cash; credit Notes Receivable
   c. debit Accounts Receivable; credit Cash
   d. debit Notes Receivable; credit Cash
8. What entry is required in the company's accounts to record outstanding checks?
   a. debit Cash; credit Accounts Payable
   b. debit Accounts Receivable; credit Cash
   c. debit Accounts Payable; credit Cash
   d. No entry is required.
9. Journal entries based on the bank reconciliation are required on the company's books for:
   a. additions to the balance according to the company's records
   b. deductions from the balance according to the company's records
   c. both a and b
   d. both additions to and deductions from the balance according to the bank's records

10. The entry to record the replenishment of the petty cash fund includes a debit to various expense and asset accounts and a credit to:

a. Cash

b. Petty Cash

c. Accounts Receivable

d. various liability accounts

TRUE/FALSE

Instructions: Indicate whether each of the following statements is true or false by placing a check mark in the appropriate column.

	True	False
1. The Sarbanes-Oxley Act of 2002 was passed by Congress because of a public outcry related to financial frauds and scandals.	____	____
2. Internal controls are guaranteed to prevent employee theft and misuse of assets.	____	____
3. In a bank reconciliation, checks issued that have not been paid by the bank are added to the balance according to the bank statement.	____	____
4. Bank memorandums not recorded by the company require entries in the company's accounts.	____	____
5. For a greater degree of internal control, the bank reconciliation should be prepared by an employee who does not engage in or record cash transactions with the bank.	____	____
6. If there is a debit balance in the cash short and over account at the end of the fiscal period, this represents income to be included in "Miscellaneous general income" in the income statement.	____	____
7. It is common practice for businesses to require that every payment of cash be evidenced by a check signed by the owner.	____	____
8. After vouchers are paid, it is customary to file them in numerical sequence in the paid voucher file.	____	____
9. Petty Cash should be debited when the petty cash fund is replenished.	____	____
10. A voucher system is a set of methods and procedures for authorizing and recording liabilities and cash payments.	____	____

Exercise 8-1

A comparison of the bank statement and the accompanying canceled checks and memorandums with the records of Pearl Co. for the month of September of the current year revealed the following reconciling items:

(1) A check drawn for $25 had been erroneously charged by the bank for $250.

(2) The bank collected $1,920 on a note left for collection. The face of the note was $1,800.

(3) Bank service charges for September totaled $28.

(4) Check No. 231, written to Stanley Optical Warehouse for $2,500, and Check No. 236, written to Stella's Janitorial Service for $100, were outstanding.

(5) A deposit of $5,250 made on September 30 was not recorded on the bank statement.

(6) A canceled check for $1,100, returned with the bank statement, had been recorded erroneously in the check register as $1,000. The check was a payment on account to Charlie's Optical Supply.

Instructions: In the following general journal, prepare any necessary entries that Pearl Co. should make as a result of these reconciling items. The accounts have not been closed.

JOURNAL PAGE

	DATE		DESCRIPTION	POST. REF.	DEBIT	CREDIT	
1							1
2							2
3							3
4							4
5							5
6							6
7							7
8							8
9							9
10							10
11							11
12							12
13							13
14							14
15							15
16							16
17							17
18							18

EXERCISE 8-2

Instructions: In the general journal provided below, prepare the entries to record the following transactions:

(1) Established a petty cash fund of $400.

(2) Replenished the fund, based on the following summary of petty cash receipts. (The amount of cash in the fund is now $128.34.)
Office supplies, $80.25
Miscellaneous selling expense, $115.33
Miscellaneous administrative expense, $78.05

JOURNAL PAGE

DATE		DESCRIPTION	POST. REF.	DEBIT	CREDIT

PROBLEM 8-1

On September 30 of the current year, Dumont Co.'s checkbook showed a balance of $7,540, and the bank statement showed a balance of $8,510. A comparison of the bank statement and Dumont's records as of September 30 revealed the following:

(a) A deposit of $1,900, mailed to the bank by Dumont on September 29, was not included in the bank statement of September 30.

(b) The following checks were outstanding: Check No. 255 for $325, Check No. 280 for $100, Check No. 295 for $700.

(c) Check No. 289 in payment of a voucher had been written for $140 and had been recorded at that amount by the bank. However, Dumont had recorded it in the check register as $410.

(d) A check for $910 received from a customer was deposited in the bank. The bank recorded it at the correct amount, but Dumont recorded it at $190.

(e) Included with the bank statement was a credit memorandum for $780, representing the proceeds of a $700 note receivable left at the bank for collection. This had not been recorded on Dumont's books.

(f) Included with the bank statement was a debit memorandum for $25 for service charges that had not been recorded on Dumont's books.

Instructions:

(1) Complete the bank reconciliation below.

(2) In the general journal on the following page, prepare the entry or entries that Dumont should make as a result of the bank reconciliation.

Dumont Co.
Bank Reconciliation
September 30, 20--

Balance according to bank statement	$
Add:	
Deduct:	
Adjusted balance	$
Balance according to company's records	$
Add:	
Deduct:	
Adjusted balance	$

(2) **JOURNAL** PAGE

DATE		DESCRIPTION	POST. REF.	DEBIT	CREDIT

CHAPTER

9 Receivables

QUIZ AND TEST HINTS

The following hints may be helpful to you in preparing for a quiz or a test over the material covered in Chapter 9.

1. You should be able to prepare journal entries for writing off an uncollectible account receivable and reinstating the account if it is later collected. You should be able to prepare these entries for both the direct write-off method and the allowance method of accounting for uncollectible accounts. You should also be able to describe and explain the differences between these two methods of accounting for uncollectible accounts, including when it is acceptable to use the direct write-off method.
2. You should be able to determine the amount of the adjusting entry for uncollectible receivables (the allowance method) for both estimation methods presented in the chapter (percent of sales and analysis of receivables). Note that the percent of sales method is the easiest to use since the amount of the entry is the same as the estimate of the uncollectible sales. The analysis of receivables method requires the entry to be made for an amount that will result in the estimated balance of the allowance account.
3. You should be able to determine the due date, interest, and maturity value of a note receivable. You should also be able to prepare journal entries for the receipt and collection of a note receivable.
4. You may be tested on a problem requiring a series of general journal entries that encompass both uncollectible accounts receivable and notes receivable. The materials presented in this Study Guide and the Illustrative Problem in the text provide an excellent review.
5. Study the new terminology introduced in this chapter for possible multiple-choice, matching, or true/false questions. Review the "Key Terms" section at the end of the chapter and be sure you understand each term. Do the Matching and Fill-in-the-Blank exercises included in this Study Guide.
6. Review the GPS graphic at the beginning of the chapter and the "At A Glance" section at the end of the chapter. Read and review each of the Key Points and related Learning Outcomes. For each Learning Outcome that has an Example Exercise, locate the Example Exercise in the chapter and be sure that you understand the solution and can work a similar item on a test.

If you have any questions about an Example Exercise, read the section of the chapter immediately preceding the Example Exercise.

7. If your instructor covers the Financial Analysis and Interpretation item at the end of the chapter, you should know how to compute and interpret changes in the accounts receivable turnover and days' sales in receivables ratios.

8. If your instructor covers Appendix 1, Discounting Notes Receivable, you should be able to compute the proceeds from discounting a notes receivable. You should also be able to prepare the journal entries for discounting a note and the journal entries if a discounted note is dishonored. Study and review the illustrations in Appendix 1 in preparation for such test questions.

MATCHING

Instructions: Match each of the statements below with its proper term. Some terms may not be used.

A.	accounts receivable	**H.**	dishonored note receivable
B.	accounts receivable turnover	**I.**	maturity value
C.	aging the receivables	**J.**	notes receivable
D.	allowance method	**K.**	number of days' sales in receivables
E.	bad debt expense	**L.**	promissory note
F.	contra asset	**M.**	receivables
G.	direct write-off method		

____ **1.** All money claims against other entities, including people, business firms, and other organizations.

____ **2.** A receivable created by selling merchandise or services on credit.

____ **3.** Amounts customers owe, for which a formal, written instrument of credit has been issued.

____ **4.** The operating expense incurred because of the failure to collect receivables.

____ **5.** The method of accounting for uncollectible accounts that provides an expense for uncollectible receivables in advance of their write-off.

____ **6.** The method of accounting for uncollectible accounts that recognizes the expense only when accounts are judged to be worthless.

____ **7.** The process of analyzing the accounts receivable and classifying them according to various age groupings, with the due date being the base point for determining age.

____ **8.** The amount that is due at the maturity or due date of a note.

____ **9.** A note that the maker fails to pay on the due date.

____ **10.** An estimate of the length of time the accounts receivable have been outstanding.

____ **11.** Measures how frequently during the year the accounts receivable are being converted to cash.

____ **12.** A written promise to pay a sum of money on demand or at a definite time.

FILL IN THE BLANK—PART A

Instructions: Answer the following questions or complete the statements by writing the appropriate words or amounts in the answer blanks.

1. All money claims against other entities, including people, business firms, and other organizations are called ____________________.
2. A(n) __________ ____________________ is a formal, written instrument of credit that has been received for the amount a customer owes.
3. The ____________________ method of accounting for uncollectible accounts provides an expense for uncollectible receivables in advance of their write-off.
4. The ____________ ______ ____________________ is a process of analyzing the accounts receivable and classifying them according to various age groupings, with the due date being the base point for determining age.
5. Allowance for Doubtful Accounts has a debit balance of $1,500 at the end of the year, before adjustments. Sales for the year amounted to $740,000, and sales returns and allowances amounted to $25,000. If uncollectible accounts expense is estimated at 1% of net sales, the amount of the appropriate adjusting entry will be ______________.
6. Allowance for Doubtful Accounts has a debit balance of $2,500 at the end of the year, before adjustments. Sales for the year amounted to $950,000, and sales returns and allowances amounted to $20,000. If the analysis of the accounts in the customers' ledger indicates doubtful accounts of $30,000, the amount of the appropriate adjusting entry will be ______________.
7. The maturity value of a $300,000, 90-day, 12% note receivable is ______________.
8. The due date of a 90-day note receivable dated July 12 is ____________________.
9. A note that the maker fails to pay on the due date is referred to as a(n) ____________________ note.
10. ________________ ____________________ ________________ measures how frequently during the year the accounts receivable are being converted to cash.

FILL IN THE BLANK—PART B

Instructions: Answer the following questions or complete the statements by writing the appropriate words or amounts in the answer blanks.

1. A(n) ________________ receivable is created by selling merchandise or services on credit.
2. The operating expense incurred because of the failure to collect receivables is recorded as ______________________ _________________ expense.
3. The _______________ ______________-_______ method of accounting for uncollectible accounts recognizes an expense only when accounts are judged to be worthless.
4. At the end of the fiscal year, after the accounts are closed, Accounts Receivable has a balance of $350,000 and Allowance for Doubtful Accounts has a credit balance of $40,000. The expected realizable value of the receivables is ________________.
5. Allowance for Doubtful Accounts has a credit balance of $800 at the end of the year, before adjustments. If an analysis of receivables indicates doubtful accounts of $11,200, the amount of the appropriate adjusting entry is ________________.
6. The amount that is due at the maturity or due date of a note is called the __________________ _____________.
7. The maturity value of a $150,000, 60-day, 15% note receivable is ________________.
8. The due date of a 120-day note receivable dated on August 18 is ______________________.
9. The ________________ ______ __________ __________ ______ __________________________ is an estimate of the length of time the accounts receivable have been outstanding, expressed in days.
10. A written promise to pay a sum of money on demand or at a definite time is called a(n) ____________________ note.

MULTIPLE CHOICE

Instructions: Circle the best answer for each of the following questions.

1. When the allowance method is used in accounting for uncollectible accounts, any uncollectible account is written off against the:
   a. allowance account
   b. sales account
   c. accounts receivable account
   d. bad debt expense account

2. When the direct write-off method is used in accounting for uncollectible accounts, any uncollectible account is written off against the:
   a. allowance account
   b. sales account
   c. accounts receivable account
   d. bad debt expense account

3. What is the type of account and normal balance of Allowance for Doubtful Accounts?
   a. asset, debit
   b. asset, credit
   c. contra asset, debit
   d. contra asset, credit

4. Assume that the allowance account has a credit balance of $170 at the end of the year, before adjustments. If the estimate of uncollectible accounts based on aging the receivables is $3,010, the amount of the adjusting entry for uncollectible accounts would be:
   a. $170
   b. $2,840
   c. $3,010
   d. $3,180

5. Assume that the allowance account has a debit balance of $250 at the end of the year, before adjustments. If the estimate of uncollectible accounts based on sales for the period is $2,200, the amount of the adjusting entry for uncollectible accounts would be:
   a. $250
   b. $1,950
   c. $2,200
   d. $2,450

6. After the accounts are adjusted and closed at the end of the fiscal year, Accounts Receivable has a balance of $430,000 and Allowance for Doubtful Accounts has a balance of $25,000. What is the expected realizable value of the accounts receivable?
   a. $25,000
   b. $405,000
   c. $430,000
   d. $455,000
7. On a promissory note, the one making the promise to pay is called the:
   a. payee
   b. creditor
   c. maker
   d. noter
8. The amount that is due on a note at the maturity or due date is called the:
   a. terminal value
   b. face value
   c. book value
   d. maturity value
9. The due date of a 90-day note dated July 1 is:
   a. September 28
   b. September 29
   c. September 30
   d. October 1
10. A 60-day, 12% note for $15,000, dated May 1, is received from a customer on account. The maturity value of the note is:
    a. $14,700
    b. $15,000
    c. $15,300
    d. $16,200

TRUE/FALSE

Instructions: Indicate whether each of the following statements is true or false by placing a check mark in the appropriate column.

	Statement	True	False
1.	The method of accounting which provides in advance for receivables deemed uncollectible is called the allowance method.	____	____
2.	The process of analyzing the receivable accounts in order to estimate the uncollectibles is sometimes called aging the receivables.	____	____
3.	The direct write-off method of accounting for uncollectible receivables provides for uncollectible accounts in the year of sale.	____	____
4.	Estimation of uncollectible accounts based on the analysis of receivables emphasizes the current net realizable value of the receivables.	____	____
5.	The allowance method of accounting for uncollectible receivables emphasizes the matching of bad debt expense with the related sales.	____	____
6.	The term *notes* includes all money claims against people, organizations, or other debtors.	____	____
7.	Accounts and notes receivable originating from sales transactions are sometimes called trade receivables.	____	____
8.	Companies with a large amount of receivables normally use the allowance method of accounting for uncollectible accounts.	____	____
9.	When a note is received from a customer from a previous sale on account, it is recorded by debiting Notes Receivable and crediting Sales.	____	____
10.	Jacob Co. issues a 90-day, 12% note on May 13; the due date of the note is August 11.	____	____

EXERCISE 9-1

Coco Co. uses the direct write-off method of accounting for uncollectibles. On August 31, 20--, Coco deemed that an amount of $550 due from Don Shore was uncollectible and wrote it off. On October 8, 20--, Shore paid the $550.

Instructions:

(1) Prepare the entry to write off the account on August 31.

(2) Prepare the entry to reinstate the account on October 8, and to record the cash received.

JOURNAL

PAGE

	DATE		DESCRIPTION	POST. REF.	DEBIT	CREDIT	
1							1
2							2
3							3
4							4
5							5
6							6
7							7
8							8
9							9
10							10
11							11
12							12
13							13
14							14
15							15
16							16
17							17
18							18
19							19
20							20

Exercise 9-2

Star Co. uses the allowance method of accounting for uncollectibles. On March 31, 20--, Star deemed that an amount of $3,150 due from Jane Eades was uncollectible and wrote it off. On May 8, 20--, Eades paid the $3,150.

Instructions:

(1) Prepare the entry to write off the account on March 31.

(2) Prepare the entry to reinstate the account on May 8, and to record the cash received.

JOURNAL

PAGE

	DATE		DESCRIPTION	POST. REF.	DEBIT	CREDIT	
1							1
2							2
3							3
4							4
5							5
6							6
7							7
8							8
9							9
10							10
11							11
12							12
13							13
14							14
15							15
16							16
17							17
18							18
19							19
20							20

EXERCISE 9-3

Instructions: Using the basic formula for interest and assuming a 360-day year, compute the interest on the following notes.

1. $8,000 at 12% for 30 days .... $ ________
2. $3,500 at 6% for 60 days .... $ ________
3. $2,000 at 12% for 90 days .... $ ________
4. $8,000 at 9% for 30 days .... $ ________
5. $7,500 at 6% for 60 days .... $ ________
6. $12,000 for 90 days at 9% .... $ ________
7. $5,250 for 120 days at 12% .... $ ________

EXERCISE 9-4

The following data regarding the current assets of Walton Company were selected from the accounting records after adjustment at the end of the current fiscal year:

Accounts Receivable	$35,000
Allowance for Doubtful Accounts	1,200
Cash	37,500
Interest Receivable	9,900
Notes Receivable	20,000

Instructions: Prepare the Current Assets section of the balance sheet for Walton Company.

PROBLEM 9-1

Instructions: Prepare the appropriate general journal entries for each of the following situations.

(1) Net sales for the year are $800,000, bad debt expense is estimated at 3% of net sales, and the allowance account has a $425 credit balance before adjustment. Prepare the adjusting entry at year end for the uncollectibles.

(2) Based on an analysis of accounts in the customers' ledger, estimated uncollectible accounts total $6,280, and the allowance account has a $325 credit balance before adjustment. Prepare the adjusting entry at year end for the uncollectibles.

(3) A $3,500 account receivable from Bentley Co. is written off as uncollectible. The allowance method is used.

(4) A $1,235 account receivable from Apple Co., which was written off three months earlier, is collected in full. The allowance method is used.

JOURNAL PAGE

	DATE		DESCRIPTION	POST. REF.	DEBIT	CREDIT	
1							1
2							2
3							3
4							4
5							5
6							6
7							7
8							8
9							9
10							10
11							11
12							12
13							13
14							14
15							15
16							16
17							17
18							18
19							19
20							20
21							21

PROBLEM 9-2

Instructions: Prepare the general journal entries to record the following transactions. (Omit explanations.)

(1) Pequot Co. received a 60-day, 12% note for $8,000 from a customer, Dave Davidson, in settlement of Davidson's account.

(2) Davidson failed to pay the note in (1) at maturity.

(3) Ten days after the maturity of the note in (1), Davidson paid Pequot in full, including interest at 11% for this 10-day period.

(4) Pequot received a 90-day, 10% note for $3,000 from a customer, Sue Smith, in settlement of Smith's account.

(5) The note in (4) was dishonored at maturity.

JOURNAL

PAGE

	DATE		DESCRIPTION	POST. REF.	DEBIT	CREDIT	
1							1
2							2
3							3
4							4
5							5
6							6
7							7
8							8
9							9
10							10
11							11
12							12
13							13
14							14
15							15
16							16
17							17
18							18
19							19
20							20
21							21
22							22
23							23
24							24

CHAPTER

10 Fixed Assets and Intangible Assets

Quiz and Test Hints

The following hints may be helpful to you in preparing for a quiz or a test over the material covered in Chapter 10.

1. The chapter emphasizes the computation of depreciation. You should be able to compute depreciation using each of the three methods: straight-line, units-of-production, and double-declining-balance. If your instructor lectures on the sum-of-the-years-digits method of depreciation in the appendix to the chapter, you should also be prepared to compute depreciation under this method.
2. A common question on quizzes and tests involves the recording of fixed asset disposals. You should be able to prepare general journal entries for disposals, including the sale of fixed assets.
3. The chapter introduces a significant amount of new terminology. These terms lend themselves to numerous multiple-choice and matching questions. Review the "Key Terms" section at the end of the chapter and be sure you understand each term. Do the Matching and Fill-in-the-Blank exercises included in this Study Guide.
4. You should expect some questions on depletion of natural resources. The computation of depletion is relatively simple and is similar to the units-of-production depreciation method. This section of the chapter lends itself to multiple-choice and true-false questions.
5. You should expect some questions related to intangible assets. The computation of amortization of patents is relatively simple, and it is similar to the straight-line depreciation method. Copyrights, trademarks, and goodwill are not amortized, but are written down for impairments. This section of the chapter lends itself to multiple-choice and true-false questions.
6. Review the GPS graphic at the beginning of the chapter and the "At A Glance" section at the end of the chapter. Read and review each of the Key Points and related Learning Outcomes. For each Learning Outcome that has an Example Exercise, locate the Example Exercise in the chapter and be sure that you understand the solution and can work a similar item on a test. If you have any questions about an Example Exercise, read the section of the chapter immediately preceding the Example Exercise.

7. If your instructor covers the Financial Analysis and Interpretation item at the end of the chapter, you should know how to compute and interpret changes in the fixed asset turnover ratio.

8. If your instructor covers Appendix 2, Exchanging Similar Fixed Assets, you should be able to prepare journal entries for exchanges of similar assets that have economic substance. Study and review the illustrations in Appendix 2 in preparation for such test questions.

MATCHING

Instructions: Match each of the statements below with its proper term. Some terms may not be used.

A. accelerated depreciation method
B. amortization
C. book value
D. capital expenditures
E. capital leases
F. copyright
G. depletion
H. depreciation
I. double-declining-balance method
J. fixed asset turnover ratio
K. fixed assets
L. goodwill
M. intangible assets
N. operating leases
O. patents
P. ratio of fixed assets to total assets
Q. residual value
R. revenue expenditures
S. straight-line method
T. trademark
U. units-of-production method

____ **1.** Long-term or relatively permanent tangible assets that are used in the normal business operations.

____ **2.** The systematic periodic transfer of the cost of a fixed asset to an expense account during its expected useful life.

____ **3.** The estimated value of a fixed asset at the end of its useful life.

____ **4.** A method of depreciation that provides for equal periodic depreciation expense over the estimated life of a fixed asset.

____ **5.** A method of depreciation that provides for depreciation expense based on the expected productive capacity of a fixed asset.

____ **6.** A method of depreciation that provides periodic depreciation expense based on the declining book value of a fixed asset over its estimated life.

____ **7.** The cost of a fixed asset minus accumulated depreciation on the asset.

____ **8.** A depreciation method that provides for a higher depreciation amount in the first year of the asset's use, followed by a gradually declining amount of depreciation.

____ **9.** The costs of acquiring fixed assets, adding to a fixed asset, improving a fixed asset, or extending a fixed asset's useful life.

____ **10.** Costs that benefit only the current period or costs incurred for normal maintenance and repairs of fixed assets.

____ **11.** Leases that include one or more provisions that result in treating the leased assets as purchased assets in the accounts.

____ **12.** Leases that do not meet the criteria for capital leases and thus are accounted for as operating expenses.

____ **13.** The process of transferring the cost of natural resources to an expense account.

____ **14.** Long-term assets that are useful in the operations of a business, are not held for sale, and are without physical qualities.

____ **15.** The periodic transfer of the cost of an intangible asset to expense.

____ **16.** An intangible asset that is created from such favorable factors as location, product quality, reputation, and managerial skill.

____ **17.** Exclusive rights to produce and sell goods with one or more unique features.

____ **18.** An exclusive right to publish and sell a literary, artistic, or musical composition.

____ **19.** A name, term, or symbol used to identify a business and its products.

____ **20.** A financial ratio that provides a measure indicating the ability of a company to generate revenues from its fixed assets.

FILL IN THE BLANK—PART A

Instructions: Answer the following questions or complete the statements by writing the appropriate words or amounts in the answer blanks.

1. Long-term or relatively permanent tangible assets that are used in the normal business operation are called ____________ assets.
2. Surveying fees incurred in connection with securing title of land for use by a business is debited to the ____________ account.
3. The cost of a special foundation incurred in connection with the acquisition of a secondhand machine would be debited to the ______________ account.
4. The estimated value of a fixed asset at the end of its useful life is called ______________ value.
5. The __________-______-____________________ method is a method of depreciation that provides for depreciation expense based on the expected productive capacity of a fixed asset.
6. The cost of a fixed asset minus accumulated depreciation on the asset is called the ____________ value.
7. A useful life of 4 years is equivalent to a straight-line depreciation rate of __________.
8. Equipment acquired on the first day of the current fiscal year for $50,000 has an estimated life of 4 years or 25,000 hours and a residual value of $5,000. Depreciation for the current year using the straight-line method is ______________.

9. Equipment acquired on the first day of the current fiscal year for $50,000 has an estimated life of 4 years or 25,000 hours and a residual value of $5,000. Depreciation for the current year using the double-declining-balance method is ______________.

10. Equipment acquired on the first day of the current fiscal year for $50,000 has an estimated life of 4 years or 25,000 hours and a residual value of $5,000. The equipment was used for 7,000 hours during the current year. Depreciation for the current year using the units-of-production method is ______________.

11. The costs of acquiring fixed assets, adding to a fixed asset, improving a fixed asset, or extending a fixed asset's useful life are called ______________ expenditures.

12. Costs that benefit only the current period or costs incurred for normal maintenance and repairs are called ______________ ______________________.

13. ________________ leases treat the leased assets as purchased assets for the accounts.

14. The process of transferring the cost of natural resources to an expense account is called ____________________.

15. ______________________________ is the periodic transfer of a cost of an intangible asset to expense.

16. ____________________ are exclusive rights to produce and sell goods with one or more unique features.

17. The cost of a patent is amortized by debiting Amortization Expense—Patents and crediting ____________________.

18. A name, term, or symbol used to identify a business and its products is called a(n) ______________________.

Fill in the Blank—Part B

Instructions: Answer the following questions or complete the statements by writing the appropriate words or amounts in the answer blanks.

1. The cost of razing an unwanted building on land purchased for use by a business is debited to the _____________ account.

2. The systematic, periodic transfer of the cost of a fixed asset to expense during its expected useful life is called ______________________.

3. The __________________-_______________ method is a method of depreciation that provides for equal periodic depreciation expense over the estimated life of a fixed asset.

4. The ____________ ____________-____________ method is a method of depreciation that provides declining periodic depreciation expense over the estimated life of a fixed asset.

5. A useful life of 5 years is equivalent to a straight-line depreciation rate of __________.

6. Equipment acquired on the first day of the current fiscal year for $80,000 has an estimated life of 5 years or 25,000 hours and a residual value of $10,000. Depreciation for the current year using the straight-line method is ____________.

7. Equipment acquired on the first day of the current fiscal year for $80,000 has an estimated life of 5 years or 25,000 hours and a residual value of $10,000. Depreciation for the current year using the double-declining-balance method is ____________.

8. Equipment acquired on the first day of the current fiscal year for $80,000 has an estimated life of 5 years or 25,000 hours and a residual value of $10,000. The equipment was used for 6,000 hours during the current year. Depreciation for the current year using the units-of-production method is ____________.

9. Depreciation methods that provide for a higher depreciation amount in the first year of the asset's use, followed by a gradually declining amount of depreciation, are referred to as ____________ depreciation methods.

10. Costs that benefit only the current period or costs incurred for normal maintenance and repairs of fixed assets are called ____________ expenditures.

11. The costs of acquiring fixed assets, adding to a fixed asset, improving a fixed asset, or extending a fixed asset's useful life are called ____________ ____________.

12. ____________ leases do not meet the criteria for capital leases and thus are accounted for as operating expenses.

13. Long-term assets that are useful in the operations of a business, are not held for sale, and are without physical qualities are called ____________ assets.

14. ____________ is an intangible asset of a business that is created from such favorable factors as location, product quality, reputation, and managerial skill.

15. A(n) ____________ is an exclusive right to publish and sell a literary, artistic, or musical composition.

16. Depletion expense related to a mineral ore deposit is recorded by debiting Depletion Expense and crediting ____________ ____________.

17. Research and development costs are normally accounted for as _______________ _____________________ _______________ in the period in which they are incurred.

18. The ____________ ____________ ______ ratio provides a measure of the revenue-generating efficiency of fixed assets.

MULTIPLE CHOICE

Instructions: Circle the best answer for each of the following questions.

1. If unwanted buildings are located on land acquired for a plant site, the cost of their removal, less any salvage recovered, should be charged to the:
   a. expense accounts
   b. building account
   c. land account
   d. accumulated depreciation account

2. The depreciation method used most often in the financial statements is the:
   a. straight-line method
   b. double-declining-balance method
   c. units-of-production method
   d. MACRS method

3. The depreciation method that would provide the highest reported net income in the early years of an asset's life would be:
   a. straight-line
   b. double-declining-balance
   c. MACRS
   d. units of production

4. Equipment with an estimated useful life of 5 years and an estimated residual value of $1,000 is acquired at a cost of $15,000. Using the double-declining-balance method, what is the amount of depreciation for the first year of use of the equipment?
   a. $2,600
   b. $3,000
   c. $5,600
   d. $6,000

5. Equipment that cost $20,000 was originally estimated to have a useful life of 5 years and a residual value of $2,000. The equipment has been depreciated for 2 years using straight-line depreciation. During the third year it is estimated that the remaining useful life is 2 years (instead of 3) and that the residual value is $1,000 (instead of $2,000). The depreciation expense on the equipment in year 3 using the straight-line method would be:
   a. $5,500
   b. $5,900
   c. $6,000
   d. $7,500
6. Assume that a drill press is rebuilt during its sixth year of use so that its useful life is extended 5 years beyond the original estimate of 10 years. In this case, the cost of rebuilding the drill press is:
   a. a revenue expenditure
   b. a capital expenditure
   c. a contra-expense
   d. an expense
7. Equipment was purchased on January 3, 2008, for $100,000 and was depreciated using the straight-line method based upon an 8-year life and $12,000 residual value. The equipment was sold on December 31, 2012, for $40,000. What is the gain on the sale of the equipment?
   a. $5,000
   b. $11,000
   c. $45,000
   d. $55,000
8. Rights to a mineral deposit estimated at 50,000,000 tons were acquired for $45,000,000. During the year, 20,000,000 tones were mined. The depletion for the year is:
   a. $9,000,000
   b. $18,000,000
   c. $20,000,000
   d. $45,000,000
9. In a lease contract, the party who legally owns the asset is the:
   a. contractor
   b. operator
   c. lessee
   d. lessor

10. Which of the following items would not be considered an intangible asset?
   a. mineral ore deposits
   b. patent
   c. copyright
   d. goodwill

TRUE/FALSE

Instructions: Indicate whether each of the following statements is true or false by placing a check mark in the appropriate column.

	True	False
1. The double-declining-balance method provides for a higher depreciation charge in the first year of use of the asset, followed by a gradually declining periodic charge.	____	____
2. The method of depreciation which yields a depreciation charge that varies with the amount of asset usage is known as the units-of-production method.	____	____
3. In using the double-declining-balance method, the asset should not be depreciated below the net book value.	____	____
4. Accelerated depreciation methods are most appropriate for situations in which the decline in productivity or earning power of the asset is proportionately greater in the early years of its use than in later years.	____	____
5. MACRS depreciation methods permit the use of asset lives that are often much shorter than the actual useful life.	____	____
6. When a fixed asset is sold, proper accounting treatment prohibits recognition of a gain or loss.	____	____
7. A lease that transfers ownership of the leased asset to the lessee at the end of the lease term should be classified as an operating lease.	____	____
8. Long-lived assets that are without physical characteristics but useful in the operations of a business are classified as fixed assets.	____	____
9. Fully depreciated assets should be retained in the accounting records until disposal has been authorized and they are removed from service.	____	____
10. Intangible assets are usually reported on the balance sheet in the current asset section.	____	____

EXERCISE 10-1

A fixed asset acquired on January 2 at a cost of $420,000 has an estimated useful life of 8 years. Assuming that it will have a residual value of $20,000, determine the depreciation for each of the first two years (a) by the straight-line method and (b) by the double-declining-balance method.

(a) Straight-line method	Depreciation
Year 1	____________
Year 2	____________

(b) Double-declining-balance method	Depreciation
Year 1	____________
Year 2	____________

EXERCISE 10-2

Bidwell Co. uses the units-of-production method for computing the depreciation on its machines. One machine, which cost $88,000, is estimated to have a useful life of 22,000 hours and no residual value. During the first year of operation, this machine was used a total of 5,200 hours. Record the depreciation of this machine on December 31, the end of the first year. (Omit explanation.)

JOURNAL PAGE

	DATE		DESCRIPTION	POST. REF.	DEBIT	CREDIT	
1							1
2							2
3							3
4							4
5							5
6							6
7							7
8							8
9							9
10							10

EXERCISE 10-3

On March 8, Tilly's Wholesale decides to sell for $2,000 cash some fixtures for which it paid $4,000 and on which it has taken total depreciation of $2,500 to date of sale. Record this sale. (Omit explanation.)

JOURNAL PAGE

	DATE		DESCRIPTION	POST. REF.	DEBIT	CREDIT	
1							1
2							2
3							3
4							4
5							5
6							6
7							7
8							8
9							9
10							10

EXERCISE 10-4

Mine-It Co. paid $2,400,000 for some mineral rights in Idaho. The deposit is estimated to contain 800,000 tons of ore of uniform grade. Record the depletion of this deposit on December 31, the end of the first year, assuming that 80,000 tons are mined during the year. (Omit explanation.)

JOURNAL PAGE

	DATE		DESCRIPTION	POST. REF.	DEBIT	CREDIT	
1							1
2							2
3							3
4							4
5							5
6							6
7							7
8							8
9							9
10							10

EXERCISE 10-5

Stables Co. acquires a patent at the beginning of its calendar (fiscal) year for $100,000. Although the patent will not expire for another ten years, it is expected to be of value for only five years. Record the amortization of this patent at the end of the fiscal year. (Omit explanation.)

JOURNAL PAGE

	DATE		DESCRIPTION	POST. REF.	DEBIT	CREDIT	
1							1
2							2
3							3
4							4
5							5
6							6
7							7
8							8
9							9
10							10

PROBLEM 10-1

Bishop Company purchased equipment on January 1, 20XA, for $80,000. The equipment is expected to have a useful life of 4 years or 15,000 operating hours and a residual value of $5,000. The equipment was used 3,400 hours in 20XA, 4,000 hours in 20XB, 6,000 hours in 20XC, and 1,600 hours in 20XD.

Instructions: Determine the amount of depreciation expense for the years ended December 31, 20XA, 20XB, 20XC, and 20XD, for each method of depreciation in the table below.

Year	Straight-Line	Double-Declining-Balance	Units-of-Production
20XA			
20XB			
20XC			
20XD			
Total			

PROBLEM 10-2

Getco Co. has a sales representative who must travel a substantial amount. A car for this purpose was acquired January 2 four years ago at a cost of $20,000. It is estimated to have a total useful life of 4 years or 100,000 miles and no residual value.

Instructions:

(1) Record the annual depreciation on Getco's car at the end of the first and third years of ownership using the straight-line method and a December 31 year end.

(2) Record the annual depreciation on Getco's car at the end of the first and third years of ownership using the double-declining-balance method and a December 31 year end.

(3) Record the annual depreciation on Getco's car at the end of the first and third years of ownership using the units-of-production method, assuming no residual value, and using a December 31 year end. The car was driven 35,000 miles in the first year and 28,000 miles in the third year.

JOURNAL PAGE

	DATE		DESCRIPTION	POST. REF.	DEBIT	CREDIT	
1							1
2							2
3							3
4							4
5							5
6							6
7							7
8							8
9							9
10							10
11							11
12							12
13							13
14							14
15							15
16							16
17							17
18							18
19							19
20							20
21							21

Problem 10-3
Appendix 1

Bishop Company purchased equipment on January 1, 20XA, for $80,000. The equipment is expected to have a useful life of 4 years or 15,000 operating hours and a residual value of $5,000. The equipment was used 3,400 hours in 20XA, 4,000 hours in 20XB, 6,000 hours in 20XC, and 1,600 hours in 20XD.

Instructions: Determine the amount of depreciation expense for the years ended December 31, 20XA, 20XB, 20XC, and 20XD, for the method of depreciation in the table below.

Year	Sum-of-the-Years-Digits
20XA	
20XB	
20XC	
20XD	
Total	

PROBLEM 10-4
APPENDIX 1

Getco Co. has a sales representative who must travel a substantial amount. A car for this purpose was acquired January 2 four years ago at a cost of $20,000. It is estimated to have a total useful life of 4 years or 100,000 miles and no residual value.

Instructions: Record the annual depreciation on Getco's car at the end of the first and second years of ownership using the sum-of-the-years-digits method, assuming no residual value, and using a December 31 year end. (Omit explanation.)

JOURNAL PAGE

	DATE		DESCRIPTION	POST. REF.	DEBIT	CREDIT	
1							1
2							2
3							3
4							4
5							5
6							6
7							7
8							8
9							9
10							10
11							11
12							12
13							13

PROBLEM 10-5
APPENDIX 2

(1) Braso Co. is planning to trade in its present truck for a new model on April 30 of the current year. The existing truck was purchased May 1 three years ago at a cost of $15,000, and accumulated depreciation is $12,000 through April 30 of the current year. The new truck has a list price of $20,700. Ralston Motors agrees to allow Braso $3,500 for the present truck, and Braso agrees to pay the balance of $17,200 in cash.

Instructions: Record the exchange in general journal form assuming that the exchange has economic substance. (Omit explanation.)

JOURNAL PAGE

	DATE		DESCRIPTION	POST. REF.	DEBIT	CREDIT	
1							1
2							2
3							3
4							4
5							5
6							6
7							7
8							8
9							9

(2) Assume the same facts as in (1), except that the allowance on the present truck is $1,000 and Braso agrees to pay the balance of $19,700 in cash.

Instructions: Record the exchange assuming that the exchange has economic substance.

JOURNAL PAGE

	DATE		DESCRIPTION	POST. REF.	DEBIT	CREDIT	
1							1
2							2
3							3
4							4
5							5
6							6
7							7
8							8
9							9

CHAPTER

11 Current Liabilities and Payroll

QUIZ AND TEST HINTS

The following hints may be helpful to you in preparing for a quiz or a test over the material covered in Chapter 11.

1. Most instructors will ask some questions related to notes payable. You should be able to compute interest and prepare the necessary journal entries, including an adjusting entry for accrued interest. Also, carefully review the discounting of notes.
2. A major focus of this chapter is on the computation of payroll. You should be able to compute total earnings, social security and Medicare tax, state and federal unemployment tax, and net pay and prepare the necessary journal entries. Be careful to calculate social security tax on only the income subject to social security tax, and Medicare tax on all earnings. In addition, don't forget that the payroll tax expense includes the employer's portion of social security and Medicare tax. Review the chapter illustrations related to these computations.
3. The journal entries for vacation pay, pensions, and warranty expense are fairly easy to do. Spend a few minutes reviewing these entries.
4. You should be familiar with the new terminology introduced in this chapter, especially terms related to payroll. Review the "Key Terms" section at the end of the chapter and be sure you understand each term. Do the Matching and Fill-in-the-Blank exercises included in this Study Guide.
5. Review the GPS graphic at the beginning of the chapter and the "At A Glance" section at the end of the chapter. Read and review each of the Key Points and related Learning Outcomes. For each Learning Outcome that has an Example Exercise, locate the Example Exercise in the chapter and be sure that you understand the solution and can work a similar item on a test. If you have any questions about an Example Exercise, read the section of the chapter immediately preceding the Example Exercise.
6. The Illustrative Problem is a good overall review of the types of journal entries you might have to prepare on a test or a quiz. Try to work the problem without looking at the solution. Check your answer. If you made any errors, review those sections of the chapter. If you still don't understand the answer, ask your instructor for help.

7. If your instructor covers the Financial Analysis and Interpretation item at the end of the chapter, you should know how to compute and interpret changes in the quick ratio.

MATCHING

Instructions: Match each of the statements below with its proper term. Some terms may not be used.

A.	defined benefit plan	**H.**	gross pay
B.	defined contribution plan	**I.**	net pay
C.	discount	**J.**	payroll
D.	discount rate	**K.**	payroll register
E.	employee's earnings record	**L.**	proceeds
F.	FICA tax	**M.**	quick assets
G.	fringe benefits	**N.**	quick ratio

____ **1.** A detailed record of each employee's earnings.

____ **2.** A multicolumn form used to assemble and summarize payroll data at the end of each payroll period.

____ **3.** A pension plan that promises employees a fixed annual pension benefit at retirement, based on years of service and compensation levels.

____ **4.** Gross pay less payroll deductions; the amount the employer is obligated to pay the employee.

____ **5.** The net amount available from discounting a note payable.

____ **6.** A pension plan that requires a fixed amount of money to be invested for the employee's behalf during the employee's working years.

____ **7.** Benefits provided to employees in addition to wages and salaries.

____ **8.** The rate used in computing the interest to be deducted from the maturity value of a note.

____ **9.** The total earnings of an employee for a payroll period.

____ **10.** Cash, cash equivalents, and receivables that can be quickly converted into cash.

____ **11.** The total amount paid to employees for a certain period.

____ **12.** Federal Insurance Contributions Act tax used to finance federal programs for old-age and disability benefits (social security) and health insurance for the aged (Medicare).

____ **13.** A financial ratio that measures the ability to pay current liabilities within a short period of time.

____ **14.** The interest deducted from the maturity value of a note.

Fill in the Blank—Part A

Instructions: Answer the following questions or complete the statements by writing the appropriate words or amounts in the answer blanks.

1. The maturity value of a 90-day, 12%, $30,000 note payable is ________________.
2. In buying equipment, a business issues a $90,000, 180-day note dated January 17, which the seller discounts at 12%. The cost of the equipment would be recorded at ________________.
3. The total earnings of an employee for a payroll period are called __________ pay.
4. ________ ________ is the amount the employer is obligated to pay the employee after payroll deductions.
5. ________________ ____________________ ____________________ ________ tax is used to finance federal programs for old-age and disability benefits (social security) and health insurance for the aged (Medicare).
6. A(n) ____________________ ________________ ______________ is a detailed record of each employee's earnings.
7. Employer's payroll taxes become liabilities when the related employee payroll is __________.
8. A pension plan that promises employees a fixed annual pension benefit based on years of service and compensation levels is called a(n) ________________ ________________ plan.
9. Rights to benefits that employees earn during their term of employment but take effect after they retire are called ______________________________ benefits.
10. The ___________ ratio measures the ability to pay current liabilities within a short period of time.

Fill in the Blank—Part B

Instructions: Answer the following questions or complete the statements by writing the appropriate words or amounts in the answer blanks.

1. The maturity value of a 120-day, 9%, $75,000 note payable is ________________.
2. In buying a building, a business issues a $240,000, 120-day note dated August 3, which the seller discounts at 10%. The cost of the building would be recorded at ________________.
3. The interest deducted from the maturity value of a note is called the ____________________.

4. The ____________________ rate is used in computing the interest to be deducted from the maturity value of a note.

5. Gross pay less payroll deductions is _________ pay.

6. A(n) ________________ ________________ is a multicolumn form used to assemble and summarize payroll data at the end of each payroll period.

7. The employer's matching portion of the Federal Insurance Contribution Act (FICA) tax that represents the contribution to health insurance for senior citizens is credited to ___________________ ________ Payable.

8. _________________ is the total amount paid to employees for a certain period.

9. Benefits provided to employees in addition to wages and salaries are called ______________ benefits.

10. A pension plan that requires a fixed amount of money to be invested for the employee's behalf during the employee's working years is called a(n) _________________ ______________________ plan.

MULTIPLE CHOICE

Instructions: Circle the best answer for each of the following questions.

1. The interest charged by the bank, at the rate of 12%, on a 90-day, non-interest-bearing note payable for $75,000 is:
   a. $1,000
   b. $2,250
   c. $3,000
   d. $9,000

2. The cost of a product warranty should be included as an expense:
   a. in the period of the sale of the product
   b. in the period of the collection of the cash from the sale of the product
   c. in the future period when the product is repaired or replaced
   d. in the future period when the cost of repairing the product is paid

3. An employee's rate of pay is $8 per hour, with time and a half for hours worked in excess of 40 during a week. If the employee works 50 hours during a week and has social security tax withheld at a rate of 6.0%, Medicare tax withheld at a rate of 1.5%, and federal income tax withheld at a rate of 15%, the employee's net pay for the week is:
   a. $440
   b. $374
   c. $341
   d. $310

4. An employee receives an hourly rate of $18, with time and a half for all hours worked in excess of 40 during a week. Payroll data for the current week are as follows: hours worked, 45; federal income tax withheld, $350; cumulative earnings for year prior to current week, $49,700; social security tax rate, 6.0%; Medicare tax rate, 1.5%. What is the gross pay for the employee?
   a. $475
   b. $505
   c. $720
   d. $855
5. Prior to the last weekly payroll period of the calendar year, the cumulative earnings of employees A and B are $99,800 and $21,000, respectively. Their earnings for the last completed payroll period of the year are $1,000 each. The amount of earnings subject to social security tax is $100,000, and the tax rate is 6%. All earnings are subject to Medicare tax at 1.5%. Assuming that the payroll will be paid on December 29, what will be the employer's total FICA tax (social security and Medicare) for this payroll period on the two salary amounts of $1,000 each?
   a. $75
   b. $90
   c. $102
   d. $150
6. Payroll taxes levied against employees become liabilities:
   a. when earned by the employee
   b. at the end of an accounting period
   c. the first of the following month
   d. at the time the liability for the employee's wages is paid
7. Which of the following items would not be considered a fringe benefit?
   a. vacations
   b. employee pension plans
   c. health insurance
   d. FICA benefits
8. For proper matching of revenues and expenses, the estimated cost of fringe benefits must be recognized as an expense of the period the:
   a. employee earns the benefit
   b. employee is paid the benefit
   c. fringe benefit contract is signed
   d. fringe benefit contract becomes effective

9. The inputs into a payroll system may be classified as either constants or variables. All of the following are variables except for:
   a. number of hours worked
   b. vacation credits
   c. number of income tax withholding allowances
   d. number of days sick leave with pay

10. Hemlock Company has a schedule of payments due on a note payable as follows:

2010	$25,000
2011	30,000
2012	40,000

How much should be disclosed as a current liability on December 31, 2009?
   a. $0
   b. $25,000
   c. $70,000
   d. $95,000

TRUE/FALSE

Instructions: Indicate whether each of the following statements is true or false by placing a check mark in the appropriate column.

	True	False
1. The total earnings of an employee for a payroll period are called gross pay.	____	____
2. Only employers are required to contribute to the Federal Insurance Contributions Act program.	____	____
3. All states require that unemployment compensation taxes be withheld from employees' pay.	____	____
4. Most employers are also subject to federal and state payroll taxes based on the amount earned by their employees, not the amount paid.	____	____
5. The amounts withheld from employees' earnings have an effect on the firm's debits to the salary or wage expense accounts.	____	____
6. All payroll taxes levied against employers become liabilities at the time the related remuneration is paid to employees.	____	____
7. Depending on when it is to be paid, vacation liability may be classified in the balance sheet as either a current liability or a long-term liability.	____	____

		True	False
8.	To properly match revenues and expense, employees' vacation pay should be accrued as a liability as the vacation rights are earned.	____	____
9.	Current installments on debt should not be disclosed as a current liability in order to match the disclosure method for property, plant, and equipment.	____	____
10.	In order for revenues and expenses to be matched properly, a liability to cover the cost of a product warranty must be recorded in the period when the product is repaired.	____	____
11.	Potential liabilities that may arise in the future because of past transactions are called contingent liabilities.	____	____
12.	All changes in the constants of the payroll system, such as changes in pay rates, should be properly authorized in writing........	____	____
13.	The net periodic pension cost of a defined benefit plan is debited to Pension Expense, the amount funded is credited to Cash, and any unfunded amount is credited to Unfunded Pension Revenue.	____	____
14.	Examples of postretirement benefits from an employer may include dental care, eye care, medical care, life insurance, tuition assistance, or tax services........	____	____
15.	The rate used by a bank in discounting a note is called the prime rate.	____	____

EXERCISE 11-1

Instructions: In each of the following situations, determine the correct amount.

(1) An employee of a firm operating under the Federal Wage and Hour Law worked 50 hours last week. If the hourly rate of pay is $14, what is the employee's gross earnings for the week?

(2) During the current pay period, an employee earned $2,000. Prior to the current period, the employee earned (in the current year) $99,500. If the social security tax is 6.0% on the first $100,000 of annual earnings and the Medicare tax rate is 1.5% on all earnings, what is the total amount of FICA tax to be withheld from the employee's pay this period?

(3) During the current pay period, an employee earned $3,000. Prior to the current period, the employee earned (in the current year) $137,800. Using the social security and Medicare tax rates and bases in (2), compute the total amount to be withheld from the employee's pay this period.

(4) Using the rates and maximum bases in (2), compute the total amount of social security and Medicare tax withheld from the pay of an employee who has earned $10,000 during the year but has actually received only $9,700, with the remaining $300 to be paid in the next year.

Exercise 11-2

Instructions: Prepare the general journal entries to record each of the following items for Wiler Co. for the year ended December 31. (Omit explanations.)

(1) Accrued employee vacation pay at the end of the year is $3,225.

(2) The estimated product warranty liability at the end of the year is 3% of sales of $150,000.

(3) A partially funded pension plan is maintained for employees at an annual cost of $40,000. At the end of the year, $27,500 is paid to the fund trustee and the remaining accrued pension liability is recognized.

JOURNAL PAGE

DATE		DESCRIPTION	POST. REF.	DEBIT	CREDIT

Problem 11-1

The weekly gross payroll of O'Brien Co. on December 7 amounts to $50,000, distributed as follows: sales salaries, $34,000; office salaries, $16,000. The following amounts are to be withheld: social security tax, $3,000; Medicare tax, $750; employees' income tax, $7,500; union dues, $900; and United Way, $450.

Instructions: Omitting explanations, prepare general journal entries to:

(1) Record the payroll.

(2) Record the payment of the payroll.

(3) Record the employer's payroll taxes. Assume that the entire payroll is subject to social security tax at 6.0%, Medicare tax at 1.5%, federal unemployment tax at 0.8%, and state unemployment tax at 5.4%.

(4) Record the employer's payroll taxes. Assume that $40,000 of payroll is subject to social security tax at 6.0% and $50,000 is subject to Medicare tax at 1.5%. Assume that none of the payroll is subject to federal or state unemployment tax.

JOURNAL

PAGE

	DATE		DESCRIPTION	POST. REF.	DEBIT	CREDIT	
1							1
2							2
3							3
4							4
5							5
6							6
7							7
8							8
9							9
10							10
11							11
12							12
13							13
14							14
15							15
16							16
17							17
18							18
19							19
20							20
21							21
22							22
23							23
24							24
25							25
26							26
27							27
28							28
29							29
30							30
31							31
32							32

PROBLEM 11-2

Instructions: For the employees listed below, compute the individual taxes indicated as well as total taxes by type and by employee. Assume the social security tax rate is 6.0% on the first $100,000 of annual earnings, the Medicare tax rate is 1.5% on all earnings, the state unemployment tax rate is 5.4% on a maximum of $7,000, and the federal unemployment tax rate is .8% on a maximum of $7,000.

		Employee FICA Withholding		Employer's Taxes				
Employee	Annual Earnings	Social Security Tax	Medicare Tax	Social Security Tax	Medicare Tax	State Unemployment	Federal Unemployment	Total
Avery	$ 12,000							
Johnson	5,000							
Jones	59,000							
Smith	73,000							
Wilson	141,000							
Total	$290,000							

Problem 11-3

Instructions: Prepare the general journal entries to record the following transactions. (Omit explanations.)

(1) Audrey Newman issued a 90-day, 12% note for $2,000 to Mayday Co. for a $2,000 overdue account.

(2) Newman paid the note in (1) at maturity.

(3) Paula Wheat borrowed $8,000 from the bank and gave the bank a 90-day, 11% note.

(4) Wheat paid the note in (3) at maturity.

(5) Randy Lucky borrowed $6,000 from the bank, giving a 60-day, non-interest-bearing note that was discounted at 9%.

(6) Lucky paid the note recorded in (5) at maturity.

JOURNAL

PAGE

	DATE		DESCRIPTION	POST. REF.	DEBIT	CREDIT	
1							1
2							2
3							3
4							4
5							5
6							6
7							7
8							8
9							9
10							10
11							11
12							12
13							13
14							14
15							15
16							16
17							17
18							18
19							19
20							20
21							21
22							22
23							23
24							24

CHAPTER

12 Accounting for Partnerships and Limited Liability Corporations

QUIZ AND TEST HINTS

The following hints may be helpful to you in preparing for a quiz or a test over the material covered in Chapter 12.

1. Note the similarity between a partnership and a limited liability company (LLC). LLCs use slightly different terms, such as members' equity, but employ similar accounting approaches.
2. You should be able to prepare journal entries for the formation and the dissolution of a partnership or LLC. Pay particular attention to the payment of a bonus on the admission of a new partner.
3. Expect at least one question involving distribution of partnership net income among the partners (or LLC members). This question may involve salary allowances and interest allowances on partners' capital balances. Remember, if the partnership agreement does not indicate how income is shared among the partners, it is shared equally. Also, be able to prepare the journal entries distributing a partnership net income or loss. The entry for distributing net income debits Income Summary and credits the partners' capital accounts.
4. If your instructor assigned a homework problem involving partnership liquidation or covered it in class, you may see a question in a quiz or test related to liquidating a partnership. You should understand how to account for gains, losses, and satisfying partner deficiencies in the liquidating process. The final distribution must be according to the final capital balances of the partners, not according to the income-sharing ratio. Review the chapter illustrations and the Illustrative Problem at the end of the chapter.
5. You should be familiar with the new terminology introduced in this chapter. Review the "Key Terms" section at the end of the chapter and be sure you understand each term. Do the Matching and Fill-in-the-Blank exercises included in this Study Guide.
6. Review the GPS graphic at the beginning of the chapter and the "At A Glance" section at the end of the chapter. Read and review each of the Key Points and related Learning Outcomes. For each Learning Outcome that has an Example Exercise, locate the Example Exercise in the chapter and be sure that you understand the solution and can work a similar item on a test.

If you have any questions about an Example Exercise, read the section of the chapter immediately preceding the Example Exercise.

7. If your instructor covers the Financial Analysis and Interpretation item at the end of the chapter, you should know how to compute and interpret changes in the ratio of revenue per employee.

MATCHING

Instructions: Match each of the statements below with its proper term. Some terms may not be used.

A. deficiency
B. limited liability company
C. liquidation
D. partnership
E. partnership agreement
F. realization
G. statement of members' equity
H. statement of partnership equity
I. statement of stockholders' equity

____ **1.** A summary of the changes in each partner's capital of a partnership that have occurred during a specific period of time.

____ **2.** A business form consisting of one or more persons or entities filing an operating agreement with a state to conduct business with limited liability to the owners, yet treated as a partnership for tax purposes.

____ **3.** The formal written contract creating a partnership.

____ **4.** The debit balance in the owner's equity account of a partner.

____ **5.** The sale of assets when a partnership is being liquidated.

____ **6.** A summary of the changes in each member's equity of a limited liability company that have occurred during a specific period of time.

____ **7.** The winding-up process when a partnership goes out of business.

____ **8.** An unincorporated business form consisting of two or more persons conducting business as co-owners for profit.

FILL IN THE BLANK—PART A

Instructions: Answer the following questions or complete the statements by writing the appropriate words or amounts in the answer blanks.

1. A(n) ______________________ is a business owned by a single individual.
2. Limited liability is a feature of ________________ ________________ ____________________ form of business organization.
3. The characteristic of ______________ ______________ means the acts of any partner can bind, or obligate, the entire partnership.
4. If the partnership agreement is silent, partnership income is divided ______________ among the partners.
5. A method for recognizing differences in partner ability or effort in dividing partnership income is a(n) _____________ ____________________.
6. If Dunn and Street share income at the ratio of 2:3, Dunn would be credited with income of ______________ out of total partnership income of $150,000.
7. A partnership's assets should be stated at ____________ ____________ ____________ when a new partner is admitted.
8. If Hastings, with a $60,000 capital account, admits Cortez to a 20% interest in a partnership for a $20,000 investment, then the bonus paid to Hastings is ______________.
9. If Mann, with a $20,000 capital account, admits Owens to a 40% interest in a partnership for a $10,000 investment, then a bonus is paid to ___________.
10. In liquidation, cash is distributed to partners according to their ____________ ________________.
11. If Burns and Kraft sell $42,000 book value of noncash assets for $30,000 in liquidating a partnership, then Burns' capital account will decline by ____________ if the income-sharing ratio is 3:1.
12. If cash is not collected from a deficient partner upon liquidation, then the deficiency becomes a(n) __________ to the partnership and is divided among the remaining partners' capital accounts according to their ______________-______________ ____________.

FILL IN THE BLANK—PART B

Instructions: Answer the following questions or complete the statements by writing the appropriate words or amounts in the answer blanks.

1. A(n) ____________________, ________________ ________________ ____________________, and ____________________ are nontaxable (flow-through) business entities.
2. A partnership is created by contract, known as the ____________________ ____________________.
3. A major disadvantage of a partnership is the feature of ________________ ________________.
4. The ________________ _______ ________________ ____________ discloses changes in member's equity for a limited liability corporation.
5. A method for recognizing differences in partner investments is by awarding ________________ on partner capital balances when dividing income between partners.
6. If Todd and Mellon shared partnership income in the ratio of 1:3, Mellon would be credited with income of ______________ out of a total partnership income of $200,000.
7. Upon admitting a new partner, the __________ or __________ in adjusting assets to current values should be divided among the capital accounts of the existing partners according to their income-sharing ratio.
8. If Collins, with a $30,000 capital account, admits McCain to a 40% interest in a partnership for a $50,000 investment, then the bonus paid to Collins is ______________.
9. If Long, with a $80,000 capital account, admits Bradley to a 50% interest in a partnership for a $100,000 investment, then a bonus is paid to ___________.
10. Prior to liquidating a partnership, cash must be ________________ from the sale of assets.
11. A debit balance in a partner's capital account upon liquidation is termed a(n) ____________________.
12. If Howe and Martin sell $75,000 book value of noncash assets for $120,000 in liquidating a partnership, then Martin's capital account will increase by ______________ if the income-sharing ratio is 1:2.

MULTIPLE CHOICE

Instructions: Circle the best answer for each of the following questions.

1. If a partnership agreement is silent on dividing net income or net losses, the partners divide income/losses:
   a. according to their original capital investments
   b. equally
   c. according to skills possessed by each partner
   d. on the basis of individual time devoted to the business
2. Which of the following is not an advantage of a partnership?
   a. It is possible to bring together more capital than in a sole proprietorship.
   b. Partners' income taxes may be less than the income taxes would be on other forms of organization.
   c. It is possible to bring together more managerial skills than in a sole proprietorship.
   d. Each partner has limited liability.
3. Which features of a limited liability company provide it advantages over a partnership?
   a. unlimited liability, taxed as a separate entity
   b. limited life, nontaxable (flow-through) entity
   c. limited liability, nontaxable (flow-through) entity
   d. limited liability, taxed as a separate entity
4. When a new partner is admitted to a partnership by a contribution of assets to the partnership:
   a. neither the total assets nor the total owner's equity of the business is affected
   b. only the total assets are affected
   c. only the owner's equity is affected
   d. both the total assets and the total owner's equity are increased
5. Boxer and Campbell have capital accounts of $25,000 and $35,000, respectively. Hansen contributes $40,000 for a 30% interest. What is the total bonus to Boxer and Campbell?
   a. $0
   b. $10,000
   c. $20,000
   d. $40,000

6. Columbo, Dexter, and Flamingo share income and losses in the ratio of 1:2:2 according to their partnership agreement. The partnership income is $80,000. How much income is allocated to Dexter's capital account?

a. $16,000

b. $26,666

c. $32,000

d. $40,000

7. Haley and Zeff share income and losses in the ratio of 2:3 according to their partnership agreement. Prior to admitting Brown, $90,000 of inventory is revalued to a current market value of $75,000. What is the impact of the revaluation on Zeff's capital account?

a. There is no impact because the revaluation is not realized.

b. a $6,000 debit

c. a $9,000 debit

d. a $22,500 debit

8. Ford, Hill, and Patterson share income and losses at the ratio of 1:2:3. At the final stages of liquidating the partnership, it is determined that Patterson has a capital deficiency of $60,000, and thus, there is insufficient cash to pay the remaining partners equal to their capital accounts. What share of the deficiency will be allocated to Ford, assuming no additional cash is collected from Patterson?

a. $10,000

b. $20,000

c. $30,000

d. $40,000

9. If there is a loss on the sale of noncash assets when a partnership goes out of business, the loss should be divided among the partners:

a. according to their original capital investments

b. according to their current capital balances

c. according to their income-sharing ratio

d. equally

10. Changes in partner capital accounts for a period of time are reported in the:

a. Statement of Owner's Equity

b. Statement of Cash Flows

c. Statement of Partnership Equity

d. Statement of Members' Equity

TRUE/FALSE

Instructions: Indicate whether each of the following statements is true or false by placing a check mark in the appropriate column.

	True	False
1. Partners are legally employees of the partnership, and their capital contributions are considered a loan.	____	____
2. Each partner is individually liable to creditors for debts incurred by the partnership.	____	____
3. Salary allowances are treated as divisions of partnership net income and are credited to the partners' capital accounts.	____	____
4. The property invested in a partnership by a partner remains identified as that partner's property.	____	____
5. A partner's claim against the assets of the partnership in the event of dissolution is measured by the amount of the partner's initial investment.	____	____
6. At the time a partnership is formed, the market values of the assets should be considered in determining each partner's investment.	____	____
7. In the absence of an agreement for income or loss distributions among the partners, the partners should share income equally, even if there are differences in their capital contributions.	____	____
8. Regardless of whether partners' salaries and interest are treated as expenses of the partnership or as a division of net income, the total amount allocated to each partner will not be affected.	____	____
9. A partnership is required to pay federal income taxes.	____	____
10. Any change in the personnel of the ownership results in a dissolution of a partnership.	____	____
11. A new partner may be admitted to a partnership without the consent of the current partners.	____	____
12. A partner's interest may be disposed of without the consent of the remaining partners.	____	____
13. When a new partner is admitted by purchasing an interest from one or more of the existing partners, the purchase price is recorded in the accounts of the partnership.	____	____

		True	False
14.	It is appropriate to adjust the old partnership assets to current market values at the time a new partner is admitted. ...	____	____
15.	At the time a new partner is admitted, a bonus may be paid to the incoming partner.	____	____
16.	A person may be admitted to a partnership by purchasing an interest from one or more of the existing partners. The only entry required by the partnership is to transfer owner's equity amounts from the capital accounts of the selling partner(s) to the capital account of the new partner............	____	____
17.	As cash is realized from the sale of assets during the liquidation of a partnership, the cash is applied first to the payment of the claims of the limited partners.	____	____
18.	If the distribution of the loss on the sale of noncash assets when a partnership goes out of business causes a partner's account to have a debit balance, this balance represents a claim of the partnership against the partner.	____	____
19.	If a deficiency of a partner is uncollectible, this represents a loss that is written off against the capital balances of the remaining partners...	____	____
20.	The most common error that occurs in liquidating a partnership is allocating gains and losses on realization of assets incorrectly among the partners..............................	____	____

EXERCISE 12-1

Ruth Cutco and Darrell Robbs formed a partnership. Cutco invested $100,000 cash and merchandise valued at $80,000. Robbs invested $10,000 cash, land valued at $115,000, equipment valued at $45,000, and merchandise valued at $5,000.

Instructions: Prepare the entries to record the investments of Cutco and Robbs on the partnership books. Use the current date.

JOURNAL PAGE

	DATE		DESCRIPTION	POST. REF.	DEBIT	CREDIT	
1							1
2							2
3							3
4							4
5							5
6							6
7							7
8							8
9							9
10							10
11							11
12							12
13							13
14							14
15							15
16							16
17							17
18							18
19							19
20							20
21							21
22							22
23							23
24							24
25							25
26							26
27							27
28							28

Exercise 12-2

Ann Hartly, Barry Smetz, and Lynette Grasso are partners, having capitals of $100,000, $55,000, and $35,000, respectively. They share net income equally.

Instructions: Prepare the entries to record each of the following situations. (Omit explanations.) Each situation is independent of one another.

(1) On June 30, John Schafer is admitted to the partnership by purchasing one-fifth of the respective capital interests of the three partners. He pays $30,000 to Hartly, $15,000 to Smetz, and $10,000 to Grasso.

JOURNAL PAGE

	DATE		DESCRIPTION	POST. REF.	DEBIT	CREDIT	
1							1
2							2
3							3
4							4
5							5
6							6
7							7
8							8
9							9
10							10

(2) On July 1, Laura Masko is admitted to the partnership for an investment of $50,000, and the parties agree to pay a bonus of $21,000 to Masko.

JOURNAL PAGE

	DATE		DESCRIPTION	POST. REF.	DEBIT	CREDIT	
1							1
2							2
3							3
4							4
5							5
6							6
7							7
8							8
9							9
10							10

EXERCISE 12-3

Arway, Batts, and Carlone are partners, having capital balances of $65,000, $55,000, and $40,000, respectively. The partners share net income equally. Carlone has decided to leave the partnership.

Instructions: Prepare the entries to record each of the following situations. (Omit explanations.) Each situation is independent of one another.

(1) The partners agree that the inventory of the partnership should be increased by $12,750 to recognize its fair market value. Arway buys Carlone's interest in the partnership for $53,000.

JOURNAL PAGE

	DATE		DESCRIPTION	POST. REF.	DEBIT	CREDIT	
1							1
2							2
3							3
4							4
5							5
6							6
7							7
8							8
9							9

(2) The partners agree that the inventory of the partnership should be increased by $6,000 to recognize its fair market value. The partnership pays Carlone cash for her interest, as reflected by the balance in her capital account.

JOURNAL PAGE

	DATE		DESCRIPTION	POST. REF.	DEBIT	CREDIT	
1							1
2							2
3							3
4							4
5							5
6							6
7							7
8							8
9							9

PROBLEM 12-1

On January 2 of the current year, Bulley and Scram formed a partnership in which Bulley invested $300,000 and Scram invested $700,000. During the year, the partnership had a net income of $200,000.

Instructions: Show how this net income would be distributed under each of the following conditions.

(1) The partnership agreement says nothing about the distribution of net income.

Bulley's share	$
Scram's share	
Total	$

(2) The partnership agreement provides that Bulley and Scram are to share net income in a 2:3 ratio, respectively.

Bulley's share	$
Scram's share	
Total	$

(3) The partnership agreement provides that Bulley and Scram are to share net income in accordance with the ratio of their original capital investments.

Bulley's share	$
Scram's share	
Total	$

(4) The partnership agreement provides that Bulley is to be allowed a salary of $30,000 and Scram a salary of $50,000, with the balance of net income distributed equally.

Division of Net Income	Bulley	Scram	Total
Salary allowance	$	$	$
Remaining income			
Net income	$	$	$ 200,000

(5) The partnership agreement provides that interest at 5% is to be allowed on the beginning capital and that the balance is to be distributed equally.

Division of Net Income	Bulley	Scram	Total
Interest allowance	$	$	$
Remaining income			
Net income	$	$	$ 200,000

(6) The partnership agreement provides that Bulley is to be allowed a salary of $15,000 and Scram a salary of $25,000; that interest at 5% is to be allowed on beginning capital; and that the balance is to be distributed equally.

Division of Net Income	Bulley	Scram	Total
Salary allowance	$	$	$
Interest allowance			
Remaining income			
Net income	$	$	$ 200,000

(7) The partnership agreement provides that Bulley is to be allowed a salary of $80,000 and Scram a salary of $78,000; that interest at 5% is to be allowed on beginning capital; and that the balance is to be distributed equally.

Division of Net Income	Bulley	Scram	Total
Salary allowance	$	$	$
Interest allowance			
Total	$	$	$
Excess of allowances over income			
Net income	$	$	$ 200,000

PROBLEM 12-2

Tropical Products, LLC consists of two members, Baskin and Robbins, who share in all income and losses according to a 3:1 income-sharing ratio. Dreyer has been asked to join the LLC. Prior to admitting Dreyer, the assets of Tropical Products were revalued to reflect their current market values. The revaluation resulted in the value of processing equipment being increased by $20,000. Prior to the revaluation, the member equity balances for Baskin and Robbins were $385,000 and $195,000, respectively.

Instructions:

(1) Provide the journal entry for the asset revaluation.

JOURNAL PAGE

	DATE		DESCRIPTION	POST. REF.	DEBIT	CREDIT	
1							1
2							2
3							3
4							4
5							5
6							6
7							7
8							8
9							9

(2) Provide the journal entry and supporting calculations for the bonus under the following independent assumptions.

(a) Dreyer purchased a 20% interest in Tropical Products, LLC for $100,000.

JOURNAL PAGE

	DATE		DESCRIPTION	POST. REF.	DEBIT	CREDIT	
1							1
2							2
3							3
4							4
5							5
6							6

(Provide supporting calculations on the following page.)

Supporting calculations:

(b) Dreyer purchased a 15% interest in Tropical Products, LLC for $180,000.

JOURNAL PAGE

	DATE		DESCRIPTION	POST. REF.	DEBIT	CREDIT	
1							1
2							2
3							3
4							4
5							5
6							6

Supporting calculations:

PROBLEM 12-3

Prior to the liquidation of the partnership of Triste, Sandpipe, and Hinkle, the ledger contained the following accounts and balances:

Cash	$100,000
Noncash Assets	$300,000
Liabilities	$120,000
Triste, Capital	$90,000
Sandpipe, Capital	$60,000
Hinkle, Capital	$130,000

Assume that the noncash assets are sold for $400,000. Triste, Sandpipe, and Hinkle share profits in a 30:50:20 ratio.

Instructions:

(1) Complete the following schedule showing the sale of assets, payment of liabilities, and distribution of the remaining cash to the partners.

					Capital	
	Cash +	Noncash Assets =	Liabilities +	Triste (30%) +	Sandpipe (50%) +	Hinkle (20%)
Balances before realization	$100,000	$300,000	$120,000	$90,000	$60,000	$130,000
Sale of noncash assets and division of gain						
Balances after realization						
Payment of liabilities						
Balances after payment of liabilities........						
Distribution of cash to partners						
Final balances						

(2) Assume that the noncash assets are sold for $130,000 and that the partner with a debit balance pays the entire deficiency. Complete the following schedule showing the sale of assets, payment of liabilities, and distribution of the remaining cash to the partners.

				Capital		
	Cash +	Noncash Assets =	Liabilities +	Triste (30%) +	Sandpipe (50%) +	Hinkle (20%)
Balances before realization	$100,000	$300,000	$120,000	$90,000	$60,000	$130,000
Sale of noncash assets and division of loss						
Balances after realization						
Payment of liabilities						
Balances after payment of liabilities						
Receipt of deficiency..................						
Balances...................						
Distribution of cash to partners.........						
Final balances						

(3) Prepare the journal entries to record the liquidation of the partnership based on the facts in (2). Use the current date. (Omit explanations.)

JOURNAL

PAGE

	DATE		DESCRIPTION	POST. REF.	DEBIT	CREDIT	
1							1
2							2
3							3
4							4
5							5
6							6
7							7
8							8
9							9
10							10
11							11
12							12
13							13
14							14
15							15
16							16
17							17
18							18
19							19
20							20
21							21
22							22
23							23
24							24
25							25
26							26
27							27
28							28
29							29
30							30
31							31
32							32
33							33

CHAPTER

13 Corporations: Organization, Capital Stock Transactions, and Dividends

QUIZ AND TEST HINTS

The following hints may be helpful to you in preparing for a quiz or a test over the material covered in Chapter 13.

1. Many new terms related to the corporate form of organization are introduced in this chapter that may be tested using true/false or multiple-choice questions. Review the "Key Terms" section at the end of the chapter and be sure you understand each term. Do the Matching and Fill-in-the-Blank exercises included in this Study Guide.
2. You should be able to compute the amount of dividends allocated between preferred stock and common stock.
3. You should be able to prepare journal entries for the issuance of par and no-par stock, treasury stock transactions, and cash and stock dividends. Expect at least one problem requiring such entries.
4. It is unlikely that you will be required to prepare a journal entry for organization expenses. However, you may be asked a multiple-choice question related to organization expenses.
5. Review the GPS graphic at the beginning of the chapter and the "At A Glance" section at the end of the chapter. Read and review each of the Key Points and related Learning Outcomes. For each Learning Outcome that has an Example Exercise, locate the Example Exercise in the chapter and be sure that you understand the solution and can work a similar item on a test. If you have any questions about an Example Exercise, read the section of the chapter immediately preceding the Example Exercise.
6. If your instructor covers the Financial Analysis and Interpretation item at the end of the chapter, you should know how to compute and interpret changes in the dividend yield ratio.

MATCHING

Instructions: Match each of the statements below with its proper term. Some terms may not be used.

A.	cash dividend	**J.**	retained earnings statement
B.	common stock	**K.**	stated value
C.	discount	**L.**	statement of stockholders' equity
D.	dividend yield	**M.**	stock
E.	earnings per share	**N.**	stock dividend
F.	outstanding stock	**O.**	stock split
G.	par	**P.**	stockholders
H.	preferred stock	**Q.**	treasury stock
I.	premium		

____ **1.** Shares of ownership of a corporation.

____ **2.** The owners of a corporation.

____ **3.** The stock in the hands of stockholders.

____ **4.** A value, similar to par value, approved by the board of directors of a corporation for no-par stock.

____ **5.** The stock outstanding when a corporation has issued only one class of stock.

____ **6.** The monetary amount printed on a stock certificate.

____ **7.** A class of stock with preferential rights over common stock.

____ **8.** The excess of the issue price of a stock over its par value.

____ **9.** The excess of the par value of a stock over its issue price.

____ **10.** A cash distribution of earnings by a corporation to its shareholders.

____ **11.** A distribution of shares of stock to its stockholders.

____ **12.** Stock that a corporation has once issued and then reacquires.

____ **13.** A statement summarizing significant changes in stockholders' equity that have occurred during a period.

____ **14.** A reduction in the par or stated value of a common stock and the issuance of a proportionate number of additional shares.

____ **15.** A ratio that is often used by investors and creditors in evaluating a company's profitability.

FILL IN THE BLANK—PART A

Instructions: Answer the following questions or complete the statements by writing the appropriate words or amounts in the answer blanks.

1. Shares of ownership of a corporation are called ____________.
2. The owners' equity in a corporation is reported on the balance sheet under the caption ________________________ ____________.
3. Net income retained in a corporation is reported on the balance sheet as ________________ ________________.
4. The stockholders' equity section of a balance sheet is composed of preferred $7 stock, $250,000; discount on preferred stock, $25,000; common stock, $750,000; premium on common stock, $100,000; retained earnings, $190,000; treasury stock, $80,000. The total paid-in capital is ______________.
5. Stock in the hands of stockholders is called ____________________ stock.
6. When a corporation has issued only one class of stock, it is called ________________ stock.
7. A class of stock that receives preferential rights, but whose dividend rights are usually limited to a certain amount is referred to as __________________________ stock.
8. A company has outstanding stock that is composed of 10,000 shares of $5, $50 par preferred stock and 150,000 shares of $10 par common stock. No dividends have been paid thus far in the current year. A total of $45,000 in dividends is to be distributed. The total amount of dividends to be paid on the common stock is ________________.
9. When the issuance price of a stock exceeds its par value, the stock is said to have been issued at a(n) ________________.
10. Land is acquired by issuing 5,000 shares of $20 par common stock with a current market price of $32 per share. The land should be recorded at a cost of ________________.
11. If a corporation issues stock and then reacquires the stock, the stock reacquired is referred to as ________________ stock.
12. A company purchases 500 shares of its $50 par common stock for $32,500 cash. The effect (increase, decrease, or none) of this purchase on the company's retained earnings is ____________________ (indicate amount and effect).
13. A(n) ____________________ is a cash distribution of earnings by a corporation to its shareholders.
14. A balance sheet indicated 20,000 shares of common stock authorized, 8,000 shares issued, and 1,500 shares of treasury stock. If a cash dividend of $5 per share is declared on the common stock, the total amount of the dividend is ________________.

15. The effect of a stock dividend on the stockholders' equity of a corporation's balance sheet is to increase paid-in capital and decrease ________________ ________________.

FILL IN THE BLANK—PART B

Instructions: Answer the following questions or complete the statements by writing the appropriate words or amounts in the answer blanks.

1. The owners of a corporation are the ________________________.
2. Capital contributed to a corporation by the stockholders and others is reported on the balance sheet as ___________-______ capital.
3. A debit balance in the retained earnings account is called a(n) ________________.
4. A value, similar to par value, approved by the board of directors of a corporation for no-par stock is called ________________ value.
5. A class of stock with preferential rights over common stock is called ____________________ stock.
6. Costs incurred in organizing a corporation are debited to the _____________ _____________ account.
7. A company has outstanding stock that is composed of 25,000 shares of $3, $100 par preferred stock and 150,000 shares of $10 par common stock. No dividends have been paid thus far in the current year. A total of $110,000 in dividends is to be distributed. The total amount of dividends to be paid on the common stock is _______________.
8. When the par value of a stock exceeds its issuance price, the stock is said to have been issued at a(n) ________________.
9. A company purchases 500 shares of its $50 par common stock for $32,500 cash. The effect (increase, decrease, or none) of this purchase on the company's paid-in capital is ________________________ (indicate amount and effect).
10. The stockholders' equity section of a balance sheet is composed of preferred $7 stock, $250,000; discount on preferred stock, $25,000; common stock, $750,000; premium on common stock, $100,000; retained earnings, $100,000 deficit; treasury stock, $80,000. The total stockholder's equity is ________________.
11. A(n) _____________ _____________ is the reduction in the par or stated value of common stock and the issuance of a proportionate number of additional shares.
12. A corporation announced a 5-for-1 stock split of its $100 par value stock, which is currently trading for $180. The estimated market value of the stock after the split is _______________.

13. A(n) _____________ ____________________ is a distribution of shares of stock to its stockholders.

14. The _____________ value is the monetary amount printed on a stock certificate.

15. The __________________ ___________ is a ratio computed by dividing the annual dividends paid per share of common stock by the market price per share at a specific date, and it indicates the rate of return to stockholders in terms of cash dividend distributions.

MULTIPLE CHOICE

Instructions: Circle the best answer for each of the following questions.

1. Which of the following is not a characteristic of the corporate form of organization?
   - **a.** ownership represented by shares of stock
   - **b.** separate legal existence
   - **c.** unlimited liability of stockholders
   - **d.** earnings subject to the federal income tax

2. The amount printed on a stock certificate is known as:
   - **a.** stated value
   - **b.** premium
   - **c.** discount
   - **d.** par value

3. Assume that a corporation has outstanding 5,000 shares of $6 cumulative preferred stock of $100 par and no dividends have been paid for the preceding four years. What is the amount of preferred dividends that must be declared in the current year before a dividend can be declared on common stock?
   - **a.** $30,000
   - **b.** $90,000
   - **c.** $120,000
   - **d.** $150,000

4. When a corporation purchases its own stock, what account is debited for the cost of the stock?
   - **a.** Common Stock Subscribed
   - **b.** Treasury Stock
   - **c.** Preferred Stock
   - **d.** Common Stock Receivable

5. The excess of the proceeds from selling treasury stock over its cost should be credited to:
   a. Retained Earnings
   b. Premium on Capital Stock
   c. Gain from Sale of Treasury Stock
   d. Paid-In Capital from Sale of Treasury Stock
6. The claims of the __________ must first be satisfied upon liquidation of a corporation.
   a. preferred stockholders
   b. partners
   c. common stockholders
   d. creditors
7. A company with 20,000 authorized shares of $20 par common stock issued 12,000 shares at $50. Subsequently, the company declared a 5% stock dividend on a date when the market price was $60 per share. What is the amount transferred from the retained earnings account to paid-in capital accounts as a result of the stock dividend?
   a. $36,000
   b. $30,000
   c. $12,000
   d. $6,000
8. The charter of a corporation provides for the issuance of 100,000 shares of common stock. Assume that 60,000 shares were originally issued and 5,000 were subsequently reacquired. What is the number of shares outstanding?
   a. 5,000
   b. 55,000
   c. 60,000
   d. 100,000
9. The entry to record the issuance of common stock at a price above par would include a credit to:
   a. Donated Capital
   b. Retained Earnings
   c. Treasury Stock
   d. Paid-In Capital in Excess of Par—Common Stock

10. A corporation purchases 10,000 shares of its own $20 par common stock for $35 per share, recording it at cost. What will be the effect on total stockholders' equity?

a. increase, $200,000

b. increase, $350,000

c. decrease, $200,000

d. decrease, $350,000

TRUE/FALSE

Instructions: Indicate whether each of the following statements is true or false by placing a check mark in the appropriate column.

	True	False
1. The stockholders of a corporation have unlimited liability....	____	____
2. A corporation may acquire, own, and dispose of property in its corporate name..........	____	____
3. The two main sources of stockholders' equity are paid-in capital and long-term debt.	____	____
4. The common stockholders have a greater chance of receiving regular dividends than do preferred stockholders. ...	____	____
5. The board of directors has the sole authority to distribute earnings to the stockholders in the form of dividends.	____	____
6. The specified minimum stockholders' contribution that a corporation is required by law to retain for protection of its creditors is called legal capital.	____	____
7. Dividend rights are normally limited to a certain amount for preferred stock.	____	____
8. When par stock is issued for more than par, the excess of the contract price over par is termed a premium.	____	____
9. Sales of treasury stock result in a net decrease in paid-in capital.........	____	____
10. Expenditures incurred in organizing a corporation, such as legal fees, taxes, fees paid to the state, and promotional costs, are charged to an intangible asset account entitled Goodwill..........	____	____
11. A commonly used method for accounting for the purchase and resale of treasury stock is the derivative method.	____	____

	True	False
12. A major objective of a stock split is to increase stockholders' equity.	____	____
13. Paid-in capital and retained earnings are two major subdivisions of stockholders' equity.	____	____
14. A liability for a dividend is normally recorded in the accounting records on the date of record.	____	____
15. An accounting entry is required to record a stock dividend.	____	____

EXERCISE 13-1

Prepare the entries in general journal form to record each of the following unrelated transactions. (Omit explanations.)

(1) Cannuck Corp. issued 20,000 shares of no-par common stock for cash at $35 per share.

JOURNAL PAGE

	DATE		DESCRIPTION	POST. REF.	DEBIT	CREDIT	
1							1
2							2
3							3
4							4
5							5
6							6
7							7

(2) Dunlo Corp. issued 20,000 shares of $25 par common stock for cash at $25 per share.

JOURNAL PAGE

	DATE		DESCRIPTION	POST. REF.	DEBIT	CREDIT	
1							1
2							2
3							3
4							4
5							5
6							6
7							7

(3) Erickson Corp. issued 20,000 shares of $50 par common stock for cash at $60 per share.

JOURNAL PAGE

	DATE		DESCRIPTION	POST. REF.	DEBIT	CREDIT	
1							1
2							2
3							3
4							4
5							5
6							6
7							7

(4) Felix Corp. issued 10,000 shares of $10 par common stock in exchange for new manufacturing equipment with a fair market value of $145,000.

JOURNAL PAGE

	DATE		DESCRIPTION	POST. REF.	DEBIT	CREDIT	
1							1
2							2
3							3
4							4
5							5
6							6
7							7

(5) Huddley Corp. issued 10,000 shares of $25 par preferred stock for cash at $30 per share.

JOURNAL PAGE

	DATE		DESCRIPTION	POST. REF.	DEBIT	CREDIT	
1							1
2							2
3							3
4							4
5							5
6							6
7							7

EXERCISE 13-2

Journalize the following transactions of Copper Corp. (Omit explanations.)

(1) On February 20, Copper declared a $60,000 cash dividend.

(2) On March 22, Copper paid the cash dividend declared on February 20.

(3) On December 15, Copper declared a 5% stock dividend on 160,000 shares of $20 par value common stock with a market value of $25 per share.

(4) On January 14, Copper issued the stock certificates for the stock dividend declared on December 15.

(5) On February 20, Copper declared a 2-for-1 stock split, exchanging 380,000 shares of $10 par common stock for 190,000 shares of $20 par common stock.

JOURNAL PAGE

DATE		DESCRIPTION	POST. REF.	DEBIT	CREDIT

Exercise 13-3

Prepare the entries in general journal form to record each of the following treasury stock transactions of Pinell Corp. using the cost basis method. (Omit explanations.)

(1) On October 1, Pinell purchased 2,000 shares of treasury stock at $75.

(2) On October 31, Pinell sold 800 shares of the treasury stock it purchased on October 1 at $82.

(3) On November 20, Pinell sold 100 shares of the treasury stock it purchased on October 1 at $70.

JOURNAL PAGE

	DATE		DESCRIPTION	POST. REF.	DEBIT	CREDIT	
1							1
2							2
3							3
4							4
5							5
6							6
7							7
8							8
9							9
10							10
11							11
12							12
13							13
14							14
15							15
16							16
17							17
18							18
19							19
20							20
21							21
22							22
23							23
24							24
25							25
26							26
27							27

PROBLEM 13-1

Pattering Corp. has 4,000 shares of $10 par common stock outstanding and 1,000 shares of $100 par 8% cumulative preferred stock outstanding. Pattering expects to pay annual dividends of $7,000, $9,000, $28,000, and $48,000 respectively for the next four years.

Instructions: By completing the following form, indicate how the dividends should be distributed to the preferred stock and common stock.

		Preferred Dividends		Common Dividends	
Year	Total Dividends	Total	Per Share	Total	Per Share
1	$ 7,000				
2	9,000				
3	28,000				
4	48,000				

PROBLEM 13-2

The stockholders' equity of Southland Corp. consists of 100,000 shares of $25 par stock, additional paid-in capital of $1,500,000, and retained earnings of $6,440,000. Theodore Rafael owns 1,000 of the outstanding shares.

Instructions:

(1) In Column A below, fill in the blanks with the appropriate figures based on the data given.

(2) In Column B, fill in the blanks with the appropriate figures based on the data given, but after a $1.50 per share cash dividend has been declared and paid.

(3) In Column C, fill in the blanks with the appropriate figures based on the data given, but after a 5% stock dividend has been declared and distributed. The market value of Southland Corp.'s stock is $30. (Ignore the instructions in (2) when making these calculations.)

	A	B	C
	Before Any Dividend	After Cash Dividend	After Stock Dividend
a. Total number of shares outstanding			
b. Total par value of shares outstanding			
c. Total additional paid-in capital			
d. Total retained earnings			
e. Total stockholders' equity			
f. Amount required to pay a $1.50 per share cash dividend next year. (Assume no further changes in the capital structure.)			
g. Percentage of total stock owned by Rafael			
h. Total number of shares owned by Rafael			
i. Total par value of Rafael's shares ...			
j. Total equity of Rafael's shares			

PROBLEM 13-3

The following accounts and their balances appear in the ledger of Charleston Corporation on December 31, the end of the current fiscal year.

Common Stock, $25 par	$2,500,000
Paid-In Capital in Excess of Par—Common Stock	500,000
Paid-In Capital in Excess of Par—Preferred Stock	375,000
Paid-In Capital in Excess of Par—Treasury Stock	4,000
Preferred $10 Stock, $100 par	750,000
Retained Earnings	1,000,000
Treasury Stock—Common	50,000

Instructions: Prepare the stockholders' equity section of the balance sheet as of December 31, the end of the current year. Ten thousand shares of preferred and 150,000 shares of common stock are authorized. One thousand shares of common stock are held as treasury stock.

CHAPTER

14 Long-Term Liabilities: Bonds and Notes

QUIZ AND TEST HINTS

The following hints may be helpful to you in preparing for a quiz or a test over the material covered in Chapter 14.

1. Study the new terminology introduced in this chapter. Review the "Key Terms" section at the end of the chapter and be sure you understand each term. As a review of the key terms, do the Matching and Fill-in-the-Blank exercises included in this Study Guide.
2. It is unlikely that you will see a problem related to the Financing Corporations section of the chapter. Instead, you should focus primarily on being able to prepare the various journal entries illustrated throughout the chapter. The Illustrative Problem is a good study aid for reviewing the various journal entries.
3. Be ready to prepare entries for the issuance of bonds at face value, at a discount, and at a premium; for discount and premium amortization; and for bond redemption.
4. Review the GPS graphic at the beginning of the chapter and the "At A Glance" section at the end of the chapter. Read and review each of the Key Points and related Learning Outcomes. For each Learning Outcome that has an Example Exercise, locate the Example Exercise in the chapter and be sure that you understand the solution and can work a similar item on a test. If you have any questions about an Example Exercise, read the section of the chapter immediately preceding the Example Exercise.
5. If your instructor covers the Financial Analysis and Interpretation item at the end of the chapter, you should know how to compute and interpret the number of times interest charges are earned ratio.
6. If your instructor covers Appendix 1, Present Value Concepts and Pricing Bonds Payable, you should be familiar with present value terminology and how to use the present value tables in Exhibits 5 and 6. You should also be able to compute the present value of a bond. Study and review the illustrations in Appendix 1 in preparation for such test questions.

7. If your instructor covers Appendix 2, Effective Interest Rate Method of Amortization, you should be to compute the amortization of a bond discount and premium using the effective interest rate method. You should also be able to prepare journal entries for amortizing a bond discount and premium using this method. Study and review the illustrations in Appendix 2 in preparation for such test questions.

MATCHING

Instructions: Match each of the statements below with its proper term. Some terms may not be used.

A.	bond	**I.**	effective rate of interest
B.	bond indenture	**J.**	installment notes
C.	carrying amount	**K.**	mortgage notes
D.	contract rate	**L.**	number of times interest charges earned
E.	discount	**M.**	premium
F.	dividend yield	**N.**	serial bonds
G.	earnings per share	**O.**	term bonds
H.	effective interest rate method		

____ **1.** A form of an interest-bearing note used by corporations to borrow on a long-term basis.

____ **2.** Measures the income earned by each share of common stock.

____ **3.** Bonds that mature on several dates.

____ **4.** The contract between a corporation issuing bonds and the bond-holders.

____ **5.** The periodic interest to be paid on the bonds that is identified in the bond indenture; expressed as a percentage of the face amount of the bond.

____ **6.** The excess of the face amount of bonds over their issue price.

____ **7.** The excess of the issue price of bonds over their face amount.

____ **8.** The balance of the bonds payable account (face amount of the bonds) less any unamortized discount or plus any unamortized pre-mium.

____ **9.** The market rate of interest at the time bonds are issued.

____ **10.** A debt that requires the borrower to make equal periodic payments to the lender for the term of the debt.

____ **11.** An installment note that is secured by the assets of the borrower.

____ **12.** A ratio that measures the risk that interest payments to debtholders will continue to be made if earnings decrease.

FILL IN THE BLANK—PART A

Instructions: Answer the following questions or complete the statements by writing the appropriate words or amounts in the answer blanks.

1. A corporation issuing bonds enters into a contract with the bondholders. This contract is known as a(n) ____________ ____________.
2. In computing earnings per share on common stock, any ____________ dividends should be subtracted from net income.
3. A corporation reserves the right to redeem ____________ bonds before they mature.
4. Bonds issued on the general credit of the issuing corporation are called ____________ ____________.
5. The ____________ rate determines the periodic interest paid on a bond.
6. When the market rate of interest on bonds is lower than the contract rate, the bonds will sell at a(n) ____________.

7–8. The two methods for amortizing a bond discount are the ____________-____________ method and the ____________ ____________ ____________ method.

9. The balance of the bonds payable account (face amount of the bonds) less any unamortized discount or plus any unamortized premium is called the ____________ ____________.
10. If the balances of Bonds Payable and Discount on Bonds Payable are $400,000 and $12,000, respectively, the carrying amount of the bonds is ____________.
11. If $2,000,000 of bonds are sold at 101½, the amount of cash received is ____________.

12–13. The entry to record a payment on an installment note debits Notes Payable and ____________ and credits ____________.

14. Jones Company has redeemed bonds at 102. The bonds have a face value of $600,000 and an unamortized premium of $10,000. Jones Company will record a gain (or loss) on redemption of ____________ (indicate amount and gain or loss).
15. River Company had interest expenses of $2,500,000 and income before tax of $29,000,000. The number of times interest charges are earned is ____________.

FILL IN THE BLANK—PART B

Instructions: Answer the following questions or complete the statements by writing the appropriate words or amounts in the answer blanks.

1. A corporation reported $120,000 of net income and has outstanding 10,000 shares of $1 preferred stock, par of $50, and 50,000 shares of $100 par common stock. The earnings per share is ______________.

2. All of Sand Company's bonds mature at the same time. These are known as ______________ bonds.

3. Bonds that may be exchanged for other securities are called ____________________ bonds.

4. When the contract rate of interest on bonds equals the market rate of interest, the bonds sell at ____________________.

5. When the contract rate of interest on bonds is lower than the market rate of interest, the bonds sell at a(n) ______________.

6. When amortizing a discount on bonds payable, the amount of the discount amortization on bonds payable ______________ (increases or decreases) Interest Expense.

7. When amortizing a premium on bonds payable, the amount of the premium amortization on bonds payable ______________ (increases or decreases) Interest Expense.

8. A firm redeemed bonds at 95. The bonds have a face value of $500,000 and an unamortized discount of $15,000. The firm will record a gain (or loss) on redemption of ______________________ (indicate amount and gain or loss).

9. If Bonds Payable has a balance of $5,000,000 and Premium on Bonds Payable has a balance of $45,000, the carrying amount of the bonds is ______________.

10–12. On April 1, Avery Company issued $4,000,000, 5-year, 12% bonds for $4,280,000 with semiannual interest payable on March 31 and September 30. If the effective rate of interest is 10%, determine the following:

10. The interest paid on September 30 is ______________.

11. The amount of premium amortized on September 30, using the straight-line method is ______________.

12. The accrued interest payable on December 31 is ______________.

13. In No. 10, the total amount of annual interest expense ________________________ (increases, decreases, or remains the same) over the life of the bonds as the premium on bonds payable is amortized.

14. A debt that requires the borrower to make equal periodic payments to the lender for the term of the note is called a(n) ______________ note.

15. Canary Company had interest expenses of $500,000 and income before tax of $250,000. The number of times interest charges are earned is ______________.

Multiple Choice

Instructions: Circle the best answer for each of the following questions.

1. The ratio that measures the income earned by each share of common stock is:
   - **a.** number of times interest charges are earned
   - **b.** dividend yield
   - **c.** earnings per share
   - **d.** dividend per share
2. A bond that gives the bondholder a right to exchange the bond for other securities under certain conditions is called a:
   - **a.** convertible bond
   - **b.** sinking bond
   - **c.** term bond
   - **d.** debenture bond
3. Bonds that are issued on the basis of the general credit of the corporation are called:
   - **a.** callable bonds
   - **b.** convertible bonds
   - **c.** debenture bonds
   - **d.** term bonds
4. If the market rate of interest is less than the coupon rate of interest, the bonds will sell for a:
   - **a.** discount
   - **b.** face value
   - **c.** maturity value
   - **d.** premium
5. The entry to record the amortization of a discount on bonds payable is:
   - **a.** debit Bonds Payable; credit Interest Expense
   - **b.** debit Interest Expense; credit Discount on Bonds Payable
   - **c.** debit Discount on Bonds Payable; credit Interest Expense
   - **d.** debit Discount on Bonds Payable; credit Bonds Payable
6. Under the straight-line method of bond discount amortization, as a bond payable approaches maturity, the total yearly amount of interest expense will:
   - **a.** increase
   - **b.** decrease
   - **c.** remain the same
   - **d.** increase or decrease, depending on the size of the original discount

7. Bonds Payable has a balance of $900,000 and Discount on Bonds Payable has a balance of $45,000. The carrying amount of the bonds is:
   a. $45,000
   b. $855,000
   c. $900,000
   d. $945,000
8. The entry to record the amortization of a premium on bonds payable is:
   a. debit Bonds Payable; credit Interest Expense
   b. debit Interest Expense; credit Premium on Bonds Payable
   c. debit Premium on Bonds Payable; credit Interest Expense
   d. debit Premium on Bonds Payable; credit Bonds Payable
9. A bond issue with a face value of $800,000 on which there is unamortized premium of $30,000 is redeemed for $790,000. The gain or loss on the redemption of the bonds is a:
   a. $10,000 gain
   b. $20,000 gain
   c. $40,000 loss
   d. $40,000 gain
10. From the first to the final payment, interest expense on an installment note payable behaves as follows:
    a. decreases
    b. decreases
    c. remains the same
    d. decreases and then increases

TRUE/FALSE

Instructions: Indicate whether each of the following statements is true or false by placing a check mark in the appropriate column.

	True	False
1. The interest rate specified on the bond indenture is called the contract rate or effective rate.	____	____
2. If the market rate is lower than the contract rate, the bonds will sell at a discount.	____	____
3. The amortization of a premium on a bonds payable increases interest expense.	____	____
4. At the maturity date, the carrying amount of a bond payable will equal its face value.	____	____
5. The straight-line method of allocating bond discount provides for a constant amount of interest expense each period.	____	____
6. Bonds that may be exchanged for other securities under certain conditions are called callable bonds.	____	____
7. A corporation's earnings per share can be affected by whether it finances its operations with common stock, preferred stock, or bonds.	____	____
8. If the price paid to redeem bonds is below the bond carrying value, the difference is recorded as a gain.	____	____
9. The balance in a discount on bonds payable account is reported in the balance sheet as a deduction from the related bonds payable.	____	____
10. An installment note secured by a pledge of the borrower's assets is called a debenture note.	____	____

EXERCISE 14-1

(1) Star Corp. issued $500,000 of 10-year, 12% bonds on June 1 of the current year with interest payable on June 1 and December 1. Journalize the entries to record the following selected transactions for the current year:

June 1. Issued the bonds for cash at face amount.
Dec. 1. Paid the interest on the bonds.

JOURNAL PAGE

	DATE		DESCRIPTION	POST. REF.	DEBIT	CREDIT	
1							1
2							2
3							3
4							4
5							5
6							6
7							7
8							8

(2) On April 1, Turner Inc. issued $1,000,000 of 10-year, 11% bonds, with interest payable semiannually on April 1 and October 1 at an effective interest rate of 12%, receiving cash of $942,645. Journalize the entries to record the following selected transactions for the current year:

Apr. 1. Sold the bonds.
Oct. 1. Made first interest payment and amortized discount for six months using the straight-line method.

JOURNAL PAGE

	DATE		DESCRIPTION	POST. REF.	DEBIT	CREDIT	
1							1
2							2
3							3
4							4
5							5
6							6
7							7
8							8
9							9
10							10
11							11

(3) On March 1, Sullivan Inc. issued $700,000 of 10-year, 11% bonds at an effective interest rate of 10%, receiving $743,625. Interest is payable semi-annually on March 1 and September 1. Journalize the entries to record the following selected transactions for the current year.

Mar. 1. Sold the bonds.

Sept. 1. Made first interest payment and amortized premium for six months using the straight-line method.

JOURNAL PAGE

	DATE		DESCRIPTION	POST. REF.	DEBIT	CREDIT	
1							1
2							2
3							3
4							4
5							5
6							6
7							7
8							8
9							9
10							10
11							11
12							12

Exercise 14-2

Grimes Co. issued $5,000,000 of 10-year bonds at face value on January 1 of the current year.

Instructions:

(1) Assume the bonds are called at 101. Prepare the entry to record the redemption of the bonds.

JOURNAL PAGE

	DATE		DESCRIPTION	POST. REF.	DEBIT	CREDIT	
1							1
2							2
3							3
4							4
5							5

(2) Assume the bonds are purchased on the open market at 98. Prepare the entry to record the redemption of the bonds.

JOURNAL PAGE

	DATE		DESCRIPTION	POST. REF.	DEBIT	CREDIT	
1							1
2							2
3							3
4							4
5							5

EXERCISE 14-3

On the first day of the fiscal year, Johnson Company obtained a $60,000, eight-year, 5% installment note from City Bank. The note requires annual payments of $9,283, with the first payment occurring on the last day of the fiscal year. The first payment consists of interest of $3,000 and principal repayment of $6,283.

Instructions:

(1) Journalize the entries to record the following:

(a) Issued the installment notes for cash on the first day of the fiscal year.

(b) Paid the first annual payment on the note.

JOURNAL PAGE

	DATE		DESCRIPTION	POST. REF.	DEBIT	CREDIT	
1							1
2							2
3							3
4							4
5							5
6							6
7							7
8							8
9							9
10							10
11							11
12							12

(2) Determine the amount of bond interest expense for the first year.

PROBLEM 14-1

On December 31 of the current fiscal year, Palus Inc. issued $500,000 of 10-year, 11% bonds. The bonds were dated December 31 of the same year. Interest on the bonds is payable on June 30 and December 31 of each year.

Instructions:

Record the following transactions. (Omit explanations and round to the nearest dollar.)

(1) The bonds were sold for $531,161 on December 31 of the current year. The market rate of interest on this date was 10%.

(2) Interest was paid on June 30, and the related amount of bond premium was amortized, based on the straight-line method.

(3) Interest was paid on December 31, and the related amount of bond premium was amortized, based on the straight-line method.

(4) On December 31 (bonds are one year old), one-half of the bonds were redeemed at 103.

JOURNAL PAGE

	DATE		DESCRIPTION	POST. REF.	DEBIT	CREDIT	
1							1
2							2
3							3
4							4
5							5
6							6
7							7
8							8
9							9
10							10
11							11
12							12
12							13
14							14
15							15
16							16
17							17
18							18
19							19
20							20
21							21
22							22

PROBLEM 14-2

On January 1 of the current fiscal year, Block Co. issued $1,000,000 of 10-year, 10% bonds. The bonds were dated January 1 of the same year. Interest on the bonds is payable on June 30 and December 31 of each year.

Instructions:

Record the following transactions. (Omit explanations and round to the nearest dollar.)

(1) The bonds were sold for $885,295 on January 1 of the current year. The market rate of interest on that date was 12%.

(2) Interest was paid on June 30, and the related amount of bond discount was amortized, based on the straight-line method.

(3) Interest was paid on December 31, and the related amount of bond discount was amortized, based on the straight-line method.

(4) On December 31 (bonds are one year old), one-half of the bonds were redeemed at 98.

JOURNAL PAGE

DATE	DESCRIPTION	POST. REF.	DEBIT	CREDIT

PROBLEM 14-3
APPENDIX 1

Jackson Inc. issued $2,000,000 of 10-year, 11% bonds with interest payable semiannually.

Instructions:

(1) Compute (a) the cash proceeds and (b) the amount of premium or discount from the sale of the bonds if the effective interest rate is 11%. Use the following present value factors:

Present value of $1 for 20 periods at 5½%	0.3427
Present value of an annuity of $1 for 20 periods at 5½%	11.9504

(2) Compute (a) the cash proceeds and (b) the amount of premium or discount from the sale of the bonds if the effective interest rate is 12%. Use the following present value factors:

Present value of $1 for 20 periods at 6%	0.3118
Present value of an annuity of $1 for 20 periods at 6%	11.4699

(3) Compute (a) the cash proceeds and (b) the amount of premium or discount from the sale of the bonds if the effective interest rate is 10%. Use the following present value factors:

Present value of $1 for 20 periods at 5 %	0.3769
Present value of an annuity of $1 for 20 periods at 5 %	12.4622

PROBLEM 14-4
APPENDIX 2

Gallatin Corporation issued $30,000,000 of five-year, 15% bonds at an effective interest rate of 13%, with interest payable semiannually, receiving cash of $32,156,768.

Instructions:

(1) Determine the amount of premium to be amortized for the first semiannual interest payment period, using the interest method. (Round to the nearest dollar.)

(2) Determine the amount of premium to be amortized for the second semi-annual interest payment period, using the interest method. (Round to the nearest dollar.)

(3) Determine the amount of bond interest expense for the first year.

PROBLEM 14-5
APPENDIX 2

Billings Corporation issued $20,000,000 of five-year, 11% bonds at an effective interest rate of 14%, with interest payable semiannually, receiving cash of $17,892,938.

Instructions:

(1) Determine the amount of premium to be amortized for the first semiannual interest payment period, using the interest method. (Round to the nearest dollar.)

(2) Determine the amount of premium to be amortized for the second semi-annual interest payment period, using the interest method. (Round to the nearest dollar.)

(3) Determine the amount of bond interest expense for the first year.

CHAPTER

15 Investments and Fair Value Accounting

QUIZ AND TEST HINTS

The following hints may be helpful to you in preparing for a quiz or a test over the material covered in Chapter 15.

1. This chapter introduces investments and fair value accounting terminology that you should know. Review the "Key Terms" section at the end of the chapter and be sure you understand each term. Do the Matching and Fill-in-the-Blank exercises included in this Study Guide.
2. You should be able to prepare journal entries for the types of investment transactions illustrated in the chapter. Review the chapter illustrations. The Illustrative Problem at the end of the chapter is an excellent review of the types of entries you might have to prepare.
3. Review the GPS graphic at the beginning of the chapter and the "At A Glance" section at the end of the chapter. Read and review each of the Key Points and related Learning Outcomes. For each Learning Outcome that has an Example Exercise, locate the Example Exercise in the chapter and be sure that you understand the solution and work a similar item on a test. If you have any questions about an Example Exercise, read the section of the chapter immediately preceding the Example Exercise.
4. If your instructor covers the Financial Analysis and Interpretation item at the end of the chapter, you should know how to compute and interpret the dividend yield.
5. If your instructor covers Appendix 1, Accounting for Held-to-Maturity Investments, you may be required to prepare journal entries for the purchase of bonds as a held-to-maturity investment. In addition, you should be able to prepare the journal entries for the amortization of a premium or discount on the bond purchase.
6. If your instructor covers Appendix 2, Comprehensive Income, you should expect to see some true/false, matching, or multiple-choice questions on comprehensive income and its reporting on the financial statements. Review Appendix 2 and pay close attention to terminology.

MATCHING

Instructions: Match each of the statements below with its proper term. Some terms may not be used.

A. available-for-sale securities
B. business combination
C. consolidated financial statements
D. cost method
E. debt securities
F. equity method
G. equity securities
H. fair value
I. held-to-maturity securities
J. investee
K. investments
L. investor
M. operating income
N. other income (loss)
O. parent company
P. subsidiary company
Q. trading securities
R. unrealized gain or loss

____ **1.** Notes and bonds that pay interest and have a fixed maturity.

____ **2.** Preferred and common stock that represent ownership in a company and do not have a fixed maturity date.

____ **3.** Debt and equity securities purchased primarily to earn additional revenue.

____ **4.** The company investing in another company's stock.

____ **5.** The company whose stock is purchased.

____ **6.** The accounting method for investments of less than 20% of the investee's outstanding stock.

____ **7.** The section of the income statement in which a gain or loss on a debt or stock investment is reported.

____ **8.** A purchase of more than 50% ownership of the outstanding stock of another company.

____ **9.** A corporation owning all or a majority of the voting stock of another corporation.

____ **10.** A corporation whose majority of stock is owned by another corporation.

____ **11.** The combined financial statements of a parent and subsidiary corporation.

____ **12.** Debt and equity securities that are purchased and sold to earn short-term profits from changes in their market prices.

____ **13.** The price that would be received for selling an asset or paying off a liability.

____ **14.** The change in fair value of the portfolio (group) of trading securities.

____ **15.** Debt investments, such as notes or bonds, that a company intends to hold until their maturity date.

____ **16.** Debt and equity securities that are not classified as trading or held-to-maturity securities.

FILL IN THE BLANK—PART A

Instructions: Answer the following questions or complete the statements by writing the appropriate words or amounts in the answer blanks.

1. A company may invest in ________________ ________________ by replacing worn-out equipment.

2. Strategic long-term investments in another company are often made for purposes of a reduction of costs, replacement of management, expansion, or ________________.

3. When bonds are purchased between interest dates, in addition to debiting the bond investment account, the ______________ ______________ account is also debited.

4. When less than 20% of outstanding stock of the investee is owned by the investor, the degree of control that the investor has over the investee is ________________.

5. Investments of less than 20% of the investee's outstanding stock are accounted for using the ___________ method.

6. When less than 20% of outstanding stock of the investee is owned by the investor, the payment of dividends by the investee is recorded by the investor by debiting the cash account and crediting the ________________ ________________ account.

7. If the proceeds from the sale of a stock investment exceed the book value (cost) of the stock investment, a ___________ is recorded.

8. The gain or loss on sale of stock investments is reported on the income statement as ______________ ______________.

9. Under the equity method, the investor records its share of any dividends received from the investee as a credit to the ________________ account.

10. Under the equity method, the investor reports its share of the net income of the investee in the ______________ ______________ section of the income statement.

11. A corporation that is controlled by another corporation that owns more than 50% of its outstanding stock is called a ________________ company.

12. A portfolio of trading securities that costs $75,000 has a fair market value of $90,000. The fair value of the trading securities is recorded by debiting ________________ ________________ for Trading Investments and crediting Unrealized Gain on Trading Investments for $15,000.

13. An unrealized gain or loss on trading investments is reported on the ________________ ________________.

14. ______________-___-________________ securities are debt investments, such as notes or bonds, that a company intends to hold until their maturity date.

15. Held-to-maturity bond investments are reported on the balance sheet at their ______________ ______________.

16. Unrealized gains and losses of available-for-sale investments are reported as part of ________________ ________________ on the balance sheet.

17. A portfolio of available-for-sale securities that costs $80,000 has a fair market value of $85,000. The fair value of the trading securities is recorded by debiting ________________ ________________ for Available-for-Sale Investments and crediting Unrealized Gain on Available-for-Sale Investments for $5,000.

18. Trading securities are reported in the ____________ asset section of the balance sheet.

FILL IN THE BLANK—PART B

Instructions: Answer the following questions or complete the statements by writing the appropriate words or amounts in the answer blanks.

1. A company invests in temporary investments primarily to earn ________________ revenue, receive dividends, or realize gains from increases in the market price of the security.

2. Most companies invest excess cash in bonds as investments to earn ________________ ________________.

3. If the proceeds from the sale of a bond investment exceed the book value (cost) of the bonds, a ______________ is recorded.

4. When 20%–50% of outstanding stock of the investee is owned by the investor, the degree of control that the investor has over the investee is ________________ ________________.

5. Investments between 20% and 50% of the investee's outstanding stock are accounted for using the ______________ method.

6. When 20%–50% of outstanding stock of the investee is owned by the investor, the payment of dividends by the investee is recorded by the investor by debiting the cash account and crediting the ____________________ account.

7. If the proceeds from the sale of a stock investment are less than the book value (cost) of the stock investment, a ______________ is recorded.

8. Under the equity method, the investor records its share of the net income of the investee as a debit to the ____________________ account.

9. Taylor Co. owns 35% of Livingston Corporation. During the past year, Livingston Corporation reported $140,000 of net income. Taylor Co. would record (if any) ____________________ as its share of Livingston Corporation's net income.

10. A corporation owning all or a majority of the voting stock of another corporation is called a ____________________ company.

11. The individual financial statements of a parent and subsidiary are normally combined into ______________________ financial statements.

12. A portfolio of trading securities that costs $75,000 has a fair market value of $90,000. The fair value of the trading securities is recorded by debiting ____________________ ____________________ for Trading Investments and crediting Unrealized Gain on Trading Investments for $15,000.

13. An unrealized gain or loss on trading investments is reported in the ______________ ____________________ section of the income statement.

14. Held-to-maturity securities are primarily purchased to earn ______________ ____________________.

15. ______________ - ____ - __________ ____________________ are debt and equity securities that are not classified as trading or held-to-maturity securities.

16. Unrealized gains and losses of available-for-sale securities are reported on the ________________ ______________.

17. A portfolio of available-for-sale securities that costs $300,000 has a fair market value of $260,000. The fair value of the trading securities is recorded by debiting ____________________ ______________ on Available-for-Sale Investments and crediting Valuation Allowance for Available-for-Sale Investments for $40,000.

18. The price that would be received for selling an asset or paying off a liability is called ______________ ________________.

MULTIPLE CHOICE

Instructions: Circle the best answer for each of the following questions.

1. Which of the following is not a strategic purpose of a long-term investment in another company's common stock?
   a. expansion
   b. integration
   c. interest revenue
   d. reduction of costs
2. An investment in bonds with a book value of $125,700 is sold for $132,000. The gain or loss on the sale of the bond investments is:
   a. loss of $6,300
   b. gain of $6,300
   c. loss of $125,700
   d. gain of $132,000
3. An investor is assumed to have a degree of control of significant influence over the investee when the investor owns what percentage of the outstanding common stock of the investee?
   a. less than 20%
   b. between 20% and 50%
   c. between 51% and 80%
   d. between 80% and 100%
4. When an investor owns between 20% and 50% of the outstanding common stock of the investee, the investor should account for its investment in the investee using the:
   a. cost method
   b. equity method
   c. purchase method
   d. investment method
5. Charmayne Corp. owns 40% of the outstanding common stock of Nichols Inc., which reported $300,000 net income and paid dividends of $120,000 during the year. The entry by Charmayne Corp. to record its share of the net income of the investee using the equity method is:
   a. debit Cash, $48,000; credit Investment in Nichols Inc., $48,000
   b. debit Investment in Nichols Inc., $120,000; credit Dividend Revenue, $120,000
   c. debit Investment in Nichols Inc., $120,000; credit Income of Nichols Inc., $120,000
   d. debit Investment in Nichols Inc., $300,000; credit Income of Nichols Inc., $300,000

6. Which of the following is not a classification for valuing and reporting debt and equity securities?
   a. available-for-sale securities
   b. held-to-maturity securities
   c. bond securities
   d. trading securities
7. Debt and equity securities that are purchased and sold to earn short-term profits from changes in their market prices are called:
   a. available-for-sale securities
   b. held-to-maturity securities
   c. speculative securities
   d. trading securities
8. Changes in fair value of trading securities are recognized as:
   a. extraordinary gains or losses
   b. operating gains or losses
   c. realized gains or losses
   d. unrealized gains or losses
9. The balance of the valuation allowance for trading investments is reported in the financial statements as:
   a. an addition to or a deduction from the balance of the investments in trading securities in the current asset section of the balance sheet
   b. an addition to or a deduction from the balance of the investments in trading securities in the noncurrent asset section of the balance sheet
   c. an unrealized gain or loss on the income statement
   d. an addition to or a deduction from stockholders' equity
10. How are unrealized gains or losses for available-for-sale securities reported on the financial statements?
   a. on the income statement as other income or loss
   b. on the income statement as part of operating income
   c. on the balance sheet as an addition to or a deduction from investments
   d. on the balance sheet as an addition to or a deduction from stockholders' equity

TRUE/FALSE

Instructions: Indicate whether each of the following statements is true or false by placing a check mark in the appropriate column.

	Statement	True	False
1.	An investor corporation that owns 15% of the outstanding common stock of the investee corporation is assumed to have significant influence over the investee corporation.	____	____
2.	A corporation that owns 30% of the outstanding common stock of an investee corporation should use the equity method to account for its investment.	____	____
3.	Under the cost method, dividends received by the investor corporation are debited to Cash and credited to Dividend Revenue.	____	____
4.	Under the equity method, the investor's share of the net income of the investee corporation is credited to the investment account.	____	____
5.	The combined financial statements of a parent corporation and its subsidiary are called consolidated financial statements...	____	____
6.	Trading securities consist only of equity securities that are purchased and sold to earn short-term profits from changes in their market prices.	____	____
7.	An unrealized gain or loss on trading investments is reported on the income statement separately or as part of other income (losses).	____	____
8.	Held-to-maturity securities are debt securities that a company intends to hold until their maturity date......................	____	____
9.	An unrealized gain or loss on available-for-sale investments is reported on the income statement separately or as part of other income (losses).	____	____
10.	There is a current trend for the Financial Accounting Standards Board (FASB) to adopt accounting principles using fair values for valuing and reporting assets and liabilities. ..	____	____

EXERCISE 15-1

The following are selected bond investment transactions for Madison Inc.:

a. Purchased for cash $270,000 of Meriweather Co. 7% bonds at 100 plus accrued interest of $3,150.
b. Received first semiannual interest.
c. Sold $180,000 of the bonds at 102 plus accrued interest of $2,250.

Instructions: Prepare journal entries to record the preceding transactions.

JOURNAL PAGE

	DATE		DESCRIPTION	POST. REF.	DEBIT	CREDIT	
1							1
2							2
3							3
4							4
5							5
6							6
7							7
8							8
9							9
10							10
11							11
12							12
13							13
14							14
15							15
16							16
17							17
18							18
19							19
20							20

Exercise 15-2

On February 20, 5,000 shares of Rhymer Company are acquired at a price of $51 per share plus a $250 brokerage fee. On September 10, a $1.10 per share dividend was received on the Rhymer Company stock. On October 5, 2,000 shares of the Rhymer Company stock were sold for $45 per share less a $100 brokerage fee.

Instructions: Using the cost method, prepare the journal entries for the purchase, dividend, and sale of the stock.

JOURNAL

PAGE

	DATE		DESCRIPTION	POST. REF.	DEBIT	CREDIT	
1							1
2							2
3							3
4							4
5							5
6							6
7							7
8							8
9							9
10							10
11							11
12							12
13							13
14							14
15							15
16							16
17							17
18							18
19							19
20							20

Exercise 15-3

On January 9, Pruett Company acquired 40% of the outstanding stock of Tolley Company for $130,000. For the year ending December 31, Tolley Company earned income of $60,000 and paid dividends of $20,000.

Instructions: Using the equity method, prepare the entries for Pruett Company for the purchase of the stock, share of Tolley income, and dividends received from Tolley Company.

JOURNAL PAGE

	DATE		DESCRIPTION	POST. REF.	DEBIT	CREDIT	
1							1
2							2
3							3
4							4
5							5
6							6
7							7
8							8
9							9
10							10
11							11
12							12
13							13
14							14
15							15
16							16
17							17
18							18
19							19
20							20

EXERCISE 15-4

On January 1, 2010, Valuation Allowance for Investments had a credit balance of $1,000. On December 31, 2010, the cost of the trading securities portfolio was $26,200 and the fair value was $30,000.

Instructions: Prepare the December 31, 2010, adjusting journal entry to record the unrealized gain or loss on trading investments.

JOURNAL PAGE

	DATE		DESCRIPTION	POST. REF.	DEBIT	CREDIT	
1							1
2							2
3							3
4							4
5							5
6							6
7							7
8							8
9							9
10							10
11							11
12							12
13							13
14							14
15							15
16							16
17							17
18							18
19							19
20							20

Exercise 15-5

On January 1, 2010, Valuation Allowance on Available-for-Sale Securities had a debit balance of $4,000. On December 31, 2010, the cost of the available-for-sale securities was $90,000 and the fair value was $92,500.

Instructions: Prepare the adjusting entry to record the unrealized gain or loss for available-for-sale securities on December 31, 2010.

JOURNAL PAGE

	DATE		DESCRIPTION	POST. REF.	DEBIT	CREDIT	
1							1
2							2
3							3
4							4
5							5
6							6
7							7
8							8
9							9
10							10
11							11
12							12
13							13
14							14
15							15
16							16
17							17
18							18
19							19
20							20

PROBLEM 15-1

The following selected investment transactions were completed by Oconee Inc. during its first year of operations.

Jan. 23	Purchased 2,400 shares of Smith Company stock as an available-for-sale security at $23 per share plus an $ 240 brokerage commission.
Feb. 6	Purchased $20,000, 8% U.S. Treasury bonds at par value plus accrued interest. The bonds pay interest on January 1 and July 1. The bonds were classified as held-to-maturity securities.
Mar. 10	Purchased 3,800 shares of Jones Company stock as a trading security at $48 per share plus a $304 brokerage commission.
May 31	Purchased 100,000 shares of Hill Company at $37 per share plus a $4,000 brokerage commission. Hill Company has 400,000 common shares issued and outstanding. The equity method was used for this investment.
July 1	Received semiannual interest on bonds purchased on February 6.
Aug. 9	Sold 2,400 shares of Jones Company stock at $61 per share less a $180 brokerage commission.
Oct. 5	Received $0.80 per share dividend on Smith Company stock.
Nov. 11	Received $1.10 per share dividend on Hill Company stock.
Dec. 31	Accrued interest on February 6 bonds.
Dec. 31	Hill Company earnings were $946,000 for the year.
Dec. 31	Fair values were:

Smith Company	$30
Jones Company	43
Hill Company	40

Instructions: Prepare journal entries for the preceding transactions.

JOURNAL

PAGE

	DATE		DESCRIPTION	POST. REF.	DEBIT	CREDIT	
1							1
2							2
3							3
4							4
5							5
6							6
7							7
8							8
9							9
10							10
11							11
12							12
13							13
14							14
15							15
16							16
17							17
18							18
19							19
20							20
21							21
22							22
23							23
24							24
25							25
26							26
27							27
28							28
29							29
30							30
31							31
32							32
33							33
34							34
35							35
36							36

JOURNAL

PAGE

	DATE		DESCRIPTION	POST. REF.	DEBIT	CREDIT	
1							1
2							2
3							3
4							4
5							5
6							6
7							7
8							8
9							9
10							10
11							11
12							12
13							13
14							14
15							15
16							16
17							17
18							18
19							19
20							20
21							21
22							22
23							23
24							24
25							25
26							26
27							27
28							28
29							29
30							30
31							31
32							32
33							33
34							34
35							35
36							36

CHAPTER

16 Statement of Cash Flows

QUIZ AND TEST HINTS

The following hints may be helpful to you in preparing for a quiz or a test over the material covered in Chapter 16.

1. Study the new terminology introduced in this chapter. Review the "Key Terms" section at the end of the chapter and be sure you understand each term. Do the Matching and Fill-in-the-Blank exercises included in this Study Guide.
2. You should be able to classify different types of cash flows as operating, investing, or financing activities. Test questions on this material often appear in a true/false or multiple-choice format.
3. Instructors may emphasize the indirect method, the direct method, or both methods of preparing the statement of cash flows. Adjust your studying to the method or methods that your instructor emphasized during class lectures and in homework assignments. You should be able to prepare a statement of cash flows using one or both methods. Often, instructors will include a partially completed statement of cash flows on an examination and require students to complete it. The Illustrative Problem is a good study aid for both the indirect and direct methods.
4. The statement of cash flows can be prepared by evaluating the changes in the noncash balance sheet accounts. Changes in the noncash current accounts are adjustments to net income in determining cash flows from operating activities under the indirect method. While changes in long-term assets are usually investing activities, changes in long-term liabilities and stockholders' equity paid in capital accounts are usually financing activities. The cash dividends are also financing activities.
5. Review the GPS graphic at the beginning of the chapter and the "At A Glance" section at the end of the chapter. Read and review each of the Key Points and related Learning Outcomes. For each Learning Outcome that has an Example Exercise, locate the Example Exercise in the chapter and be sure that you understand the solution and can work a similar item on a test. If you have any questions about an Example Exercise, read the section of the chapter immediately preceding the Example Exercise.

6. If your instructor covers the Financial Analysis and Interpretation item at the end of the chapter, you should know how to compute and interpret changes in free cash flow.

7. The spreadsheet (work sheet) for preparing the statement of cash flows for the indirect method appears in the Appendix to the chapter. Study the Appendix if your instructor has expressed a preference for use of this spreadsheet (work sheet) in preparing the statement of cash flows.

MATCHING

Instructions: Match each of the statements below with its proper term. Some terms may not be used.

A. cash flows from financing activities
B. cash flows from investing activities
C. cash flows from operating activities
D. direct method
E. free cash flow
F. indirect method
G. statement of cash flows

____ **1.** The section of the statement of cash flows that reports cash flows from transactions affecting the equity and debt of the business.

____ **2.** The section of the statement of cash flows that reports cash flows from transactions affecting investments in noncurrent assets.

____ **3.** A summary of the major cash receipts and cash payments for a period.

____ **4.** A method of reporting the cash flows from operating activities as the difference between the operating cash receipts and the operating cash payments.

____ **5.** The section of the statement of cash flows that reports the cash transactions affecting the determination of net income.

____ **6.** A method of reporting the cash flows from operating activities as the net income from operations adjusted for all deferrals of past cash receipts and payments and all accruals of expected future cash receipts and payments.

____ **7.** The amount of operating cash flow remaining after replacing current productive capacity.

FILL IN THE BLANK—PART A

Instructions: Answer the following questions or complete the statements by writing the appropriate words or amounts in the answer blanks.

1. The financial statement that reports a firm's major cash inflows and outflows for a period is the __________________ ______ __________ __________.

2. The two alternative methods of reporting operating activities in the statement of cash flows are the _____________ and _____________ methods.

3–7. Indicate the section of the statement of cash flows in which each of the following would appear (answer operating activities, investing activities, or financing activities):

3. Depreciation expense on equipment would appear under ________________ activities.

4. Sale of long-term investments would appear under ________________ activities.

5. Sale of equipment would appear under ________________ activities.

6. Issuance of bonds would appear under ________________ activities.

7. Sale of patents would appear under ________________ activities.

8–10. This year, Young Company issued 500,000 shares of common stock, inventory increased by $20,000, and a new asset was purchased for $1,000,000. For each of these events, indicate whether net cash flows increased or decreased:

8. Common stock issued. Net cash flows ________________.

9. Inventory increased. Net cash flows ________________.

10. New asset purchased. Net cash flows ________________.

11. Cash dividends of $35,000 were declared during the year. Cash dividends payable were $8,000 and $8,750 at the beginning and end of the year, respectively. The amount of cash flows for payment of dividends during the year is ______________.

12. The net income from operations was $75,000, and the only revenue or expense item not affecting cash was depreciation expense of $27,000. The amount of net cash flows from operating activities that would appear on the statement of cash flows is ______________.

13. A corporation purchased and retired 3,000 shares of its $50 par common stock, originally issued at par, for $65. Cash flows amounted to ______________.

14. If a fixed asset having a book value of $54,000 is sold (for cash) at a gain of $6,000, the total amount reported as a cash flow is ______________.

15. The $47,000 net income for the year included a loss of $2,500 on the sale of land. Exclusive of the effect of other adjustments, the amount of net cash flows from operating activities is ______________.

16. A corporation issued $1,000,000 of bonds payable at 104. Cash flow from this transaction was ______________.

17. If 15,000 shares of $20 par common stock were issued at 22, the amount to be reported in the cash flows from financing activities section of the statement of cash flows would be ______________.

18. Cash flows resulting from the redemption of debt securities are classified in the statement of cash flows as related to ______________ activities.

19. Jones Company had cash flow from operations of $75,000. This year, dividends paid amounted to $6,000, and the company purchased $9,000 in spare parts for machines used on the factory floor. Jones Company's free cash flow is ______________.

20. A cash flow term for which an amount should not be reported in the financial statements because it could mislead readers is _________ _________ _______ _________.

FILL IN THE BLANK—PART B

Instructions: Answer the following questions or complete the statements by writing the appropriate words or amounts in the answer blanks.

1. The __________________ method of analyzing operating cash flows begins with net income and adjusts it for revenues and expenses that do not involve the receipt or payment of cash.

2. The statement of cash flows groups cash flow activities as financing, investing, or ________________.

3. When the ______________ method of reporting cash flows is used, a supplemental schedule reconciling net income and net cash flow from operating activities must also be prepared.

4–8. Indicate the section of the statement of cash flows in which each of the following would appear (answer operating activities, investing activities, or financing activities):

4. Retirement of long-term debt would appear under _________________ activities.

5. Sale of common stock would appear under ___________________ activities.

6. Net income would appear under ___________________ activities.

7. Payment of cash dividends would appear under __________________ activities.

8. Purchase of equipment would appear under __________________ activities.

9. ______________ investing and financing activities that will affect future cash flows are reported in a separate schedule to the statement of cash flows.

10–11. Indicate whether each of the following items would be added to or deducted from net income on the schedule reconciling net income with cash flows from operating activities:

10. Increase in inventories would be ______________ __________ net income.

11. Increase in accounts payable would be ______________ __________ net income.

12. If a loss of $15,000 is incurred in selling (for cash) store equipment having a book value of $345,000, the total amount reported as a cash flow is ______________.

13. A corporation issued $750,000 of 20-year bonds at 99½. Cash flows were ______________.

14. A corporation purchased 25,000 shares of its $100 par common stock, originally issued at par, as treasury stock for $125. Cash flows were ______________.

15. Cash dividends of $50,000 were declared during the year. Cash dividends payable were $8,500 and $12,500 at the beginning and end of the year, respectively. The amount of cash flows for the payment of dividends during the year is ______________.

16. The net loss from operations was $15,000, and the only revenue or expense item not affecting cash was depreciation expense of $35,000. The amount to be reported as net cash flow from operating activities on the statement of cash flows is ______________.

17. In preparing a statement of cash flows under the indirect method, it is efficient to analyze the ______________ ______________ account first.

18. The $55,000 net income for the year included a gain of $4,000 on the sale of equipment. Exclusive of the effect of other adjustments, the amount of net cash flows from operating activities is ______________.

19. Cash flow for interest expense is included on the statement of cash flows as an ______________ activity.

20. A measure of cash available for corporate purposes, after productive assets are maintained, is called __________ __________ __________.

MULTIPLE CHOICE

Instructions: Circle the best answer for each of the following questions.

1. Which of the following is not one of the major sections of the statement of cash flows?
   a. cash flows from financing activities
   b. cash flows from selling activities
   c. cash flows from operating activities
   d. cash flows from investing activities

2. Noncash investing and financing activities which may have a significant effect on future cash flows are reported:
   a. in the statement of cash flows
   b. in a separate schedule to accompany the statement of cash flows
   c. in the retained earnings statement
   d. in a footnote accompanying the balance sheet

3. Under the indirect method, which of the following items must be deducted from reported net income to determine net cash flow from operating activities?
   a. depreciation of fixed assets
   b. decreases in current assets
   c. decreases in current liabilities
   d. loss on sale of equipment

4. During the past year, Lockhart Inc. declared $40,000 in cash dividends. If the beginning and ending balance of the dividends payable account was $12,000 and $10,000, respectively, what amount of cash paid for dividends will appear in the cash flow from financing activities section of the statement of cash flows?
   a. $30,000
   b. $38,000
   c. $40,000
   d. $42,000

5. Under the direct method, which of the following items must be added to operating expenses reported on the income statement to determine cash payments for operating expenses?
   a. increase in accrued expenses
   b. decrease in prepaid expenses
   c. increase in income taxes payable
   d. increase in prepaid expenses

6. An example of a cash flow from a financing activity is:
   a. receipt of cash from sale of land
   b. receipt of cash from collection of accounts receivable
   c. payment of cash for acquisition of treasury stock
   d. payment of cash for new machinery

7. Which of the following items appears first on the statement of cash flows prepared using the direct method?
   a. retained earnings
   b. cash received from customers
   c. net income
   d. depreciation

8. Which of the following would not be considered a noncash investing and financing activity in preparing a statement of cash flows?
   a. withdrawal of cash by the owner of a business
   b. issuance of common stock to retire long-term debt
   c. acquisition of a manufacturing plant by issuing bonds
   d. issuance of common stock in exchange for convertible preferred stock

9. To convert the cost of merchandise sold as reported on the income statement to cash payments for merchandise, the cost of merchandise sold is increased for the:
   a. increase in inventories
   b. increase in accounts payable
   c. decrease in inventories
   d. decrease in accounts receivable

10. Cash payments for income taxes are included on the statement of cash flows as:
    a. financing activities
    b. investing activities
    c. operating activities
    d. nonoperating activities

11. A loss on the sale of land is reflected on the statement of cash flows by:
    a. adding the loss to the book value of the land to determine the cash flow from investing activities.
    b. deducting the loss from net income to determine the cash flow from operating activities.
    c. deducting the loss from the book value of the land to determine the cash flow from investing activities.
    d. both b and c

12. Caldwell Company had cash flows from operating activities of $290,000. Depreciation expense for the year was $25,000. Cash flows for dividends totaled $32,000. Cash flows used for purchasing property, plant, and equipment to maintain existing operations was $60,000. What is the free cash flow?
    a. $193,000
    b. $218,000
    c. $230,000
    d. $250,000

TRUE/FALSE

Instructions: Indicate whether each of the following statements is true or false by placing a check mark in the appropriate column.

	True	False
1. The statement of cash flows is required as part of the basic set of financial statements.	____	____
2. Cash outflows from the payment of cash dividends is a type of financing activity.	____	____
3. Cash receipts from the sale of fixed assets would be classified as a cash flow from investing activities.	____	____
4. Under the direct method, depreciation is the first noncash account balance analyzed.	____	____
5. Under the indirect method, increases in current liabilities are deducted from net income reported on the income statement in determining cash flows from operating activities.	____	____
6. Noncash investing and financing activities that may have a significant effect on future cash flows should be included in a separate schedule to the statement of cash flows.	____	____
7. The correct amount to include in cash flows from financing activities is cash dividends paid, not cash dividends declared.	____	____
8. The analysis of retained earnings provides a starting point for determining cash flows from operating activities under the indirect method.	____	____
9. The direct method provides a more accurate figure of cash flows from operating activities than does the indirect method.	____	____
10. Under the direct method, the increase in the trade receivables account is deducted from sales to determine the cash received from customers.	____	____

Exercise 16-1

Instructions: Listed in the first column below are selected transactions and account balance changes of Mason Inc. for the current year. Indicate by placing a check mark in the appropriate column(s) how each of the items would be reported in the statement of cash flows.

Item	Cash Flows From			Schedule of Noncash Investing and Financing Activities
	Operating Activities	Investing Activities	Financing Activities	
1. Decrease in prepaid expenses...........				
2. Retirement of bonds				
3. Proceeds from sale of investments....				
4. Increase in inventories.......................				
5. Issuance of common stock				
6. Purchase of equipment......................				
7. Cash dividends paid..........................				
8. Acquisition of building in exchange for bonds..				
9. Amortization of patents				
10. Amortization of discount on bonds payable				

EXERCISE 16-2

The net income reported on the income statement of Hunter Inc. for the current year was $150,000. Depreciation recorded on equipment and building amounted to $45,000 for the year. Balances of the current asset and current liability accounts at the beginning and end of the year are as follows:

	End of Year	Beginning of Year
Cash	$ 42,875	$ 36,250
Trade receivables (net)	147,500	137,500
Inventories	109,375	93,750
Prepaid expenses	9,250	11,875
Accounts payable (merchandise creditors)	57,000	40,000
Salaries payable	7,625	10,625

Instructions: Prepare the cash flows from operating activities section of the statement of cash flows using the indirect method.

EXERCISE 16-3

The income statement of Hunter Inc. for the current year is as follows:

Sales		$530,000
Cost of merchandise sold		130,000
Gross profit		$400,000
Operating expenses:		
Depreciation expense	$ 45,000	
Other operating expenses	160,000	
Total operating expenses		205,000
Income before income tax		$195,000
Income tax		45,000
Net income		$150,000

Instructions: Using the income statement presented above and the account balances provided in Exercise 16-2, prepare the cash flows from operating activities section of the statement of cash flows using the direct method.

PROBLEM 16-1

The comparative balance sheet of Stellar Inc. at December 31, 2010, appears below.

Stellar Inc.
Comparative Balance Sheet
December 31, 2010 and 2009

	2010	2009	Increase Decrease*
Assets			
Cash	$ 84,000	$ 66,000	$ 18,000
Trade receivables (net)	156,000	144,000	12,000
Inventories	300,000	306,000	6,000*
Prepaid expenses	12,000	14,400	2,400*
Land	80,000	96,000	16,000*
Building	360,000	360,000	0
Accumulated depreciation—building	(120,000)	(91,200)	(28,800)
Equipment	180,000	102,000	78,000
Accumulated depreciation—equipment	(72,000)	(70,800)	(1,200)
Total assets	$980,000	$926,400	$ 53,600
Liabilities			
Accounts payable	$216,000	$208,800	$ 7,200
Dividends payable	24,000	21,600	2,400
Bonds payable	240,000	300,000	60,000*
Total liabilities	$480,000	$530,400	$ 50,400*
Stockholders' Equity			
Common stock	$140,000	$120,000	$ 20,000
Retained earnings	360,000	276,000	84,000
Total stockholders' equity	$500,000	$396,000	$104,000
Total liabilities and stockholders' equity	$980,000	$926,400	$ 53,600

The following additional data were taken from the records of Stellar Inc.:

a. Equipment costing $96,000 was purchased, and fully depreciated equipment costing $18,000 was discarded.

b. Net income, including gain on sale of land, was $114,000. Depreciation expense on equipment was $19,200; on building, $28,800.

c. Bonds payable of $60,000 were retired at face value.

d. A cash dividend of $30,000 was declared.

e. Land costing $36,000 was sold for $54,000, resulting in an $18,000 gain on the sale.

f. Land was acquired by issuing common stock, $20,000.

Instructions: Complete the following statement of cash flows using the indirect method of reporting cash flows from operating activities.

Stellar Inc.
Statement of Cash Flows
For Year Ended December 31, 2010

Cash flows from operating activities:		
Net income, per income statement	$ ______	
Adjustments to reconcile net income to net cash flow from operating activities:		
Depreciation	______	
Gain on sale of land	______	
Changes in current operating assets and liabilities:		
Increase in trade receivables	______	
Decrease in inventories	______	
Decrease in prepaid expenses	______	
Increase in accounts payable	______	
Net cash flow from operating activities		$ ______
Cash flows from investing activities:		
Cash received from land sold	$ ______	
Less: Cash paid for purchase of equipment ..	______	
Net cash flow used for investing activities		______
Cash flows from financing activities:		
Cash used to retire bonds payable	$ ______	
Cash paid for dividends	______	
Net cash flow used for financing activities		______
Increase in cash		$ ______
Cash, January 1, 2010		______
Cash, December 31, 2010		$ ______

Schedule of Noncash Investing and Financing Activities:

Acquisition of land by issuance of common stock .... $ ______

PROBLEM 16-2

The income statement of Stellar Inc. is provided below. Stellar's comparative balance sheet data were provided in Problem 16-1.

Instructions: Complete the statement of cash flows for Stellar Inc. using the direct method of reporting cash flows from operating activities.

Stellar Inc.
Income Statement
For Year Ended December 31, 2010

Sales		$575,000
Cost of merchandise sold		225,000
Gross profit		$350,000
Operating expenses:		
Depreciation expense	$ 48,000	
Other operating expenses	172,000	
Total operating expenses		220,000
Income from operations		$130,000
Other income:		
Gain on sale of land		18,000
Income before income tax		$148,000
Income tax		34,000
Net income		$114,000

Stellar Inc.
Statement of Cash Flows
For Year Ended December 31, 2010

Cash flows from operating activities:			
Cash received from customers		$	
Deduct: Cash payments for merchandise	$		
Cash payments for operating expenses			
Cash payments for income tax			
Net cash flow from operating activities			$
Cash flows from investing activities:			
Cash received from land sold		$	
Less cash paid for purchase of equipment			
Net cash flow used for investing activities			
Cash flows from financing activities:			
Cash used to retire bonds payable		$	
Cash paid for dividends			
Net cash flow used for financing activities			
Increase in cash			$
Cash, January 1, 2010			
Cash, December 31, 2010			$

Schedule of Noncash Investing and Financing Activities:

Acquisition of land by issuance of common stock	$

Schedule Reconciling Net Income with Cash Flows from Operating Activities:

Cash flows from operating activities:	
Net income, per income statement	$
Adjustments to reconcile net income to net cash flow from operating activities:	
Depreciation	
Gain on sale of land	
Changes in current operating assets and liabilities:	
Increase in trade receivables	
Decrease in inventories	
Decrease in prepaid expenses	
Increase in accounts payable	
Net cash flow from operating activities	$

Supporting calculations:

CHAPTER

17 Financial Statement Analysis

Quiz and Test Hints

The following hints may be helpful to you in preparing for a quiz or a test over the material covered in Chapter 17.

1. When studying this chapter, you should focus primarily on the various analytical measures described and illustrated. These measures are also summarized in Exhibit 10 of the chapter. Pay special attention to each measure's computation, its use, and its classification as either a solvency or profitability measure. A good study aid for the computation of the measures is the Illustrative Problem at the end of the chapter.
2. Instructors will often include exam problems asking you to provide either a horizontal or vertical analysis. Be familiar with both of these.
3. Instructors often use true/false and multiple-choice questions to test this chapter. Such questions may require the computation of ratios or test your understanding of various terms introduced in the chapter.
4. You should be familiar with the new terminology introduced in this chapter. Review the "Key Terms" section at the end of the chapter and be sure you understand each term. Do the Matching and Fill-in-the-Blank exercises included in this Study Guide.
5. Review the GPS graphic at the beginning of the chapter and the "At A Glance" section at the end of the chapter. Read and review each of the Key Points and related Learning Outcomes. For each Learning Outcome that has an Example Exercise, locate the Example Exercise in the chapter and be sure that you understand the solution and can work a similar item on a test. If you have any questions about an Example Exercise, read the section of the chapter immediately preceding the Example Exercise.

MATCHING

Instructions: Match each of the statements below with its proper term. Some terms may not be used.

A. accounts receivable turnover
B. asset turnover
C. common-size statement
D. current ratio
E. dividend yield
F. dividends per share
G. earnings per share (EPS) on common stock
H. horizontal analysis
I. inventory turnover
J. leverage
K. Management Discussion and Analysis
L. number of days' sales in inventory
M. number of days' sales in receivables
N. number of times interest charges earned
O. price-earnings (P/E) ratio
P. profitability
Q. quick assets
R. quick ratio
S. rate earned on common stockholders' equity
T. rate earned on stockholders' equity
U. rate earned on total assets
V. ratio of fixed assets to long-term liabilities
W. ratio of liabilities to stockholders' equity
X. solvency
Y. vertical analysis

____ **1.** The percentage of increases and decreases in corresponding items in comparative financial statements.

____ **2.** The sum of cash, receivables, and marketable securities.

____ **3.** The relationship between the volume of sales and inventory, computed by dividing the average inventory by the average daily cost of goods sold.

____ **4.** The ability of a firm to pay its debts as they come due.

____ **5.** The relationship between credit sales and accounts receivable, computed by dividing the average net accounts receivable by the average daily sales on account.

____ **6.** The relationship between credit sales and accounts receivable, computed by dividing net sales on account by the average net accounts receivable.

____ **7.** The tendency of the rate earned on stockholders' equity to vary from the rate earned on total assets because the amount earned on assets acquired through the use of funds provided by creditors varies from the interest paid to these creditors.

____ **8.** A financial statement in which all items are expressed only in relative terms.

____ **9.** A measure of profitability computed by dividing net income by total stockholders' equity.

____ **10.** The ratio of the market price per share of common stock, at a specific date, to the annual earnings per share.

____ **11.** A measure of the profitability of assets, without regard to the equity of creditors and stockholders in the assets.

____ **12.** The profitability ratio of net income available to common shareholders to the number of common shares outstanding.

____ **13.** The number of sales dollars earned for each dollar of total assets calculated as the ratio of sales to total assets.

____ **14.** The percentage analysis of component parts in relation to the total of the parts in a single financial statement.

____ **15.** A measure of profitability computed by dividing net income, reduced by preferred dividend requirements, by common stockholders' equity.

____ **16.** The ratio of current assets to current liabilities.

____ **17.** The relationship between the volume of goods sold and inventory, computed by dividing the cost of goods sold by the average inventory.

____ **18.** The ability of a firm to earn income.

____ **19.** An annual report disclosure that provides an analysis of the results of operations and financial condition.

Fill in the Blank—Part A

Instructions: Answer the following questions or complete the statements by writing the appropriate words or amounts in the answer blanks.

1. Percentage analysis used to show the relationship of the component parts to the total in a single statement is called ____________ ____________.
2. __________________ ____________ focuses primarily on the relationship between operating results as reported in the income statement and resources available to the business as reported in the balance sheet.
3. The use of ratios showing the ability of an enterprise to pay its current liabilities is known as ____________ ____________ ____________.
4. ________________ is the ability of a business to meet its financial obligations as they come due.
5. ______________-________ statements are prepared in order to compare percentages of the current period with past periods, to compare individual businesses, or to compare one business with industry percentages published by trade associations or financial information services.
6. The ratio of current assets to current liabilities is called the ____________ ratio.
7. The ratio of _______ __________ ______ ___________ is a profitability measure that shows how effectively a firm utilizes its assets.
8. The ratio of the sum of cash, receivables, and marketable securities to current liabilities is called the __________ ratio.
9. ___________ ______ __________ _____ ____________ _________ is the ratio of net income available to common shareholders to the number of common shares outstanding.
10. The excess of the current assets of a business over its current liabilities is called ______________ _____________.
11. ______________ ___________________ ______________ is computed by dividing net sales by the average net accounts receivable.
12. ________________ _______________ is computed by dividing the cost of goods sold by the average inventory.
13. The ratio of __________________ _______ ______________________ ___________ is a solvency measure that indicates the margin of safety for creditors.
14. The number of times ________________ _________________ _______ _____________ is a measure of the risk that dividends to preferred stockholders may not be paid.

15. If significant amounts of nonoperating income and expense are reported on the income statement, it may be desirable to compute the ratio of ______ ______ ______ to total assets as a profitability measure.

16. The rate earned on ______ ______ focuses only on the rate of profits earned on the amount invested by common stockholders.

17. Earnings per share and ______ per share on common stock are commonly used by investors in assessing alternative stock investments.

18. All publicly held corporations are required to have a(n) ______ ______ of their financial statements.

19. The ratio of ______ ______ ______ ______-______ ______ is a solvency measure that indicates the margin of safety of the noteholders or bondholders.

20. In a vertical analysis of the income statement, each item is stated as a percent of ______ ______.

Fill in the Blank—Part B

Instructions: Answer the following questions or complete the statements by writing the appropriate words or amounts in the answer blanks.

1. The percentage analysis of increases and decreases in corresponding items in comparative financial statements is called ______ ______.

2. The ______ ______ is a profitability measure that shows the rate of return to common stockholders in terms of cash dividend distributions.

3. The ______ ______ report describes the results of an independent examination of the financial statements.

4. The ______ ______ ______ ______ ______ ______ is computed by dividing the average net accounts receivable by the average daily net sales.

5. The ______ ______ ______ ______ ______ ______ is computed by dividing the average inventory by the average daily cost of goods sold.

6. The number of times ______ ______ ______ is a measure of the risk that interest payments will not be made if earnings decrease.

7. The ______ ______ ______ ______ ______ measures the profitability of total assets, without considering how the assets are financed.

8. The ________ ___________ _____ __________________ __________ is computed by dividing net income by average total stockholders' equity.

9. The difference between the rate earned by a business on the equity of its stockholders and the rate earned on total assets is called _____________.

10. The __________-____________ ratio is computed by dividing the market price per share of common stock at a specific date by the annual earnings per share.

11. The ______________________ ___________________ _______ ________________ section of a corporate annual report includes management's analysis of the results of operations, financial condition, and significant risks.

12. ___________ ___________ are cash and other current assets that can be quickly converted to cash.

13. In a(n) ______________-_________ statement, all items are expressed as percentages.

14. ________________ ______________ focuses on the ability of a business to pay or otherwise satisfy its current and noncurrent liabilities.

15. The current ratio is sometimes called the working capital ratio or the _____________ ratio.

16. Two measures that are useful for evaluating the management of inventory are the inventory turnover and the ____________ ______ _________ _________ ______ _______________.

17. A profitability measure often quoted in the financial press and normally reported in the income statement in corporate annual reports is ______________ _______ __________.

18. All items in _______________-__________ statements are expressed only in relative terms.

19. Quick assets normally include cash, marketable securities, and _________________.

20. The Sarbanes-Oxley Act requires independent auditors to attest to management's assessment of ______________ ____________.

MULTIPLE CHOICE

Instructions: Circle the best answer for each of the following questions.

1. Statements in which all items are expressed only in relative terms (percentages of a common base) are:
   a. relative statements
   b. horizontal statements
   c. vertical statements
   d. common-size statements
2. Which one of the following measures is a solvency measure?
   a. rate earned on total assets
   b. price-earnings ratio
   c. accounts receivable turnover
   d. ratio of net sales to assets
3. Based on the following data for the current year, what is the inventory turnover?

Net sales	$6,500,000
Cost of goods sold	$4,000,000
Inventory, beginning of year	$250,000
Inventory, end of year	$345,000
Accounts receivable, beginning of year	$175,000
Accounts receivable, end of year	$297,000

   a. 26.7
   b. 16
   c. 13.4
   d. 11.6
4. Based on the following data for the current year, what is the accounts receivable turnover?

Net sales	$6,500,000
Cost of goods sold	$4,000,000
Inventory, beginning of year	$250,000
Inventory, end of year	$345,000
Accounts receivable, beginning of year	$175,000
Accounts receivable, end of year	$297,000

   a. 37.1
   b. 27.5
   c. 21.8
   d. 17

5. Which of the following sections of corporate annual reports normally includes a statement concerning future prospects and risks?
   a. independent auditor's report
   b. footnotes to the financial statements
   c. management's internal control assertion
   d. management discussion and analysis

6. A measure used in evaluating the efficiency in collecting receivables is:
   a. working capital ratio
   b. quick ratio
   c. receivables/inventory ratio
   d. number of days' sales in receivables

7. Based on the following data for the current year, compute the number of times interest charges are earned.

Income before income tax	$510,000
Interest expense	$30,000
Total assets	$4,080,000

   a. 8
   b. 17
   c. 18
   d. 136

8. Based on the following data for the current year, what is the quick ratio?

Cash	$27,000
Marketable securities	$23,000
Receivables	$90,000
Inventory	$105,000
Current liabilities	$70,000

   a. 2.0
   b. 3.5
   c. 0.7
   d. 1.5

9. In vertical analysis of the balance sheet, each asset item is stated as a percent of total:
   a. current assets
   b. assets
   c. current liabilities
   d. liabilities

10. Based on the following data for the current year, what is the earnings per share on common stock?

Net income	$460,000
Preferred dividends	$50,000
Interest expense	$24,000
Shares of common stock outstanding	50,000

a. $9.20

b. $8.68

c. $8.20

d. $7.72

11. Companies with high P/E ratios are usually associated with:

a. a high-dividend yield

b. high-profit growth

c. low long-term debt to total assets

d. strong current position

12. Based on the following data, what is the rate earned on total assets?

Net income	$240,000
Preferred dividends	$60,000
Interest expense	$120,000
Interest income	$40,000
Average total assets	$1,000,000

a. 18%

b. 28%

c. 30%

d. 36%

TRUE/FALSE

Instructions: Indicate whether each of the following statements is true or false by placing a check mark in the appropriate column.

	True	False
1. In horizontal analysis of the income statement, each item is stated as a percentage of total sales.	____	____
2. Solvency is the ability of a business to meet its financial obligations as they come due.	____	____
3. The ratio of net sales to assets provides a solvency measure that shows the margin of safety of the debtholders.	____	____
4. The quick ratio or acid-test ratio is the ratio of the sum of cash, receivables, and marketable securities to current liabilities.	____	____
5. Net sales divided by the year-end net accounts receivable gives the accounts receivable turnover.	____	____
6. Net income minus the amount required for preferred dividends divided by the average common stockholders' equity gives the rate earned on common stockholders' equity.	____	____
7. The rate earned on total assets is calculated by subtracting interest expense from net income and dividing this sum by the average total assets.	____	____
8. The tendency on the rate earned on stockholders' equity to vary disproportionately from the rate earned on total assets is referred to as financial leverage.	____	____
9. A profitability measure that shows the rate of return to common stockholders in terms of cash dividends is known as the dividend yield on common stock.	____	____
10. The excess of the current assets of an enterprise over its current liabilities and stockholders' equity is called working capital.	____	____

EXERCISE 17-1

Instructions: Using the condensed income statement information presented below, perform a vertical analysis for Delta Corp. for the years ending December 31, 2010 and 2009, stating each item as a percent of revenues.

	2010	Percent	2009	Percent
Revenues	$450,000		$389,000	
Costs and expenses:				
Cost of sales	$200,000		$176,000	
Selling and administrative expenses	100,000		73,000	
Total costs and expenses	$300,000		$249,000	
Earnings before income taxes	$150,000		$140,000	
Income taxes	34,500		32,200	
Net earnings	$115,500		$107,800	

EXERCISE 17-2

Instructions: Using the condensed balance sheet data presented below, perform a horizontal analysis for Carson Inc. on December 31, 2010. Indicate the amount and percent increase (decrease) in the columns provided.

			Increase (Decrease)	
	2010	2009	Amount	Percent
Current assets	$250,000	$219,500		
Fixed assets	435,000	401,600		
Intangible assets	43,700	46,000		
Current liabilities	88,000	80,000		
Long-term liabilities	225,000	250,000		
Common stock	214,000	167,600		
Retained earnings	200,000	170,000		

Problem 17-1

Instructions: Using the information below and on the following page, perform a horizontal analysis for Nordic Inc. by filling in the Amount and Percent columns that are provided. (Round all percents to one decimal place.)

Nordic Inc.
Comparative Income Statement
For the Years Ended December 31, 2010 and 2009

			Increase (Decrease)	
	2010	2009	Amount	Percent
Sales	$690,500	$585,000		
Sales returns and allowances	25,500	23,000		
Net sales	$665,000	$562,000		
Cost of goods sold	420,000	330,000		
Gross profit	$245,000	$232,000		
Selling expenses	$ 43,000	$ 47,700		
Administrative expenses	31,000	31,000		
Total operating expenses	$ 74,000	$ 78,700		
Operating income	$171,000	$153,300		
Other income	13,000	16,400		
	$184,000	$169,700		
Other expense	58,000	53,500		
Income before income taxes	$126,000	$116,200		
Income taxes	34,000	32,400		
Net income	$ 92,000	$ 83,800		

Nordic Inc.
Comparative Balance Sheet
December 31, 2010 and 2009

			Increase (Decrease)	
Assets	2010	2009	Amount	Percent
Cash	$ 76,000	$ 69,000		
Marketable securities	98,900	130,000		
Accounts receivable (net)	199,000	195,000		
Inventory	450,000	375,000		
Prepaid expenses	28,000	26,300		
Long-term investments	35,000	35,000		
Fixed assets (net)	871,000	835,000		
Intangible assets	18,000	22,800		
Total assets	$1,775,900	$1,688,100		
Liabilities				
Current liabilities	$ 129,000	$ 107,000		
Long-term liabilities	420,000	440,000		
Total liabilities	$ 549,000	$ 547,000		
Stockholders' Equity				
Preferred 3% stock, $100 par	$ 102,000	$ 93,000		
Common stock, $50 par	549,900	530,100		
Retained earnings	575,000	518,000		
Total stockholders' equity	$1,226,900	$1,141,100		
Total liabilities and stockholders' equity	$1,775,900	$1,688,100		

PROBLEM 17-2

Instructions: Using the information below and on the following page, perform a vertical analysis for Voyageur Inc. by filling in the Percent columns on the statements provided. (Round all percents to one decimal place.)

Voyageur Inc.
Comparative Balance Sheet
December 31, 2010 and 2009

	2010		2009	
Assets	Amount	Percent	Amount	Percent
Cash	$ 500,000		$ 425,000	
Marketable securities	200,000		185,000	
Accounts receivable (net)	680,000		575,000	
Inventory	860,000		740,000	
Prepaid expenses	104,000		95,000	
Long-term investments	450,000		410,000	
Fixed assets	6,556,000		5,420,000	
Total assets	$9,350,000	100%	$7,850,000	100%
Liabilities				
Current liabilities	$1,090,000		$1,050,000	
Long-term liabilities	2,150,000		2,050,000	
Total liabilities	$3,240,000		$3,100,000	
Stockholders' Equity				
Preferred 5% stock, $100 par	$ 350,000		$ 350,000	
Common stock, $10 par	2,550,000		2,550,000	
Retained earnings	3,210,000		1,850,000	
Total stockholders' equity	$6,110,000		$4,750,000	
Total liabilities and stockholders' equity	$9,350,000	100%	$7,850,000	100%

Voyageur Inc.
Income Statement
For the Year Ended December 31, 2010

	Amount	Percent
Sales	$12,800,000	
Sales returns and allowances	300,000	
Net sales	$12,500,000	100%
Cost of goods sold	7,550,000	
Gross profit	$ 4,950,000	
Selling expenses	$ 1,550,000	
Administrative expenses	825,000	
Total operating expenses	$ 2,375,000	
Operating income	$ 2,575,000	
Other income	125,000	
	$ 2,700,000	
Other expense (interest)	150,000	
Income before income taxes	$ 2,550,000	
Income taxes	937,000	
Net income	$ 1,613,000	

PROBLEM 17-3

Voyageur Inc. declared $250,000 of common stock dividends during 2010. The price of Voyageur's common stock on December 31, 2010 is $29.75.

Instructions: Using the data for Voyageur Inc. from Problem 17-2, determine the following amounts and ratios for 2010. (Round all ratios to one decimal point.)

	Calculation	Final Result
a. Working capital		
b. Current ratio		
c. Quick ratio		
d. Accounts receivable turnover		
e. Number of days' sales in receivables		
f. Inventory turnover		
g. Number of days' sales in inventory		
h. Ratio of fixed assets to long-term liabilities		
i. Ratio of liabilities to stockholders' equity		

	Calculation	Final Result
j. Number of times interest charges earned		
k. Number of times preferred dividends earned		
l. Ratio of net sales to assets		
m. Rate earned on total assets		
n. Rate earned on stockholders' equity		
o. Rate earned on common stockholders' equity		
p. Earnings per share on common stock		
q. Price-earnings ratio		
r. Dividends per share of common stock		
s. Dividend yield		

SOLUTIONS

CHAPTER 1

MATCHING

1. H	7. U	13. S	19. J	25. R
2. W	8. D	14. I	20. B	26. JJ
3. Y	9. M	15. F	21. EE	27. G
4. FF	10. O	16. T	22. C	28. II
5. DD	11. V	17. CC	23. N	29. X
6. K	12. P	18. E	24. GG	30. A

FILL IN THE BLANK—PART A

1. business
2. corporation
3. accounting
4. ethics
5. managerial
6. unit of measure
7. assets
8. owner's equity
9. accounting equation
10. $70,000
11. account payable
12. $130,000
13. $80,000
14. revenue
15. $15,000 net income
16. statement of owner's equity
17. $38,000 net income
18. account
19. $94,000 increase
20. statement of cash flows

FILL IN THE BLANK—PART B

1. manufacturing
2. merchandising
3. proprietorship
4. financial
5. Financial Accounting Standards Board (FASB)
6. business entity
7. liabilities
8. business transaction
9. prepaid expenses
10. account receivable
11. $80,000
12. $65,500
13. expenses
14. income statement
15. ($5,000) net loss
16. balance sheet
17. $13,500 increase
18. statement of cash flows
19. $29,000 net income
20. balance sheet

MULTIPLE CHOICE

1. a. Incorrect. General accounting is not a category of employment by accountants.
   b. Incorrect. Accountants and their staffs who provide services on a fee basis are said to be employed in public accounting.
   c. Incorrect. Independent accounting is not a category of employment by accountants.
   d. ***Correct.*** Accountants employed by a particular business firm or not-for-profit organization, perhaps as chief accountant, controller, or financial vice-president, are said to be engaged in private accounting.

2. a. Incorrect. Service businesses provide services rather than products to customers.
   b. ***Correct.*** Manufacturing businesses change basic inputs into products that are sold to individual customers.
   c. Incorrect. Merchandising businesses do not make the products, but instead they purchase them from other businesses and sell them to customers.
   d. Incorrect. A proprietorship is a form of business organization rather than a type of business.

3. a. Incorrect. The cost concept is the basis for entering the exchange price, or cost, into the accounting records.
   b. Incorrect. The objectivity concept requires that the accounting records and reports be based upon objective evidence.
   c. Incorrect. The business entity concept limits the economic data in the accounting system to data related directly to the activities of the business or entity.
   d. ***Correct.*** The unit of measure concept requires that economic data be recorded in dollars.

4. a. Incorrect. The business entity concept limits the economic data in the accounting system to data related directly to the activities of the business or entity.
b. ***Correct.*** The cost concept is the basis for recording the amounts, or cost, into the accounting records.
c. Incorrect. The matching principle emphasizes matching the expenses with the revenue generated during a period by those expenses.
d. Incorrect. Proprietorship is not a principle, but instead it is a form of business organization.

5. a. Incorrect.
b. Incorrect.
c. Incorrect.
d. ***Correct.*** The accounting equation (Assets = Liabilities + Owner's Equity) may also be expressed as Assets – Liabilities = Owner's Equity.

6. a. Incorrect.
b. Incorrect.
c. Incorrect.
d. ***Correct.*** If total liabilities increased by $20,000 during a period of time and owner's equity increased by $5,000 during the same period, total assets must increase by $25,000. That is, if the right side of the accounting equation increases by $25,000 (Liabilities + Owner's Equity), the left side of the equation must also increase by the same amount, $25,000.

7. a. Incorrect.
b. Incorrect.
c. ***Correct.*** The payment of a credit of $6,000 decreases the asset, Cash, and decreases the liability, Accounts Payable.
d. Incorrect.

8. a. Incorrect.
b. Incorrect.
c. Incorrect.
d. ***Correct.*** The amount of net income for the year is $40,000. It is computed as ending owner's equity $135,000 ($355,000 – $220,000) less beginning owner's equity $100,000 ($290,000 – $190,000) equals the change in owner's equity, $35,000. The change in owner's equity of $35,000 plus withdrawals of $30,000 less the additional investment of $25,000 equals the net income for the year, $40,000.

9. a. ***Correct.*** The amount of net income of $11,000 is determined by subtracting expenses, $59,000, from the revenues, $70,000. The owner's withdrawals, $25,000, do not affect the determination of net income.
b. Incorrect.
c. Incorrect.
d. Incorrect.

10. a. ***Correct.*** The statement of cash flows does not contain a section for cash flows from marketing activities.
b. Incorrect. The statement of cash flows contains a section for investing activities.
c. Incorrect. The statement of cash flows contains a section for financing activities.
d. Incorrect. The statement of cash flows contains a section for cash flows from operating activities.

TRUE/FALSE

1. T

2. F Accountants and their staffs who provide services on a fee basis are said to be employed in public accounting, not private accounting.

3. T

4. F The concept that expenses incurred in generating revenue should be matched against the revenue in determining net income or net loss is the matching concept, not the cost concept.

5. F The operating activities section, not the financing activities section, of the statement of cash flows includes cash transactions that enter into the determination of net income.

6. F The debts of a business are called its accounts payable, not accounts receivable.

7. F A partnership is owned by two or more individuals.

8. T

9. F A summary of the changes in the owner's equity of a business entity that have occurred during a specific period of time, such as a month or a year, is called the statement of owner's equity, not the statement of cash flows.

10. F A claim against a customer for sales made on credit is an account receivable, not an account payable.

EXERCISE 1-1

	A	L	OE		A	L	OE
1.	+	0	+	**6.**	+,–	0	0
2.	+	+	0	**7.**	+,–	0	0
3.	+	0	+	**8.**	–	–	0
4.	+	0	+	**9.**	–	–	0
5.	–	0	–	**10.**	–	0	–

PROBLEM 1-1

	Assets				=	Liabilities	+	Owner's Equity										
Trans.	Cash	+	Supplies	+	Land	=	Accts. Pay.	+	Ed Casey, Capital	–	Ed Casey, Drawing	+	Fees Earned	–	Rent Exp.	–	Supplies Exp.	–	Misc. Exp.
(1)	40,000								40,000										
(2)			2,000				2,000												
Bal.	40,000		2,000				2,000		40,000										
(3)	– 14,000				14,000														
Bal.	26,000		2,000		14,000		2,000		40,000										
(4)	– 1,800						– 1,800												
Bal.	24,200		2,000		14,000		200		40,000										
(5)	– 2,000										– 2,000								
Bal.	22,200		2,000		14,000		200		40,000		– 2,000								
(6)	– 2,800														– 2,800				
Bal.	19,400		2,000		14,000		200		40,000		– 2,000				– 2,800				
(7)							900												– 900
Bal.	19,400		2,000		14,000		1,100		40,000		– 2,000				– 2,800				– 900
(8)	10,000								10,000										
Bal.	29,400		2,000		14,000		1,100		50,000		– 2,000				– 2,800				– 900
(9)	6,000												6,000						
Bal.	35,400		2,000		14,000		1,100		50,000		– 2,000		6,000		– 2,800				– 900
(10)			– 600														– 600		
Bal.	35,400		1,400		14,000		1,100		50,000		– 2,000		6,000		– 2,800		– 600		– 900

PROBLEM 1-2

(1)

Tom's Painting Service
Income Statement
For Year Ended December 31, 20--

Sales		$27,450
Expenses:		
Supplies expense	$5,450	
Advertising expense	4,825	
Truck rental expense	1,525	
Utilities expense	700	
Misc. expense	1,400	13,900
Net income		$13,550

(2)

Tom's Painting Service
Statement of Owner's Equity
For Year Ended December 31, 20--

Investment, Jan. 1, 20--		$ 4,000
Additional investment by owner	$ 2,000	
Income for the year	13,550	
Less withdrawal	(1,000)	
Increase in owner's equity		14,550
Tom Wallace, capital, Dec. 31, 20--		$18,550

(3)

Tom's Painting Service
Balance Sheet
December 31, 20--

Assets		Liabilities	
Cash	$10,050	Accounts payable	$ 4,450
Accounts receivable	8,950	Owner's Equity	
Supplies	4,000	Tom Wallace, capital	18,550
Total assets	$23,000	Total liability & owner's equity	$23,000

CHAPTER 2

MATCHING

1. A
2. O
3. D
4. B
5. P
6. Q
7. S
8. K
9. U
10. H
11. F
12. C
13. L
14. N
15. M
16. I
17. J
18. R
19. X
20. Y
21. W
22. G
23. E
24. V
25. T

FILL IN THE BLANK—PART A

1. account
2. chart of accounts
3. revenue
4. T account
5. debits
6. debit
7. credit
8. debit
9. credit
10. liability
11. credit
12. debit
13. credit
14. journal
15. journalizing
16. double-entry accounting
17. posting
18. two-column journal
19. accounts receivable
20. transposition

Fill in the Blank—Part B

1. ledger
2. assets
3. liabilities
4. owner's equity
5. expenses
6. credits
7. balance
8. journalizing
9. drawing
10. unearned revenue
11. debit
12. debit
13. credit
14. liability
15. asset
16. debit
17. credit
18. trial balance
19. slide
20. correcting

Multiple Choice

1. a. Incorrect.
b. ***Correct.*** The receipt of cash from customers in payment of their accounts would be recorded by a debit to Cash and a credit to Accounts Receivable.
c. Incorrect.
d. Incorrect.

2. a. Incorrect. The third step in recording a transaction in a two-column journal is to list the account to be credited.
b. Incorrect. The fourth step in recording a transaction in a two-column journal is to list the amount to be credited.
c. Incorrect. The second step in recording a transaction in a two-column journal is to list the amount to be debited.
d. ***Correct.*** The first step in recording a transaction in a two-column journal is to list the account to be debited.

3. a. Incorrect. Cash is debited when the owner invests cash.
b. ***Correct.*** The drawing account of a sole proprietorship is debited when the owner withdraws cash.
c. Incorrect. Accounts Payable is debited when a liability is paid.
d. Incorrect. An expense account is debited when an expense is paid.

4. a. Incorrect.
b. Incorrect.
c. ***Correct.*** The equality of debits and credits in the ledger should be verified at the end of each accounting period by preparing a trial balance.
d. Incorrect.

5. a. ***Correct.*** Incorrectly computing an account balance will cause an inequality in the trial balance totals.
b. Incorrect. A failure to record a transaction will not cause an inequality in the trial balance totals.
c. Incorrect. Recording the same transaction more than once will not cause an inequality in the trial balance totals.
d. Incorrect. Posting a transaction to the wrong account will not cause an inequality in the trial balance totals.

6. a. Incorrect.
b. ***Correct.*** Since cash is an asset, credits to Cash result in a decrease in assets.
c. Incorrect.
d. Incorrect.

7. a. Incorrect.
b. ***Correct.*** Under the rules of double-entry accounting, debits to expense accounts signify a decrease in owner's capital.
c. Incorrect.
d. Incorrect.

8. a. Incorrect.
b. Incorrect.
c. Incorrect.
d. ***Correct.*** Under the rules of double-entry accounting, when rent is prepaid for several months in advance, the debit is to Prepaid Rent, an asset account.

9. a. Incorrect.
b. Incorrect.
c. ***Correct.*** Under the rules of double-entry accounting, when an asset is purchased on account, the credit is to Accounts Payable, a liability account.
d. Incorrect.

10. a. Incorrect.
b. ***Correct.*** Under the rules of double-entry accounting, when a payment is made to a supplier for goods previously purchased on account, the debit is to Accounts Payable, a liability account.
c. Incorrect.
d. Incorrect.

TRUE/FALSE

1. F Amounts entered on the left side of an account, regardless of the account title, are called debits or charges to the account, not credits.
2. T
3. T
4. F The balance sheet accounts, not the income statement accounts, are listed first in the chart of accounts.
5. T
6. F Every business transaction affects a minimum of two accounts, not one account.
7. F The process of recording a transaction in a journal is called journalizing, not posting.
8. F The group of accounts for a business entity is called its ledger, not a journal.
9. T
10. F A recording error caused by the erroneous rearrangement of digits, such as writing $627 as $672, is called a transposition, not a slide.

EXERCISE 2-1

	Account Debited		Account Credited	
Transaction	Type	Effect	Type	Effect
(1)	asset	+	capital	+
(2)	asset	+	liability	+
(3)	asset	+	liability	+
(4)	asset	+	revenue	+
(5)	liability	–	asset	–
(6)	expense	+	liability	+
(7)	asset	+	asset	–
(8)	drawing	+	asset	–

PROBLEM 2-1

(1)	June 1	Cash	11	5,000	
		Equipment	18	14,500	
		Vehicles	19	21,000	
		Joan Star, Capital	31		40,500

June 16	Equipment	18	5,500	
	Accounts Payable	21		5,500
28	Supplies	12	500	
	Accounts Payable	21		500
30	Accounts Payable	21	2,100	
	Cash	11		2,100

(2)

ACCOUNT *Cash* ACCOUNT NO. *11*

DATE	ITEM	POST. REF.	DEBIT	CREDIT	BALANCE DEBIT	BALANCE CREDIT
20--						
June 1		1	5,000		5,000	
30		1		2,100	2,900	

ACCOUNT *Supplies* ACCOUNT NO. *12*

DATE	ITEM	POST. REF.	DEBIT	CREDIT	BALANCE DEBIT	BALANCE CREDIT
20--						
June 28		1	500		500	

ACCOUNT *Equipment* ACCOUNT NO. *18*

DATE	ITEM	POST. REF.	DEBIT	CREDIT	BALANCE DEBIT	BALANCE CREDIT
20--						
June 1		1	14,500		14,500	
16		1	5,500		20,000	

ACCOUNT *Vehicles* ACCOUNT NO. *19*

DATE	ITEM	POST. REF.	DEBIT	CREDIT	BALANCE DEBIT	BALANCE CREDIT
20--						
June 1		1	21,000		21,000	

ACCOUNT *Accounts Payable* ACCOUNT NO. *21*

DATE	ITEM	POST. REF.	DEBIT	CREDIT	BALANCE DEBIT	BALANCE CREDIT
20--						
June 16		1		5,500		5,500
28		1		500		6,000
30		1	2,100			3,900

ACCOUNT *Joan Star, Capital* ACCOUNT NO. *31*

DATE	ITEM	POST. REF.	DEBIT	CREDIT	BALANCE DEBIT	BALANCE CREDIT
20--						
June 1		1		40,500		40,500

(3)

Star Service Company
Trial Balance
June 30, 20--

Cash	2,900	
Supplies	500	
Equipment	20,000	
Vehicles	21,000	
Accounts Payable		3,900
Joan Star, Capital		40,500
	44,400	44,400

PROBLEM 2-2

(1)

Cash

(a)	20,000	(b)	2,500
(d)	19,600	(c)	1,000
		(e)	1,100
		(g)	2,600
		(h)	5,000
		(i)	800
		(k)	240
		(l)	1,700
		(m)	2,000
		(n)	5,000
		(o)	500

Office Equipment

(a)	13,200		

Rent Expense

(b)	2,500		

Auto

(g)	13,000		

Salary Expense

(e)	1,100		

Accounts Payable

(k)	240	(f)	200
(m)	2,000	(g)	10,400
		(j)	240

Telephone Expense

(j)	240		

Auto Repairs & Maintenance Expense

(i)	800		

Office Supplies

(c)	1,000		
(f)	200		

Judy Turner, Capital

		(a)	33,200

Janitor Expense

(o)	500		

Judy Turner, Drawing

(h)	5,000		

Prepaid Insurance

(l)	1,700		

Legal Fees

		(d)	19,600

Library

(n)	5,000		

(2)

Judy Turner
Trial Balance
January 31, 20--

Account	Debit	Credit
Cash	17,160	
Office Supplies	1,200	
Prepaid Insurance	1,700	
Library	5,000	
Office Equipment	13,200	
Auto	13,000	
Accounts Payable		8,600
Judy Turner, Capital		33,200
Judy Turner, Drawing	5,000	
Legal Fees		19,600
Rent Expense	2,500	
Salary Expense	1,100	
Telephone Expense	240	
Auto Repairs & Maintenance Expense	800	
Janitor Expense	500	
	61,400	61,400

PROBLEM 2-3

(a)	Prepaid Insurance	1,000	
	Prepaid Rent		1,000
	To correct erroneous debit to prepaid rent.		
(b)	Accounts Receivable	200	
	Accounts Payable		200
	To correct erroneous credit to accounts receivable.		
(c)	Drawing	3,000	
	Cash		3,000
	To correct erroneous entry debiting cash and crediting drawing.		

CHAPTER 3

MATCHING

1. A
2. J
3. B
4. U
5. Q
6. H
7. G
8. T
9. V
10. C
11. D
12. P
13. M
14. N
15. E
16. I
17. F
18. L

FILL IN THE BLANK—PART A

1. accounting period
2. cash
3. revenue recognition
4. adjusting
5. prepaid expenses
6. accrued expenses
7. advertising expense
8. accumulated depreciation—equipment
9. unearned fees
10. wages payable
11. overstated
12. understated
13. understated
14. $10,700
15. $800
16. fixed assets
17. depreciation
18. book value
19. $88,700
20. adjusted

FILL IN THE BLANK—PART B

1. accrual
2. matching
3. adjusting
4. unearned revenues
5. accrued revenues
6. depreciation
7. accumulated depreciation
8. understated
9. overstated
10. interest expense
11. prepaid rent
12. depreciation expense
13. fees earned
14. balance sheet
15. revenue
16. expense
17. overstated
18. overstated
19. $1,950
20. $800

MULTIPLE CHOICE

1. a. Incorrect.
b. ***Correct.*** Entries required at the end of an accounting period to bring the accounts up to date and to assure the proper matching of revenues and expenses are called adjusting entries.
c. Incorrect.
d. Incorrect. Correcting entries correct errors in the accounting records. Entries required at the end of an accounting period to bring the accounts up to date and to assure the proper matching of revenues and expenses are called adjusting entries.

2. a. ***Correct.*** The amount of accrued but unpaid expenses at the end of the fiscal period is both an expense and a liability.
b. Incorrect. The amount of accrued but unpaid expenses at the end of the fiscal period is both an expense and a liability, not an asset.
c. Incorrect. The amount of accrued but unpaid expenses at the end of the fiscal period is both an expense and a liability, not a deferral.
d. Incorrect. The amount of accrued but unpaid expenses at the end of the fiscal period is both an expense and a liability, not a revenue.

3. a. Incorrect.
b. Incorrect.
c. ***Correct.*** If the effect of the debit portion of an adjusting entry is to increase the balance of an expense account, the effect of the credit portion of the entry is a decrease in the balance of an asset account.
d. Incorrect.

4. a. Incorrect.
b. Incorrect.
c. Incorrect.
d. ***Correct.*** If the effect of the credit portion of an adjusting entry is to increase the balance of a liability account, the effect of the debit portion of the entry is an increase in the balance of an expense account.

5. a. Incorrect.
b. ***Correct.*** The balance in the prepaid rent account before adjustment at the end of the year is $12,000, which represents three months' rent paid on December 1. The adjusting entry required on December 31 debits Rent Expense, $4,000, and credits Prepaid Rent, $4,000.
c. Incorrect.
d. Incorrect.

6. a. ***Correct.*** At the end of the preceding fiscal year, the usual adjusting entry for accrued salaries owed to employees was omitted. The error was not corrected, and the accrued salaries were included in the first salary payment in the current fiscal year. As a result, Salary Expense was overstated and net income was understated for the current year.
b. Incorrect. Salaries Payable is understated at the end of the preceding fiscal year, not the current year.
c. Incorrect. Salary Expense was overstated and net income was understated for the current fiscal year, not the preceding year.
d. Incorrect. Salary Expense and Salaries Payable were understated, rather than overstated, for the preceding year.

7. a. Incorrect.
b. Incorrect.
c. ***Correct.*** The decrease in usefulness of fixed assets as time passes is called depreciation.
d. Incorrect.

8. a. ***Correct.*** The difference between the fixed asset account and the related accumulated depreciation account is called the book value of the asset.
b. Incorrect.
c. Incorrect.
d. Incorrect.

9. a. Incorrect. Expenses will be understated, not overstated.
b. Incorrect. Net income will be overstated, not understated.
c. Incorrect. Assets will be overstated, not understated.
d. ***Correct.*** If a $250 adjustment for depreciation is not recorded, owner's equity will be overstated.

10. a. ***Correct.*** The corrected net income is computed as $50,000 less the adjusting entry for supplies expense of $500 and accrued salaries of $1,300.
b. Incorrect.
c. Incorrect.
d. Incorrect.

TRUE/FALSE

1. T
2. F When the reduction in prepaid expenses is not properly recorded, the asset accounts will be overstated, but the expense accounts will be understated, not overstated.
3. T
4. F If the adjusting entry to record accrued wages at the end of the year is omitted, net income and owner's equity will be overstated, but total assets will not be affected. Instead, liabilities will be understated.
5. T
6. T
7. T
8. F Expenses that have not been paid or revenues that have not been received are accruals, not deferrals.
9. T
10. F The amount of accrued revenue is recorded by debiting an asset account, not a liability account. The credit is to a revenue account.

EXERCISE 3-1

(1)

Cash (Dr.)	Cash (Cr.)	Prepaid Insurance (Dr.)	Prepaid Insurance (Cr.)	Insurance Expense (Dr.)	Insurance Expense (Cr.)
	May 1 5,400	May 1 5,400	Dec. 31 1,200	Dec. 31 1,200	

(2) Unexpired insurance........................ $4,200

(3) Insurance expense.......................... $1,200

EXERCISE 3-2

(1)

Cash (Dr.)	Cash (Cr.)	Salary Expense (Dr.)	Salary Expense (Cr.)	Salaries Payable (Dr.)	Salaries Payable (Cr.)
	Oct. 7 250	Oct. 7 250			Oct. 31 50
	14 250	14 250			
	21 250	21 250			
	28 250	28 250			
		31 50			

(2) Salary expense................................ $1,050

(3) Salaries payable.............................. $50

EXERCISE 3-3

Unearned Rent (Dr.)	Unearned Rent (Cr.)	Rent Revenue (Dr.)	Rent Revenue (Cr.)
Dec. 31 500	Dec. 1 6,000		Dec. 31 500

Date	Account	Debit	Credit
Dec. 31	Unearned Rent..	500	
	Rent Revenue....................................		500
	Rent earned.		

EXERCISE 3-4

Interest Receivable (Dr.)	Interest Receivable (Cr.)	Interest Revenue (Dr.)	Interest Revenue (Cr.)
Dec. 31 320			Dec. 31 320

Date	Account	Debit	Credit
Dec. 31	Interest Receivable...................................	320	
	Interest Revenue................................		320
	Accrued interest revenue.		

PROBLEM 3-1

(1)

		Debit	Credit
(a)	Salaries Expense	2,000	
	Salaries Payable		2,000
	Accrued salaries.		
(b)	Rent Expense	726	
	Prepaid Rent		726
	Rent expired.		
(c)	Supplies Expense	1,750	
	Supplies		1,750
	Supplies used.		
(d)	Depreciation Expense	400	
	Accumulated Depreciation		400
	Depreciation of tools and equipment.		
(e)	Accounts Receivable	2,100	
	Service Fees		2,100
	Accrued fees.		

(2)

Bob's Service Company
Adjusted Trial Balance
July 31, 20--

	Debit Balances	Credit Balances
Cash	9,218	
Accounts Receivable	9,377	
Supplies	1,000	
Prepaid Rent	7,986	
Tools & Equipment	21,829	
Accumulated Depreciation		1,935
Accounts Payable		7,117
Salaries Payable		2,000
Bob Jones, Capital		37,417
Bob Jones, Drawing	3,234	
Service Fees		30,799
Salary Expense	17,929	
Rent Expense	726	
Supplies Expense	1,750	
Depreciation Expense	400	
Miscellaneous Expense	5,819	
	79,268	79,268

CHAPTER 4

MATCHING

1. H
2. F
3. M
4. G
5. K
6. J
7. P
8. I
9. L
10. A
11. D
12. Q
13. S

FILL IN THE BLANK—PART A

1. end-of-period spreadsheet (work sheet)
2. note receivable
3. current liabilities
4. balance sheet
5. balance sheet
6. net income
7. net loss
8. income summary
9. owner's capital
10. income summary
11. owner's capital
12. post-closing
13. accounting cycle
14. natural business year

FILL IN THE BLANK—PART B

1. current assets
2. property, plant, and equipment
3. long-term liabilities
4. income statement
5. income statement
6. net loss
7. net income
8. closing entries
9. income summary
10. owner's capital
11. income summary
12. owner's capital
13. fiscal year
14. seasonal operations

Multiple Choice

1. a. Incorrect. Notes receivable are written claims against customers, not creditors.
   b. Incorrect. Notes receivable are written claims against customers, not owner's equity.
   c. ***Correct.*** Notes receivable are written claims against customers.
   d. Incorrect. Notes payable, not notes receivable, are written claims against assets.

2. a. Incorrect. An end-of-period spreadsheet (work sheet) extends the adjusted trial balance amounts to the Income Statement and Balance Sheet columns as well as totals the Adjustment columns and extends the adjustments to the Adjusted Trial Balance columns.
   b. Incorrect. An end-of-period spreadsheet (work sheet) totals the Adjustment columns as well as extends the adjusted trial balance amounts to the Income Statement and Balance Sheet columns and extends the work sheet adjustments to the Adjusted Trial Balance columns.
   c. Incorrect. An end-of-period spreadsheet (work sheet) extends the work sheet adjustments to the Adjusted Trial Balance columns as well as totals the Adjustment columns and extends the adjusted trial balance amounts to the Income Statement and Balance Sheet columns.
   d. ***Correct.*** An end-of-period spreadsheet (work sheet) extends the adjusted trial balance amounts to the Income Statement and Balance Sheet columns, totals the Adjustment columns, and extends the work sheet adjustments to the Adjusted Trial Balance columns.

3. a. ***Correct.*** If the Income Statement Credit column is greater than the Income Statement Debit column, a net income exists.
   b. Incorrect. If the Income Statement Credit column is greater than the Income Statement Debit column, a net income exists, not a net loss.
   c. Incorrect.
   d. Incorrect.

4. a. Incorrect. After all of the account balances have been extended to the Balance Sheet columns of the end-of-period spreadsheet (work sheet), the totals of the Debit and Credit columns are $377,750 and $387,750, respectively. The amount of net loss for the period is $10,000—the difference between the Balance Sheet Debit and Credit columns. Because the Balance Sheet Credit column is larger than the Debit column, a net loss has been incurred, rather than a net income.
   b. ***Correct.*** After all of the account balances have been extended to the Balance Sheet columns of the end-of-period spreadsheet (work sheet), the totals of the Debit and Credit columns are $377,750 and $387,750, respectively. The amount of net loss for the period is $10,000—the difference between the Debit and Credit columns. Because the Balance Sheet Credit column is larger than the Debit column, a net loss has been incurred.
   c. Incorrect. The net income or net loss is computed as the difference between the Balance Sheet Debit and Credit columns, not the total of the Debit column.
   d. Incorrect. The net income or net loss is computed as the difference between the Balance Sheet Debit and Credit column, not the total of the Credit column.

5. a. ***Correct.*** After all of the account balances have been extended to the Income Statement columns of the end-of-period spreadsheet (work sheet), the totals of the Debit and Credit columns are $62,300 and $67,600, respectively. The amount of the net income for the period is $5,300—the difference between the Debit and Credit columns. Because the Income Statement Credit column is larger than the Debit column, a net income has been incurred.
   b. Incorrect. After all of the account balances have been extended to the Income Statement columns of the end-of-period spreadsheet (work sheet), the totals of the Debit and Credit columns are $62,300 and $67,600, respectively. The amount of the net income for the period is $5,300—the difference between the Debit and Credit columns. Because the Income Statement Credit column is larger than the Debit column, a net income has been incurred, rather than a net loss.
   c. Incorrect. The net income or net loss is computed as the difference between the Income Statement Debit and Credit columns, not the total of the Debit column.
   d. Incorrect. The net income or net loss is computed as the difference between the Income Statement Debit and Credit columns, not the total of the Credit column.

6. a. Incorrect. Lisa Murray, Drawing should be closed to Lisa Murray, Capital at the end of the fiscal year, not to Income Summary.
b. Incorrect. Accumulated Depreciation—Equipment is not closed at the end of the fiscal year.
c. ***Correct.*** Sales should be closed to Income Summary at the end of the fiscal year.
d. Incorrect. Accounts Payable is not closed at the end of the fiscal year.

7. a. Incorrect. Salaries Expense is closed at the end of the fiscal year to Income Summary.
b. Incorrect. Sales is closed at the end of the fiscal year to Income Summary.
c. ***Correct.*** Lisa Murray, Drawing should be closed to Lisa Murray, Capital at the end of the fiscal year.
d. Incorrect. Accounts Receivable is not closed at the end of the fiscal year.

8. a. Incorrect. Salaries Expense is closed to Income Summary at the end of the period and does not appear in the post-closing trial balance.
b. Incorrect. Lisa Murray, Drawing is closed to Lisa Murray, Capital at the end of the period and does not appear in the post-closing trial balance.
c. Incorrect. Sales is closed to Income Summary at the end of the period and does not appear in the post-closing trial balance.
d. ***Correct.*** Lisa Murray, Capital is not closed at the end of the period and does appear in the post-closing trial balance.

9. a. Incorrect. The maximum length of an accounting period is normally greater than 6 months.
b. ***Correct.*** The maximum length of an accounting period is normally 1 year.
c. Incorrect. The maximum length of an accounting period is normally less than 2 years.
d. Incorrect. The maximum length of an accounting period is normally less than 3 years.

10. a. Incorrect.
b. Incorrect.
c. ***Correct.*** The complete sequence of accounting procedures for a fiscal period is frequently called the accounting cycle.
d. Incorrect.

TRUE/FALSE

1. F The balance of Accumulated Depreciation—Equipment is extended to the Balance Sheet columns of the end-of-period spreadsheet (work sheet), not the Income Statement columns.

2. F The difference between the Debit and Credit columns of the Income Statement section of the end-of-period spreadsheet (work sheet) is the same as the difference between the Debit and Credit columns of the Balance Sheet section. This difference is the net income or net loss for the period.

3. T

4. T

5. F The balances of the accounts reported in the balance sheet are carried from year to year and are called real or permanent accounts, not temporary accounts.

6. T

7. F If the Income Statement Debit column is greater than the Income Statement Credit column, the difference is a net loss, not a net income.

8. F A type of work sheet frequently used by accountants prior to the preparation of financial statements is called a end-of-period spreadsheet (work sheet), not a post closing trial balance. The post-closing trial balance is prepared after the closing entries have been recorded to verify the equality of the debit and credit balances.

9. T

10. T

EXERCISE 4-1

			Debit	Credit
Aug.	31	Salary Expense	1,500	
		Salaries Payable		1,500
		Accrued salaries.		
	31	Rent Expense	560	
		Prepaid Rent		560
		Rent expired.		
	31	Supplies Expense	700	
		Supplies		700
		Supplies used.		
	31	Depreciation Expense	1,000	
		Accumulated Depreciation		1,000
		Depreciation.		
	31	Accounts Receivable	3,200	
		Repair Fees		3,200
		Accrued fees.		

EXERCISE 4-2

(1)

			Post. Ref.	Debit	Credit
20--					
Mar.	31	Service Fees	50	19,225	
		Income Summary	45		19,225
	31	Income Summary	45	13,980	
		Salary Expense	58		8,550
		Supplies Expense	67		5,430

(2)

ACCOUNT *Income Summary* ACCOUNT NO. *45*

DATE		ITEM	POST. REF.	DEBIT	CREDIT	BALANCE DEBIT	BALANCE CREDIT
20--							
Mar.	31		7		19,225		19,225
	31		7	13,980			5,245

ACCOUNT *Service Fees* ACCOUNT NO. *50*

DATE		ITEM	POST. REF.	DEBIT	CREDIT	BALANCE DEBIT	BALANCE CREDIT
20--							
Mar.	15		5		4,850		4,850
	31		6		14,375		19,225
	31		7	19,225			–0–

ACCOUNT *Salary Expense* ACCOUNT NO. *58*

DATE		ITEM	POST. REF.	DEBIT	CREDIT	BALANCE DEBIT	BALANCE CREDIT
20--							
Mar.	31		5	8,550		8,550	
	31		7		8,550	–0–	

ACCOUNT *Supplies Expense* ACCOUNT NO. *67*

DATE		ITEM	POST. REF.	DEBIT	CREDIT	BALANCE DEBIT	BALANCE CREDIT
20--							
Mar.	15		5	2,430		2,430	
	25		6	1,720		4,150	
	31		6	1,280		5,430	
	31		7		5,430	–0–	

PROBLEM 4-1

(1)

Castle Shop
Income Statement
For Year Ended April 30, 20--

Service fees		$34,808
Operating expenses:		
Wages expenses	$19,376	
Supplies expense	1,200	
Depreciation expense	1,000	
Rent expense	792	
Misc. expenses	6,348	
Total operating expenses		28,716
Net income		$ 6,092

(2)

Castle Shop
Statement of Owner's Equity
For Year Ended April 30, 20--

Capital, May 1, 20--		$38,818
Income for the year	$6,092	
Less drawing for the year	3,528	
Increase in owner's equity		2,564
Capital, April 30, 20--		$41,382

(3)

Castle Shop
Balance Sheet
April 30, 20--

Assets			Liabilities		
Current assets:			Current liabilities:		
Cash	$10,056		Accounts payable	$7,764	
Accounts receivable	10,938		Wages payable	2,000	
Supplies	1,800		Unearned fees	1,500	
Prepaid rent	8,712		Total liabilities		$11,264
Total current assets		$31,506			
Property, plant, and equipment:			Owner's Equity		
Tools & equipment	$23,814		Castle, capital		41,382
Less accumulated depreciation	2,674	21,140			
Total assets		$52,646	Total liabilities and owner's equity		$52,646

PROBLEM 4-2

(1)

20--		Adjusting Entries		
Apr.	30	Supplies Expense	1,200	
		Supplies		1,200
		Supplies used.		
	30	Rent Expense	792	
		Prepaid Rent		792
		Rent expired.		
	30	Depreciation Expense	1,000	
		Accumulated Depreciation		1,000
		Depreciation.		
	30	Wages Expense	2,000	
		Wages Payable		2,000
		Accrued wages.		

	Apr. 30	Accounts Receivable	3,000	
		Service Fees		3,000
		Accrued fees.		
	30	Unearned Fees	500	
		Service Fees		500
		Fees earned.		
(2)	20--	Closing Entries		
	Apr. 30	Service Fees	34,808	
		Income Summary		34,808
	30	Income Summary	28,716	
		Wages Expense		19,376
		Miscellaneous Expense		6,348
		Supplies Expense		1,200
		Depreciation Expense		1,000
		Rent Expense		792
	30	Income Summary	6,092	
		Castle, Capital		6,092
	30	Castle, Capital	3,528	
		Castle, Drawing		3,528

CHAPTER 5

MATCHING

1. D
2. E
3. C
4. N
5. A
6. K
7. B
8. M
9. F
10. L
11. I
12. J
13. O
14. P
15. G

FILL IN THE BLANK—PART A

1. cash payments
2. special
3. internal controls
4. purchases
5. general
6. cash payments
7. general
8. accounts receivable
9. cash
10. revenue
11. general
12. supply chain management

FILL IN THE BLANK—PART B

1. cash receipts
2. accounts receivable
3. accounting
4. accounts payable
5. cash payments
6. general
7. revenue
8. cash receipts
9. fees earned
10. accounts payable
11. controlling
12. purchases
13. general
14. subsidiary
15. customer relationship management

MULTIPLE CHOICE

1. a. Incorrect. Installation is not a phase of installing or changing an accounting system.
   b. Incorrect. Verification is not a phase of installing or changing an accounting system.
   c. Incorrect. Management is not a phase of installing or changing an accounting system.
   d. ***Correct.*** The job of installing or changing an accounting system is made up of three phases: (1) analysis, (2) design, and (3) implementation.

2. a. Incorrect. The total amounts in the "Accounts Payable Cr." column of the purchases journal are posted to the general ledger, not the individual amounts.
b. Incorrect. Postings are not made to the general journal; rather, entries that do not fit in any of the special journals, such as the purchases journal, are recorded in the general journal.
c. ***Correct.*** The individual amounts in the "Accounts Payable Cr." column of the purchases journal are posted to the appropriate account in the accounts payable subsidiary ledger.
d. Incorrect. There is no such thing as an accounts payable journal.

3. a. Incorrect. The purchase of supplies on account would be recorded in the purchases journal.
b. Incorrect. The receipt of cash for services rendered would be recorded in the cash receipts journal.
c. ***Correct.*** The billing of fees earned on account would be recorded in the revenue journal.
d. Incorrect. The payment of an account payable would be recorded in the cash payments journal.

4. a. ***Correct.*** The controlling account in the general ledger that summarizes the individual accounts with creditors in a subsidiary ledger is Accounts Payable.
b. Incorrect.
c. Incorrect. Accounts Receivable is the controlling account in the general ledger that summarizes the individual subsidiary ledger accounts for customers, not creditors.
d. Incorrect.

5. a. Incorrect. Internal control policies and procedures do not necessarily provide reasonable assurance that all liabilities will be paid.
b. Incorrect. Internal control policies and procedures do not necessarily provide reasonable assurance that a net income will be earned.
c. Incorrect. Internal control policies and procedures do not necessarily provide reasonable assurance that they are being effectively applied.
d. ***Correct.*** Internal control policies and procedures provide reasonable assurance that business information is accurate.

6. a. Incorrect.
b. ***Correct.*** The controlling account for the customer's ledger is Accounts Receivable.
c. Incorrect. Accounts Payable is the controlling account for the creditor's ledger, not the customer's ledger.
d. Incorrect.

7. a. ***Correct.*** At regular intervals the amounts entered in the "Accounts Receivable Cr." column of the revenue journal are posted to the individual accounts receivable accounts.
b. Incorrect. At the end of each month, the total of the "Accounts Receivable Cr." column of the revenue journal is posted to the Accounts Receivable controlling account. The individual accounts are posted more frequently.
c. Incorrect. The Accounts Receivable control account is normally posted at the end of each month, while the individual accounts are posted more frequently.
d. Incorrect. The adjusting entries are prepared and posted at the end of each month, while the individual accounts are posted more frequently.

8. a. Incorrect. The revenue journal is a special journal for recording services provided on account.
b. ***Correct.*** The general journal is not a special journal, but instead it is an all-purpose journal for recording transactions that do not fit into any of the special journals.
c. Incorrect. The cash receipts journal is a special journal for recording receipts of cash.
d. Incorrect. The purchases journal is a special journal for recording purchases of items on account.

9. a. Incorrect. The original transactions must be entered into the computer system. Often there is a manual entry at some initial transaction point, such as at a cash register.
b. Incorrect. Adjusting entries are frequently performed manually.
c. ***Correct.*** The computerized accounting system will post transactions into the ledger automatically.
d. Incorrect. Month-end postings to the controlling accounts are unnecessary because this control is not needed in a computerized environment.

10. a. Incorrect. Supply chain management applications are used to plan and coordinated suppliers.
b. ***Correct.*** Customer relationship management software helps plan and coordinate marketing and sales efforts.
c. Incorrect. Product life-cycle management applications are used to plan and coordinate the product development and design process.
d. Incorrect. The revenue and collection cycle is a basic manual or computerized transaction processing sequence to any business.

TRUE/FALSE

1. F It is the goal of systems analysis, not systems design, to identify information needs and how the system should provide the information.
2. F Transactions involving the payment of cash for any purpose usually are recorded in a cash payments journal, not a purchases journal. The purchases journal is used to record purchases of items on account.
3. F When there are a large number of individual accounts with a common characteristic, it is common to place them in a separate ledger called a subsidiary ledger, not a detail ledger.
4. T
5. F Acquisitions on account that are not provided for in special debit columns are recorded in the purchases journal in the final set of columns called "Other Accounts Dr.", not "Misc."
6. T
7. F At the end of each month, the total of the amount column of the revenue journal is posted as a debit to Accounts Receivable, not Cash. The credit is to Fees Earned.
8. T
9. T
10. T
11. F The cost of computer hardware and software has declined, thus making computerized accounting systems more affordable to small- and medium-size businesses.
12. T
13. T
14. F Regardless whether a business uses computers to process accounting data, the concepts and methods for a manual system *are* relevant.
15. F B2C e-commerce is used to conduct purchase and sales transactions between businesses and consumers, such as with Amazon.com.

EXERCISE 5-1

Feb.	1	purchases journal
	6	cash receipts journal
	8	general journal
	11	cash payments journal
	18	revenue (sales) journal
	28	cash receipts journal

EXERCISE 5-2

REVENUE JOURNAL

DATE		INVOICE NO.	ACCOUNT DEBITED	POST. REF.	ACCTS. REC. DR. FEES EARNED CR.
20--					
Oct.	3	2883	Blanders Co.		8,250
	4	2884	Montana Co.		5,000

CASH RECEIPTS JOURNAL

DATE		ACCOUNT CREDITED	POST. REF.	OTHER ACCOUNTS CR.	ACCOUNTS REC. CR.	CASH DR.
20--						
Oct.	13	Blanders Co.			7,250	7,250
	14	Montana Co.			5,000	5,000
	25	Office Supplies		300		300
	31	Fees Earned		39,600		39,600

GENERAL JOURNAL

20--				
Oct.	8	Fees Earned	1,000	
		Accounts Receivable—Blanders Co.		1,000

EXERCISE 5-3

PURCHASES JOURNAL

DATE		ACCOUNT CREDITED	POST. REF.	ACCOUNTS PAY. CR.	STORE SUPPLIES DR.	OFFICE SUPPLIES DR.	OTHER ACCOUNTS DR.
20--							
Mar.	2	Eastside Co.		1,250	1,250		
	8	Bench Co.		600	600		
	28	James & Co.		900	800	100	

CASH PAYMENTS JOURNAL

DATE		CK. NO.	ACCOUNT DEBITED	POST. REF.	OTHER ACCOUNTS DR.	ACCOUNTS PAY. DR.	CASH CR.
20--							
Mar.	16	230	Bench Co.			600	600
	20	231	Office Supplies		250		250
	27	232	Eastside Co.			950	950

GENERAL JOURNAL

20--				
Mar.	9	Accounts Payable—Eastside Co.	300	
		Store Supplies		300

PROBLEM 5-1

(1)–(3)

REVENUE JOURNAL

DATE		INVOICE NO.	ACCOUNT DEBITED	POST. REF.	ACCTS. REC. DR. FEES EARNED CR.
20--					
Sept.	8	210	Robert Poon	✓	1,220
	12	225	Jeff Lucas	✓	750
	24	260	Pamela Stark	✓	860
	30	290	Steve Kocan	✓	2,500
					5,330
					(113)(411)

(2) and **(3)**

GENERAL LEDGER

Accounts Receivable		113		
Sept. 30	5,330			

Fees Earned				411
			Sept. 30	5,330

ACCOUNTS RECEIVABLE LEDGER

Steve Kocan		
Sept. 30	2,500	

Jeff Lucas		
Sept. 12	750	

Robert Poon		
Sept. 8	1,220	

Pamela Stark		
Sept. 24	860	

(4)

Steve Kocan	$2,500
Jeff Lucas	750
Robert Poon	1,220
Pamela Stark	860
Total accounts receivable	$5,330

PROBLEM 5-2

(1)–(3)

PURCHASES JOURNAL

DATE		ACCOUNT CREDITED	POST. REF.	ACCOUNTS PAYABLE CR.	STORE SUPPLIES DR.	OFFICE SUPPLIES. DR.	OTHER ACCOUNTS DR. ACCOUNT	POST. REF.	AMOUNT
20--									
Apr.	14	Mills Co.	✓	300	300				
	16	Quick Co.	✓	175		175			
	22	Mills Co.	✓	5,250			Store Equip.	121	5,250
	30	Mills Co.	✓	280	280				
				6,005	580	175			5,250
				(211)	(115)	(116)			(✓)

(2) and **(3)**

GENERAL LEDGER

Store Supplies		115		
Apr. 30	580			

Office Supplies				116
Apr. 30	175			

Store Equipment		121		
Apr. 22	5,250			

Accounts Payable				211
			Apr. 30	6,005

ACCOUNTS PAYABLE LEDGER

Mills Co.			Quick Co.		
	Apr. 14	300		Apr. 16	175
	22	5,250			
	30	280			

(4) Mills Co. $5,830
Quick Co. 175
Total accounts payable $6,005

PROBLEM 5-3

(1)

Store Supplies	3,650	Accounts Payable	15,890
Office Supplies	1,250		
Other Accounts	10,990		
Debit totals	15,890	Credit totals	15,890

(2)

PURCHASES JOURNAL

DATE		ACCOUNT CREDITED	POST. REF.	ACCOUNTS PAYABLE CR.	STORE SUPPLIES DR.	OFFICE SUPPLIES. DR.	OTHER ACCOUNTS DR. ACCOUNT	POST. REF.	AMOUNT
20--									
Oct.	29	Hartkemeyer Co.	✓	7,620			Store Equip.	121	7,620
	31			15,890	3,650	1,250			10,990
				(211)	(115)	(116)			

GENERAL LEDGER

Store Supplies		115	Office Supplies		116
Oct. 31	3,650		Oct. 31	1,250	

Store Equipment		121	Accounts Payable		211
Oct. 29	7,620			Oct. 31	15,890

CHAPTER 6

MATCHING

1. C	6. S	11. X	16. F	21. L	25. J
2. H	7. K	12. Y	17. N	22. P	26. A
3. M	8. U	13. D	18. Z	23. O	27. W
4. R	9. T	14. BB	19. B	24. AA	28. V
5. Q	10. E	15. G	20. I		

FILL IN THE BLANK—PART A

1. cost of merchandise sold
2. sales
3. operating expenses
4. merchandise inventory
5. periodic
6. merchandise available for sale
7. purchases return or allowance
8. sales discounts
9. credit
10. FOB shipping point
11. $50
12. $60
13. $700
14. multiple-step
15. administrative
16. loss from operations
17. other
18. inventory shrinkage
19. $240,000
20. report

FILL IN THE BLANK—PART B

1. gross profit
2. operating expenses
3. perpetual
4. physical inventory
5. purchases discounts
6. debit
7. sales return or allowance
8. trade discounts
9. FOB destination
10. $160
11. $15,100
12. $33
13. $9,900
14. $6,600
15. selling
16. income from operations
17. other income
18. single-step
19. $215,000
20. account

MULTIPLE CHOICE

1. a. Incorrect. Cost of merchandise sold is not included in the owner's equity section of the balance sheet.
   b. Incorrect. Cost of merchandise sold is not included in the other income section of the income statement.
   c. ***Correct.*** The basic differences between the financial statements of a merchandising business and a service business include reporting cost of merchandise sold on the income statement and the balance sheet as a current asset.
   d. Incorrect. An owner's equity statement is prepared for both a merchandising business and a service business.

2. a. Incorrect. The sales discount should be deducted in determining the amount the seller will received.
   b. ***Correct.*** The seller will receive $58.80, computed as $60 less the sales discount of $1.20 ($60 × 2%).
   c. Incorrect.
   d. Incorrect. $1.20 is the amount of the sales discount, not the amount received by the seller.

3. a. Incorrect. A debit memorandum is issued by the buyer, not the seller.
   b. ***Correct.*** A credit memorandum is issued by the seller when a customer is allowed a reduction from the original price for defective goods.
   c. Incorrect.
   d. Incorrect.

4. a. ***Correct.*** When the seller prepays the freight costs and the terms of sale are FOB shipping point, the seller records the payment of the freight costs by debiting Accounts Receivable. This is because freight costs are the responsibility of the buyer when the terms are FOB shipping point.
   b. Incorrect.
   c. Incorrect.
   d. Incorrect.

5. a. Incorrect.
b. Incorrect.
c. ***Correct.*** If the seller collects sales tax at the time of sale, the seller credits the tax to Sales Tax Payable.
d. Incorrect.

6. a. Incorrect. Accounts Receivable normally appears in the chart of accounts of both a merchandising and a service business.
b. Incorrect. Advertising Expense normally appears in the chart of accounts of both a merchandising and a service business.
c. ***Correct.*** Sales Returns and Allowances appears in the chart of accounts for a merchandising business but not for a service business.
d. Incorrect. Accumulated Depreciation normally appears in the chart of accounts of both a merchandising and a service business.

7. a. ***Correct.*** The excess of net revenue from sales over the cost of merchandise sold is gross profit.
b. Incorrect. Operating profit, sometimes called income from operations, is gross profit less selling and administrative expenses.
c. Incorrect.
d. Incorrect.

8. a. Incorrect. Income from operations is computed by subtracting from gross profit both selling and administrative expenses.
b. Incorrect. Income from operations is computed by subtracting from gross profit both selling and administrative (general) expenses.
c. Incorrect. Income from operations is computed by subtracting from gross profit both selling and administrative expenses.
d. ***Correct.*** Income from operations is computed by subtracting operating expenses from gross profit. Operating expenses include both selling and administrative expenses.

9. a. Incorrect.
b. Incorrect.
c. Incorrect.
d. ***Correct.*** After all adjusting entries are posted, the balances of all asset, liability, revenue, and expense accounts correspond exactly to the amounts in the financial statements.

10. a. Incorrect. Sales appears as revenue from operations.
b. ***Correct.*** In a multiple-step income statement of a merchandising business, interest revenue would appear as "other income."
c. Incorrect. Sales discounts are deducted from sales in reporting revenue from sales.
d. Incorrect. Sales returns and allowances are deducted from sales in reporting revenue from sales.

TRUE/FALSE

1. T

2. F In a perpetual inventory system, purchases of merchandise are recorded in the merchandise inventory account, not the purchases account.

3. T

4. F A discount offered the purchaser of goods as a means of encouraging payment before the end of the credit period is known as a purchases (or sales) discount, not a bank discount.

5. T

6. F If the seller is to absorb the cost of delivering the goods, the terms are stated FOB (free on board) destination, not FOB shipping point.

7. F The liability for the sales tax is incurred at the time the seller sells the merchandise, not when the seller receives payment from the buyer.

8. T

9. T
10. F The accounting cycle for a merchandising business is similar to, not significantly different from, that of a service business.
11. F The physical inventory taken at the end of the period is normally smaller, not larger, than the amount of the balance of the merchandise inventory account.
12. F Any merchandise inventory shrinkage is normally debited to the cost of merchandise sold account, not the merchandise inventory account.
13. F Expenses incurred directly and entirely in connection with the sale of merchandise are called selling expenses, not administrative expenses.
14. F Revenue from sources such as income from interest, rent, dividends, and gains resulting from the sale of fixed assets is classified as "other income," not income from operations.
15. T
16. T
17. T
18. F The traditional balance sheet arrangement of assets on the left-hand side with the liabilities and owner's equity on the right-hand side is called the account form, not the report form.
19. F After the adjusting and closing entries have been recorded and posted, the general ledger accounts that appear on the balance sheet *do* have balances. The general ledger accounts that appear in the income statement *do not* have balances. In addition, the owner's drawing account *does not* have a balance.
20. T

EXERCISE 6-1

Sales				$875,000
Cost of merchandise sold:				
Merchandise inventory, July 1, 2009			$130,000	
Purchases		$600,000		
Less: Purchases returns and allowances	$45,000			
Purchases discounts	10,000	55,000		
Net purchases		$545,000		
Add freight in		7,500		
Cost of merchandise purchased			552,500	
Merchandise available for sale			$682,500	
Less merchandise inventory, June 30, 2010			125,000	
Cost of merchandise sold				557,500
Gross profit				$317,500

EXERCISE 6-2

		Debit	Credit
(1)	Merchandise Inventory	5,000	
	Accounts Payable		5,000
(2)	Accounts Payable	5,000	
	Cash		4,900
	Merchandise Inventory		100
(3)	Merchandise Inventory	3,580	
	Accounts Payable		3,580
(4)	Accounts Payable	900	
	Merchandise Inventory		900
(5)	Accounts Payable	2,680	
	Cash		2,680

EXERCISE 6-3

	Account	Debit	Credit
(1)	Cash	3,150	
	Sales		3,150
	Cost of Merchandise Sold	2,000	
	Merchandise Inventory		2,000
(2)	Cash	2,850	
	Sales		2,850
	Cost of Merchandise Sold	1,380	
	Merchandise Inventory		1,380
(3)	Credit Card Expense	100	
	Cash		100
(4)	Accounts Receivable	4,500	
	Sales		4,500
	Accounts Receivable	150	
	Cash		150
	Cost of Merchandise Sold	3,100	
	Merchandise Inventory		3,100
(5)	Sales Returns and Allowances	400	
	Accounts Receivable		400
	Merchandise Inventory	275	
	Cost of Merchandise Sold		275
(6)	Cash	4,168	
	Sales Discounts	82	
	Accounts Receivable		4,250

EXERCISE 6-4

Date		Account	Debit	Credit
20--				
Jan.	3	Merchandise Inventory	25,000	
		Accounts Payable		25,000
	5	Accounts Payable	5,000	
		Merchandise Inventory		5,000
	12	Accounts Receivable	50,000	
		Sales		50,000
	12	Cost of Merchandise Sold	35,000	
		Merchandise Inventory		35,000
	13	Accounts Payable	20,000	
		Cash		19,600
		Merchandise Inventory		400
	15	Sales Returns and Allowances	8,000	
		Accounts Receivable		8,000
	15	Merchandise Inventory	5,600	
		Cost of Merchandise Sold		5,600
	22	Cash	41,580	
		Sales Discounts	420	
		Accounts Receivable		42,000

Exercise 6-5

Appendix 2

	Account	Debit	Credit
(1)	Purchases	5,000	
	Accounts Payable		5,000
(2)	Accounts Payable	5,000	
	Cash		4,900
	Purchases Discounts		100
(3)	Purchases	3,500	
	Freight In	80	
	Accounts Payable		3,580
(4)	Accounts Payable	900	
	Purchases Returns and Allowances		900
(5)	Accounts Payable	2,680	
	Cash		2,680

Exercise 6-6

Appendix 2

Date		Account	Debit	Credit
20--				
Jan.	3	Purchases	25,000	
		Accounts Payable		25,000
	5	Accounts Payable	5,000	
		Purchases Returns and Allowances		5,000
	12	Accounts Receivable	50,000	
		Sales		50,000
	13	Accounts Payable	20,000	
		Cash		19,600
		Purchases Discounts		400
	15	Sales Returns and Allowances	8,000	
		Accounts Receivable		8,000
	22	Cash	41,580	
		Sales Discounts	420	
		Accounts Receivable		42,000

PROBLEM 6-1

Date		Account	Debit	Credit
20--				
Sept.	3	Merchandise Inventory	8,500	
		Accounts Payable		8,500
	4	Office Supplies	800	
		Cash		800
	6	Accounts Receivable	4,000	
		Sales		4,000
	6	Cost of Merchandise Sold	3,000	
		Merchandise Inventory		3,000
	7	Accounts Payable	2,000	
		Merchandise Inventory		2,000
	10	Merchandise Inventory	5,000	
		Cash		5,000
	12	Cash	5,500	
		Sales		5,500
	12	Cost of Merchandise Sold	3,200	
		Merchandise Inventory		3,200
	13	Accounts Payable	6,500	
		Cash		6,435
		Merchandise Inventory		65
	16	Cash	3,920	
		Sales Discounts	80	
		Accounts Receivable		4,000
	20	Credit Card Expense	300	
		Cash		300
	24	Accounts Receivable	3,000	
		Sales		3,000
	24	Cost of Merchandise Sold	1,750	
		Merchandise Inventory		1,750
	26	Cash	2,200	
		Sales		2,200
	26	Cost of Merchandise Sold	1,400	
		Merchandise Inventory		1,400
	30	Sales Returns and Allowances	1,000	
		Accounts Receivable		1,000
	30	Merchandise Inventory	600	
		Cost of Merchandise Sold		600

PROBLEM 6-2

(a)

Miller Co.
Multiple-Step Income Statement
For Year Ended March 31, 20--

Revenue from sales:			
Sales		$1,016,700	
Less: Sales returns and allowances		13,010	
Net sales			$1,003,690
Cost of merchandise sold			681,060
Gross profit			$ 322,630
Operating expenses:			
Selling expenses:			
Sales salaries expense	$78,250		
Delivery expense	42,100		
Advertising expense	13,090		
Depr. expense—delivery equip.	9,050		
Misc. selling expense	13,950		
Total selling expenses		$ 156,440	
Administrative expenses:			
Office salaries expense	$55,800		
Insurance expense	16,000		
Office supplies expense	9,100		
Misc. administrative expenses	6,870		
Total administrative expenses		87,770	
Total operating expenses			244,210
Income from operations			$ 78,420
Other income:			
Interest revenue			1,020
Net income			$ 79,440

(b)

Miller Co.
Single-Step Income Statement
For Year Ended March 31, 20--

Revenues:		
Net sales		$1,003,690
Interest revenue		1,020
Total revenues		$1,004,710
Expenses:		
Cost of merchandise sold	$681,060	
Selling expenses	156,440	
Administrative expenses	87,770	
Total expenses		925,270
Net income		$ 79,440

(c)

Cost of Merchandise Sold	4,200	
Merchandise Inventory		4,200
Merchandise shrinkage.		

PROBLEM 6-3

Miller Co.
Statement of Owner's Equity
For Year Ended March 31, 20--

R. W. Miller, capital, April 1, 20--		$193,650
Net income for year	$79,440	
Less withdrawals	30,000	
Increase in owner's equity		49,440
R. W. Miller, capital, March 31, 20--		$243,090

PROBLEM 6-4

Miller Co.
Balance Sheet
March 31, 20--

Assets		
Current assets:		
Cash	$ 49,620	
Accounts receivable	107,780	
Merchandise inventory	115,800	
Office supplies	1,250	
Prepaid insurance	8,740	
Total current assets		$283,190
Property, plant, and equipment:		
Delivery equipment	$ 60,150	
Less accumulated depreciation	22,950	
Total property, plant, and equipment		37,200
Total assets		$320,390
Liabilities		
Current liabilities:		
Accounts payable	$ 75,300	
Salaries payable	2,000	
Total current liabilities		$ 77,300
Owner's Equity		
R. W. Miller, capital		243,090
Total liabilities and owner's equity		$320,390

PROBLEM 6-5

APPENDIX 2

20--				
Sept.	3	Purchases	8,500	
		Accounts Payable		8,500
	4	Office Supplies	800	
		Cash		800
	6	Accounts Receivable	4,000	
		Sales		4,000
	7	Accounts Payable	2,000	
		Purchases Returns and Allowances		2,000
	10	Purchases	5,000	
		Cash		5,000
	12	Cash	5,500	
		Sales		5,500
	13	Accounts Payable	6,500	
		Cash		6,435
		Purchases Discounts		65
	16	Cash	3,920	
		Sales Discounts	80	
		Accounts Receivable		4,000
	20	Credit Card Expense	300	
		Cash		300
	24	Accounts Receivable	3,000	
		Sales		3,000
	26	Cash	2,200	
		Sales		2,200
	30	Sales Returns and Allowances	1,000	
		Accounts Receivable		1,000

CHAPTER 7

MATCHING

1. I
2. B
3. E
4. A
5. F
6. G
7. J
8. C
9. D
10. H

FILL IN THE BLANK—PART A

1. physical inventory
2. last-in, first-out (lifo)
3. $1,270
4. lifo
5. lower-of-cost-or-market (LCM)
6. $15,000
7. understated
8. understated
9. gross profit
10. inventory turnover

FILL IN THE BLANK—PART B

1. first-in, first-out (fifo)
2. average cost
3. $1,388
4. net realizable value
5. $45
6. overstated
7. understated
8. retail inventory
9. 120.000
10. number of days' sales in inventory

Multiple Choice

1. a. ***Correct.*** The total cost of the 15 units on hand at the end of the period, as determined under a perpetual inventory system and the lifo costing method, is $80 [(5 units × $6) + (10 units × $5)].
   b. Incorrect.
   c. Incorrect.
   d. Incorrect.

2. a. Incorrect.
   b. Incorrect.
   c. Incorrect.
   d. ***Correct.*** The total cost of the 15 units on hand at the end of the period, as determined under a perpetual inventory system and the fifo costing method, is $120 (15 units × $8).

3. a. ***Correct.*** The total cost of the 15 units on hand at the end of the period, as determined under a periodic inventory system and the lifo costing method, is $80 [(5 units × $6) + (10 units × $5)].
   b. Incorrect.
   c. Incorrect.
   d. Incorrect.

4. a. Incorrect.
   b. Incorrect.
   c. Incorrect.
   d. ***Correct.*** The total cost of the 15 units on hand at the end of the period, as determined under a periodic inventory system and the fifo costing method, is $120 (15 units × $8).

5. a. Incorrect.
   b. Incorrect.
   c. ***Correct.*** The total cost of the 15 units on hand at the end of the period, as determined under a periodic inventory system and the average costing method, is $99 (15 units × $6.60).
   d. Incorrect.

6. a. Incorrect. During a period of rising prices, the fifo inventory costing method will result in the highest amount of net income.
   b. ***Correct.*** During a period of rising prices, the lifo inventory costing method will result in the lowest amount of net income.
   c. Incorrect. During a period of rising prices, the average inventory costing method will result in an amount of net income that is higher than lifo and lower than fifo.
   d. Incorrect. The perpetual inventory system is not an inventory costing method.

7. a. Incorrect. The lower of cost or market method is permitted under both the periodic and the perpetual inventory systems.
   b. Incorrect.
   c. Incorrect.
   d. ***Correct.*** If the replacement price of an item of inventory is lower than its cost, the use of the lower of cost or market method reduces gross profit for the period in which the decline occurred.

8. a. Incorrect.
   b. Incorrect.
   c. ***Correct.*** When lifo is strictly applied to a perpetual inventory system, the unit cost prices assigned to the ending inventory will not necessarily be those associated with the earliest unit costs of the period if at any time during a period the number of units of a commodity sold exceeds the number previously purchased during the same period.
   d. Incorrect.

9. a. Incorrect. If merchandise inventory at the end of the period is understated, gross profit will be understated, not overstated.
   b. Incorrect. If merchandise inventory at the end of the period is understated, owner's equity will be understated, not overstated.
   c. ***Correct.*** If merchandise inventory at the end of the period is understated, net income will be understated because cost of merchandise sold will be overstated.
   d. Incorrect. If merchandise inventory at the end of the period is understated, cost of merchandise sold will be overstated, not understated.

10. a. ***Correct.*** If merchandise inventory at the end of period 1 is overstated and at the end of period 2 is correct, gross profit in period 2 will be understated because cost of merchandise sold will be overstated in period 2.
    b. Incorrect. If merchandise inventory at the end of period 1 is overstated and at the end of period 2 is correct, assets at the end of period 2 will be correct, not overstated.
    c. Incorrect. If merchandise inventory at the end of period 1 is overstated and at the end of period 2 is correct, owner's equity at the end of period 2 will be correct, not understated.
    d. Incorrect. If merchandise inventory at the end of period 1 is overstated and at the end of period 2 is correct, cost of merchandise sold in period 2 will be overstated, not understated.

TRUE/FALSE

1. F The two principal systems of inventory accounting are periodic and perpetual. Physical is not an inventory system.
2. T
3. F If merchandise inventory at the end of the period is overstated, owner's equity at the end of the period will be overstated, not understated. This is because cost of merchandise sold will be understated, and thus net income and owner's equity will be overstated.
4. F During a period of rising prices, the inventory costing method that will result in the highest amount of net income is fifo, not lifo. This is because fifo will assign the highest costs to inventory, and thus, cost of merchandise sold will be lower than lifo.
5. T
6. T
7. F As used in the phrase "lower of cost or market," *market* is the cost to replace the merchandise on the inventory date, not the selling price.
8. F When the retail inventory method is used, inventory at retail is converted to cost by multiplying the inventory at retail by the ratio of cost to selling (retail) price for the merchandise available for sale. The denominator is the selling (retail) price for the merchandise available for sale, not the replacement cost of the merchandise available for sale.
9. T
10. F If merchandise inventory at the end of the period is understated, gross profit will be understated, not overstated. This is because cost of merchandise sold will be overstated.

EXERCISE 7-1

	Total	
	Cost	Lower of Cost or Market
Commodity A	$3,750	$3,600
Commodity B	2,760	2,760
Commodity C	1,450	1,200
Commodity D	1,440	1,290
Total	$9,400	$8,850

EXERCISE 7-2

Sales	Cost of Merchandise Sold	Gross Profit
(1) Correct	**(1)** Overstated	**(1)** Understated
(2) N/A	**(2)** $5,000	**(2)** $5,000

Net Income	Merchandise Inventory (October 31, 2007)
(1) Understated	**(1)** Understated
(2) $5,000	**(2)** $5,000

Current Assets	Total Assets	Liabilities
(1) Understated	**(1)** Understated	**(1)** Correct
(2) $5,000	**(2)** $5,000	**(2)** N/A

Owner's Equity
(1) Understated
(2) $5,000

PROBLEM 7-1

(1)

Date Purchased	Units	Price	Total Cost
November 1	12	$58	$696
Total	12		$696

(2)

Date Purchased	Units	Price	Total Cost
January 10	2	$48	$ 96
February 15	5	54	270
November 1	5	58	290
Total	12		$656

(3)

Date Purchased	Units	Price	Total Cost
November 1	12	$58	$696
Total	12		$696

(4)

Date Purchased	Units	Price	Total Cost
January 10	10	$48	$480
February 15	2	54	108
Total	12		$588

(5) Average unit cost: $\frac{\$11,485}{210} = \$54.69$

12 units in inventory @ $54.69 = $656.28

PROBLEM 7-2

	(1) Fifo	(2) Lifo	(3) Average Cost
Sales	$2,240,000	$2,240,000	$2,240,000
Purchases	$1,783,900	$1,783,900	$1,783,900
Less ending inventory	145,600	100,000	118,920
Cost of merchandise sold	$1,638,300	$1,683,900	$1,664,980
Gross profit	$ 601,700	$ 556,100	$ 575,020

Computation of Ending Inventory

	Date Purchased	Units	Price	Total Cost
Fifo:	November 1	100	$69	$ 6,900
	December 1	1,900	$73	138,700
	Total	2,000		$145,600
Lifo:	January 1	2,000	$50	$100,000

Average Cost: $\frac{\$1,783,900}{30,000} = \$59.46$

$\$59.46 \times 2,000 = \$118,920$

PROBLEM 7-3

APPENDIX

	Cost	Retail
(1) Merchandise inventory, August 1	$118,500	$170,000
Purchases in August (net)	299,125	472,500
Merchandise available for sale	$417,625	$642,500
Ratio of cost to retail $\frac{\$417,625}{\$642,500} = 65\%$		
Sales in August (net)		479,000
Merchandise inventory, August 31, at retail		$163,500
Merchandise inventory, August 31, at estimated cost ($163,500 × 65%)		$106,275

(2) Merchandise inventory, August 1		$118,500
Purchases in August (net)		299,125
Merchandise available for sale		$417,625
Sales in August (net)	$479,000	
Less estimated gross profit ($479,000 × 30%)	143,700	
Estimated cost of merchandise sold		335,300
Estimated merchandise inventory, August 31		$ 82,325

CHAPTER 8

MATCHING

1. Q
2. M
3. K
4. L
5. C
6. S
7. R
8. J
9. A
10. O
11. D
12. H
13. P

FILL IN THE BLANK—PART A

1. cash
2. remittance advice
3. voucher
4. due
5. electronics fund transfer (EFT)
6. bank reconciliation
7. deducted from
8. deducted from
9. company's records
10. compensating

FILL IN THE BLANK—PART B

1. element
2. change
3. Other income
4. voucher
5. receiving report
6. petty cash
7. added to
8. added to
9. deducted from
10. cash equivalents

MULTIPLE CHOICE

1. a. Incorrect. Since the treasurer is responsible for the custody of cash, the remittance advices should not be sent to the treasurer.
   b. Incorrect. Since the cashier's department handles cash, the remittance advices should not be sent to the cashier's department.
   c. ***Correct.*** For good internal control over cash receipts, remittance advices should be separated from cash received by mail and sent directly to the accounting department.
   d. Incorrect. Voucher clerks do not use remittance advices in carrying out their responsibilities.

2. a. Incorrect. Vouchers are not prepared by the treasurer.
   b. Incorrect. Vouchers are not paid immediately after they are prepared; they are filed and paid by the due date.
   c. Incorrect. Paid vouchers are filed numerically, not by due date.
   d. ***Correct.*** An important characteristic of the voucher system is the requirement that a voucher be prepared for each major expenditure.

3. a. Incorrect.
   b. Incorrect.
   c. Incorrect.
   d. ***Correct.*** In a bank reconciliation, NSF checks are deducted from the balance according to the company's records.

4. a. ***Correct.*** In a bank reconciliation, deposits not recorded by the bank are added to the balance according to the bank statement.
   b. Incorrect.
   c. Incorrect.
   d. Incorrect.

5. a. Incorrect.
   b. ***Correct.*** The amount of the outstanding checks is included on the bank reconciliation as a deduction from the balance per bank statement.
   c. Incorrect.
   d. Incorrect.

6. a. Incorrect.
   b. ***Correct.*** The entry required in the depositor's accounts for receipts from cash sales of $7,500, recorded incorrectly as $5,700, is a debit to Cash and a credit to Sales for $1,800.
   c. Incorrect.
   d. Incorrect.

7. a. Incorrect.
   b. ***Correct.*** The entry required in the depositor's accounts for a credit memorandum for a short-term, non-interest-bearing note collected by the bank is a debit to Cash and a credit to Notes Receivable.
   c. Incorrect.
   d. Incorrect.

8. a. Incorrect.
b. Incorrect.
c. Incorrect.
d. ***Correct.*** No entry is required in the company's accounts to record outstanding checks.

9. a. Incorrect. Journal entries based on the bank reconciliation are also required on the company's books for deductions from the balance according to the company's records.
b. Incorrect. Journal entries based on the bank reconciliation are also required on the company's books for additions to the balance according to the company's records.
c. ***Correct.*** Journal entries based on the bank reconciliation are required on the company's books for both additions to the balance according to the company's records and deductions from the balance according to the company's records.
d. Incorrect. Journal entries based on the bank reconciliation are not required on the company's books for additions to and deductions from the balance according to the bank's records.

10. a. ***Correct.*** The entry to record the replenishment of the petty cash fund includes a debit to various expense and asset accounts and a credit to Cash.
b. Incorrect.
c. Incorrect.
d. Incorrect.

TRUE/FALSE

1. T
2. F Internal controls provide reasonable assurance that employees will not steal or misuse assets, but do not guarantee against employee theft or misuse.
3. F In a bank reconciliation, checks issued that have not been paid by the bank are deducted from, not added to, the balance according to the bank statement.
4. T
5. T
6. F A debit balance in the cash short and over account at the end of the fiscal period represents a miscellaneous administrative expense not income.
7. F It is *not* common practice for businesses to require that every payment of cash be evidenced by a check signed by the owner. Some small payments of cash are often made out of a petty cash fund.
8. T
9. F When a petty cash fund is replenished, the accounts debited are determined by summarizing the petty cash receipts. Petty Cash is only debited when the fund is initially established or increased.
10. T

EXERCISE 8-1

		Debit	Credit
(2)	Cash	1,920	
	Notes Receivable		1,800
	Interest Revenue		120
(3)	Miscellaneous Administrative Expense	28	
	Cash		28
(6)	Accounts Payable—Charlie's Optical Supply	100	
	Cash		100

EXERCISE 8-2

		Debit	Credit
(1)	Petty Cash	400.00	
	Cash		400.00
(2)	Office Supplies	80.25	
	Miscellaneous Selling Expense	115.33	
	Miscellaneous Administrative Expense	78.05	
	Cash Short and Over		1.97
	Cash		271.66

PROBLEM 8-1

(1)

Dumont Co.
Bank Reconciliation
September 30, 20--

Balance according to bank statement		$ 8,510
Add deposit not recorded		1,900
		$10,410
Deduct outstanding checks:		
No. 255	$325	
No. 280	100	
No. 295	700	1,125
Adjusted balance		$ 9,285
Balance according to company's records		$ 7,540
Add: Error in recording Check No. 289	$270	
Error in a deposit	720	
Note and interest collected by bank	780	1,770
		$ 9,310
Deduct bank service charge		25
Adjusted balance		$ 9,285

(2)

		Debit	Credit
Sept. 30	Cash	1,745	
	Miscellaneous Administrative Expense	25	
	Accounts Payable		270
	Accounts Receivable		720
	Notes Receivable		700
	Interest Revenue		80

CHAPTER 9

MATCHING

1. M
2. A
3. J
4. E
5. D
6. G
7. C
8. I
9. H
10. K
11. B
12. L

FILL IN THE BLANK—PART A

1. receivables
2. note receivable
3. allowance
4. aging of receivables
5. $7,150
6. $32,500
7. $309,000
8. October 10
9. dishonored
10. accounts receivable turnover

FILL IN THE BLANK—PART B

1. account
2. bad debt
3. direct write-off
4. $310,000
5. $10,400
6. maturity value
7. $153,750
8. December 16
9. number of days' sales in receivables
10. promissory

MULTIPLE CHOICE

1. a. ***Correct.*** When the allowance method is used in accounting for uncollectible accounts, any uncollectible account is written off against the allowance account. The entry is a debit to the allowance account and a credit to the accounts receivable account.
   b. Incorrect.
   c. Incorrect.
   d. Incorrect. When the direct write-off method is used in accounting for uncollectible accounts, any uncollectible account is written off against the bad debt expense account.

2. a. Incorrect. When the allowance method is used in accounting for uncollectible accounts, any uncollectible account is written off against the allowance account.
   b. Incorrect.
   c. Incorrect.
   d. ***Correct.*** When the direct write-off method is used in accounting for uncollectible accounts, any uncollectible account is written off against the bad debt expense account. The entry is a debit to the bad debt expense account and a credit to the accounts receivable account.

3. a. Incorrect.
   b. Incorrect.
   c. Incorrect.
   d. ***Correct.*** The allowance for doubtful accounts is a contra asset account, normally with a credit balance.

4. a. Incorrect.
   b. ***Correct.*** If the allowance account has a credit balance of $170 at the end of the year before adjustments and if the estimate of uncollectible accounts based on aging the receivables is $3,010, the amount of the adjusting entry for uncollectible accounts is $2,840 ($3,010 – $170).
   c. Incorrect.
   d. Incorrect.

5. a. Incorrect.
   b. Incorrect.
   c. ***Correct.*** If the allowance account has a debit balance of $250 at the end of the year before adjustments and if the estimate of uncollectible accounts based on sales for the period is $2,200, the amount of the adjusting entry for uncollectible accounts is $2,200. The balance of the allowance account does not affect the amount of the adjusting entry when the estimate is based upon sales.
   d. Incorrect.

6. a. Incorrect.
   b. ***Correct.*** After the accounts are adjusted and closed at the end of the fiscal year, Accounts Receivable has a balance of $430,000 and Allowance for Doubtful Accounts has a balance of $25,000. The expected realizable value of the accounts receivable is $405,000 ($430,000 – $25,000).
   c. Incorrect.
   d. Incorrect.

7. a. Incorrect. The payee is the one to whose order the note is payable.
   b. Incorrect.
   c. ***Correct.*** On a promissory note, the one making the promise to pay is called the maker.
   d. Incorrect.

8. a. Incorrect.
   b. Incorrect.
   c. Incorrect.
   d. ***Correct.*** The amount that is due on a note at the maturity or due date is called the maturity value.

9. a. Incorrect.
b. ***Correct.*** The due date of a 90-day note dated July 1 is September 29, determined as follows: 30 days in July; 31 days in August; and 29 days in September.
c. Incorrect.
d. Incorrect.

10. a. Incorrect.
b. Incorrect.
c. ***Correct.*** The maturity value of a 60-day, 12% note for $15,000, dated May 1, is $15,300 computed as follows: [$15,000 + ($15,000 × 60/360 × 12%)].
d. Incorrect.

TRUE/FALSE

1. T

2. T

3. F The direct write-off method of accounting for uncollectible receivables provides for uncollectible accounts in the year when the account is determined to be worthless (uncollectible), not the year of sale.

4. T

5. T

6. F Notes do not include all money claims against people, organizations, or other debtors. An account receivable is another example of a money claim against people, organizations, or other debtors.

7. T

8. T

9. F When a note is received from a customer on account, it is recorded by debiting Notes Receivable and crediting Accounts Receivable, not Sales.

10. T

EXERCISE 9-1

	Date		Account	Debit	Credit
(1)	Aug.	31	Uncollectible Accounts Expense	550	
			Accounts Receivable—Don Shore		550
(2)	Oct.	8	Accounts Receivable—Don Shore	550	
			Bad Debt Expense		550
		8	Cash	550	
			Accounts Receivable—Don Shore		550

EXERCISE 9-2

	Date		Account	Debit	Credit
(1)	Mar.	31	Allowance for Doubtful Accounts	3,150	
			Accounts Receivable—Jane Eades		3,150
(2)	May	8	Accounts Receivable—Jane Eades	3,150	
			Allowance for Doubtful Accounts		3,150
		8	Cash	3,150	
			Accounts Receivable—Jane Eades		3,150

EXERCISE 9-3

1. $80
2. $35
3. $60
4. $60
5. $75
6. $270
7. $210

EXERCISE 9-4

Walton Company
Balance Sheet
December 31, 20--

Assets		
Current assets:		
Cash		$ 37,500
Notes receivable		20,000
Accounts receivable	$35,000	
Less allowance for doubtful accounts	1,200	33,800
Interest receivable		9,900
Total current assets		$101,200

PROBLEM 9-1

		Debit	Credit
(1)	Bad Debt Expense	24,000	
	Allowance for Doubtful Accounts		24,000
	Uncollectible accounts estimate.		
(2)	Bad Debt Expense	5,955	
	Allowance for Doubtful Accounts		5,955
	Uncollectible accounts estimate.		
(3)	Allowance for Doubtful Accounts	3,500	
	Accounts Receivable—Bentley Co.		3,500
(4)	Accounts Receivable—Apple Co.	1,235	
	Allowance for Doubtful Accounts		1,235
	Cash	1,235	
	Accounts Receivable—Apple Co.		1,235

PROBLEM 9-2

		Debit	Credit
(1)	Notes Receivable	8,000.00	
	Accounts Receivable—Dave Davidson		8,000.00
(2)	Accounts Receivable—Dave Davidson	8,160.00*	
	Interest Revenue		160.00
	Notes Receivable		8,000.00

		Debit	Credit
(3)	Cash	8,184.93	
	Interest Revenue		24.93**
	Accounts Receivable—Dave Davidson		8,160.00
(4)	Notes Receivable	3,000.00	
	Accounts Receivable—Sue Smith		3,000.00
(5)	Accounts Receivable—Sue Smith	3,075.00	
	Interest Revenue		75.00
	Notes Receivable		3,000.00

* $8,000 × 60/360 × 12% = $160; $8,000 + $160 = $8,160

** $8,160 × 10/360 × 11% = $24.93

CHAPTER 10

MATCHING

1. K
2. H
3. Q
4. S
5. U
6. I
7. C
8. A
9. D
10. R
11. E
12. N
13. G
14. M
15. B
16. L
17. O
18. F
19. T
20. J

FILL IN THE BLANK—PART A

1. fixed
2. land
3. machine
4. residual
5. units-of-production
6. book
7. 25%
8. $11,250
9. $25,000
10. $12,600
11. capital
12. revenue expenditures
13. capital
14. depletion
15. amortization
16. patents
17. Patents
18. trademark

FILL IN THE BLANK—PART B

1. land
2. depreciation
3. straight-line
4. double-declining-balance
5. 20%
6. $14,000
7. $32,000
8. $16,800
9. accelerated
10. revenue
11. capital expenditures
12. operating
13. intangible
14. goodwill
15. copyright
16. Accumulated Depletion
17. current operating expenses
18. fixed asset turnover ratio

MULTIPLE CHOICE

1. a. Incorrect.
   b. Incorrect.
   c. ***Correct.*** If unwanted buildings are located on land acquired for a plant site, the cost of their removal, less any salvage recovered, should be charged to the land account.
   d. Incorrect.

2. a. ***Correct.*** The depreciation method used most often in the financial statements is the straight-line method.
   b. Incorrect. The double-declining-balance method is the third most used method for financial statements.
   c. Incorrect. The units-of-production method is the second most used method for financial statements.
   d. Incorrect. The MACRS method is used to compute depreciation for tax purposes.

3. a. ***Correct.*** The depreciation method that would provide the highest reported net income in the early years of an asset's life would be the straight-line method.
b. Incorrect. The double-declining-balance depreciation method is an accelerated depreciation method that provides more depreciation in the early years of an asset's life.
c. Incorrect. MACRS is a depreciation method used for tax purposes that provides more depreciation in the early years of an asset's life.
d. Incorrect. The units-of-production depreciation method provides more or less depreciation in the early years of an asset's life depending upon the usage of the asset.

4. a. Incorrect.
b. Incorrect.
c. Incorrect.
d. ***Correct.*** Using the double-declining-balance method, the amount of depreciation for the first year of use of the equipment is $6,000 ($15,000 × 40%).

5. a. Incorrect.
b. ***Correct.*** The depreciation expense on the equipment in Year 3 using the straight-line method would be $5,900, computed as follows: depreciation in Years 1 and 2 is $3,600 per year [($20,000 – $2,000)/5 years]; book value at the end of Year 2 is $12,800 ($20,000 – $3,600 – $3,600); remaining depreciation is computed as $5,900 [($12,800 – $1,000)/2 years].
c. Incorrect.
d. Incorrect.

6. a. Incorrect.
b. ***Correct.*** The cost of rebuilding the drill press is a capital expenditure and should be capitalized.
c. Incorrect.
d. Incorrect.

7. a. ***Correct.*** A gain of $5,000 was recognized on the sale of the equipment as follows:

Annual depreciation [($100,000 – $12,000)/8 years]	$ 11,000
Cost of equipment	$100,000
Accumulated depreciation on Dec. 31, 2012 ($11,000 × 5)	55,000
Book value of equipment on Dec. 31, 2012	$ 45,000
Selling price	$ 50,000
Book value of the equipment on Dec. 31, 2012	45,000
Gain on sale of equipment	$ 5,000

b. Incorrect. $11,000 is the annual depreciation.
c. Incorrect. $45,000 is the book value of the equipment on December 31, 2012.
d. Incorrect. $55,000 is the accumulated depreciation on December 31, 2012.

8. a. Incorrect.
b. ***Correct.*** The depletion rate is $0.90 per ton ($45,000,000/50,000,000 tons). Multiplying the depletion rate of $0.90 per ton by the number of tons mined (20,000,000) yields the depletion of $18,000,000.
c. Incorrect.
d. Incorrect.

9. a. Incorrect.
b. Incorrect.
c. Incorrect. The lessee is the party to whom the rights to use the asset are granted by the lessor.
d. ***Correct.*** The lessor legally owns the asset.

10. a. ***Correct.*** Mineral ore deposits are natural resources with tangible characteristics.
b. Incorrect. Patents do not have tangible characteristics and are intangible assets.
c. Incorrect. Copyright do not have tangible characteristics and are intangible assets.
d. Incorrect. Goodwill does not have tangible characteristics and is an intangible asset.

TRUE/FALSE

1. T
2. T
3. F In using the double-declining-balance method, the asset should not be depreciated below the asset's residual value, not below the net book value.
4. T
5. T
6. F A sale of a fixed asset normally recognizes a gain (if the asset's book value is less than the sale price) or a loss (if the asset's book value is more than the sale price).
7. F A lease that transfers ownership of the leased asset to the lessee at the end of the lease term should be classified as a capital lease, not an operating lease.
8. F Long-lived assets that are without physical characteristics but useful in the operations of a business are classified as intangible assets, not fixed assets.
9. T
10. F Intangible assets are usually reported on the balance sheet in a separate section immediately following fixed assets, not in the current asset section.

EXERCISE 10-1

(a) Straight-line method	Depreciation
Year 1	$50,000
Year 2	$50,000

(b) Double-declining-balance method	Depreciation
Year 1	$105,000
Year 2	$78,750

EXERCISE 10-2

Dec. 31	Depreciation Expense—Equipment	20,800	
	Accumulated Depreciation—Equipment		20,800

EXERCISE 10-3

Mar. 8	Accumulated Depreciation—Fixtures	2,500	
	Cash	2,000	
	Fixtures		4,000
	Gain on Disposal of Assets		500

EXERCISE 10-4

Dec. 31	Depletion Expense	240,000	
	Accumulated Depletion—Mineral Rights		240,000

EXERCISE 10-5

Dec. 31	Amortization Expense—Patents	20,000	
	Patents		20,000

PROBLEM 10-1

	Depreciation Expense		
Year	Straight-Line	Double-Declining-Balance	Units-of-Production
20xA	$18,750	$40,000	$17,000
20xB	18,750	20,000	20,000
20xC	18,750	10,000	30,000
20xD	18,750	5,000	8,000
Total	$75,000	$75,000	$75,000

PROBLEM 10-2

(1)	Dec. 31	Depreciation Expense—Automobile	9,450*	
		Accumulated Depreciation—Automobile		5,000
		*($20,000/4)		
	Dec. 31	Depreciation Expense—Automobile	5,000	
		Accumulated Depreciation—Automobile		5,000
(2)	Dec. 31	Depreciation Expense—Automobile	10,000*	
		Accumulated Depreciation—Automobile		10,000
		*($20,000 × 50%)		
	Dec. 31	Depreciation Expense—Automobile	2,500*	
		Accumulated Depreciation—Automobile		2,500
		*[($20,000 – $10,000 – $5,000) × 50%]		
(3)	Dec. 31	Depreciation Expense—Automobile	7,000*	
		Accumulated Depreciation—Automobile		7,000
		*(35,000 miles × $0.20)		
	Dec. 31	Depreciation Expense—Automobile	5,600*	
		Accumulated Depreciation—Automobile		5,600
		*(28,000 miles × $0.20)		

PROBLEM 10-3

APPENDIX 1

Year	Sum-of-the-Years-Digits	
20XA	$30,000	[($80,000 – $5,000) × (4/10)]
20XB	22,500	[($80,000 – $5,000) × (3/10)]
20XC	15,000	[($80,000 – $5,000) × (2/10)]
20XD	7,500	[($80,000 – $5,000) × (1/10)]
Total	$75,000	

PROBLEM 10-4

APPENDIX 1

(1)	Dec. 31	Depreciation Expense—Automobile	8,000*	
		Accumulated Depreciation—Automobile		8,000
		*[$20,000 × (4/10)]		
	Dec. 31	Depreciation Expense—Automobile	6,000*	
		Accumulated Depreciation—Automobile		6,000
		*[$20,000 × (3/10)]		

PROBLEM 10-5

APPENDIX 2

(1)	Apr. 30	Accumulated Depreciation—Truck	12,000	
		Truck	20,700	
		Truck		15,000
		Cash		17,200
		Gain on Exchange of Truck		500
(2)	Apr. 30	Accumulated Depreciation—Truck	12,000	
		Truck	20,700	
		Loss on Exchange of Truck	2,000	
		Truck		15,000
		Cash		19,700

CHAPTER 11

MATCHING

1. E
2. K
3. A
4. I
5. L
6. B
7. G
8. D
9. H
10. M
11. J
12. F
13. N
14. C

FILL IN THE BLANK—PART A

1. $30,900
2. $84,600
3. gross
4. net pay
5. Federal Insurance Contributions Act (FICA)
6. employee's earnings record
7. paid
8. defined benefit
9. postretirement
10. quick

FILL IN THE BLANK—PART B

1. $77,250
2. $232,000
3. discount
4. discount
5. net
6. payroll register
7. Medicare Tax
8. payroll
9. fringe
10. defined contribution

MULTIPLE CHOICE

1. a. Incorrect.
b. ***Correct.*** The interest charged by the bank, at the rate of 12%, on a 90-day, non-interest-bearing note payable for $75,000 is $2,250 ($75,000 × 12% × 90/360).
c. Incorrect.
d. Incorrect.

2. a. ***Correct.*** The cost of a product warranty should be included as an expense in the period of the sale of the product.
b. Incorrect.
c. Incorrect.
d. Incorrect.

3. a. Incorrect. $440 is the employee's gross pay.
b. Incorrect. $374 doesn't deduct the FICA or Medicare withholdings.
c. ***Correct.*** The employee's net pay for the week is $341, computed as follows: gross pay is $440 [($8 × 40 hours) + ($12 × 10 hours)]; thus, net pay is [$440 – ($440 × 6%) – ($440 × 1.5%) – ($440 × 15%)].
d. Incorrect.

4. a. Incorrect.
b. Incorrect. The gross pay is the earnings before any deductions such as federal income tax withholding.
c. Incorrect.
d. ***Correct.*** The gross pay for the employee is $855, computed as [($18 × 40 hours) + ($27 × 5 hours)].

5. a. Incorrect.
b. Incorrect.
c. ***Correct.*** The employer's total FICA tax (social security and Medicare) for this payroll period is $102, computed as [($200 × 6%) + ($1,000 × 6%) + ($1,000 × 1.5%) + ($1,000 × 1.5%)].
d. Incorrect. The FICA tax is limited to $200 on the first employee ($100,000 – $99,800) rather than the full $1,000.

6. a. Incorrect.
b. Incorrect.
c. Incorrect.
d. ***Correct.*** Payroll taxes levied against employees become liabilities at the time the liability for the employee's wages is paid.

7. a. Incorrect. Vacations are a fringe benefit.
b. Incorrect. Employee pension plans are a fringe benefit.
c. Incorrect. Health insurance is a fringe benefit.
d. ***Correct.*** FICA benefits are not considered a fringe benefit.

8. a. ***Correct.*** For proper matching of revenues and expenses, the estimated cost of fringe benefits must be recognized as an expense of the period the employee earns the benefit.
b. Incorrect.
c. Incorrect.
d. Incorrect.

9. a. Incorrect. Number of hours worked is a variable input in a payroll system.
b. Incorrect. Vacation credits are a variable input in a payroll system.
c. ***Correct.*** Number of income tax withholding allowances is a constant in a payroll system, not a variable input.
d. Incorrect. Number of days sick leave with pay is a variable input in a payroll system.

10. a. Incorrect. A current liability for the next period's installment should be disclosed.
b. ***Correct.*** A current liability of $25,000 should be disclosed for the next period's installment.
c. Incorrect. This is the amount of the long-term liability.
d. Incorrect. This is the amount of the total liability, which should be disclosed in separate short-term and long-term portions.

TRUE/FALSE

1. T
2. F Both employers and employees are required to contribute to the Federal Insurance Contributions Act program.
3. F Not all states require that unemployment compensation taxes be withheld from employees' pay.
4. F Employers are subject to federal and state payroll taxes based on the amount paid to their employees, not the amount earned by their employees.
5. F The amounts withheld from employees' earnings do not have an effect on the firm's debits to the salary or wage expense accounts.
6. T
7. T
8. T

9. F Current installments on long-term debt *should* be disclosed as a current liability, even though the accounting for property, plant, and equipment does not have a similar disclosure convention.

10. F In order for revenues and expenses to be matched properly, a liability to cover the cost of a product warranty should be recorded in the period when the product is sold, not repaired.

11. T

12. T

13. F The net periodic pension cost of a defined benefit plan is debited to Pension Expense, the amount funded is credited to Cash, and any unfunded amount is credited to Unfunded Pension Liability, not Revenue.

14. T

15. F The rate used by a bank in discounting a note is called the discount rate, not the prime rate.

EXERCISE 11-1

(1)	$770	
(2)	$60	($500 × 6%) + (1.5% × 2,000)
(3)	$45	($3,000 × 1.5%)
(4)	$727.50	($9,700 × 7.5%)

EXERCISE 11-2

(1)	Dec. 31	Vacation Pay Expense	3,225	
		Vacation Pay Payable		3,225
		Accrued vacation pay.		
(2)	Dec. 31	Product Warranty Expense	4,500	
		Product Warranty Payable		4,500
		Estimated warranty expense.		
(3)	Dec. 31	Pension Expense	40,000	
		Cash		27,500
		Unfunded Accrued Pension Cost		12,500
		Accrued pension liability.		

PROBLEM 11-1

(1)	Dec. 7	Sales Salaries Expense	34,000	
		Office Salaries Expense	16,000	
		Social Security Tax Payable		3,000
		Medicare Tax Payable		750
		Employees Income Tax Payable		7,500
		Union Dues Payable		900
		United Way Payable		450
		Salaries Payable		37,400
(2)	Dec. 7	Salaries Payable	37,400	
		Cash		37,400
(3)	Dec. 7	Payroll Taxes Expense	6,850	
		Social Security Tax Payable		3,000
		Medicare Tax Payable		750
		State Unemployment Tax Payable		2,700
		Federal Unemployment Tax Payable		400

			Debit	Credit
(4)	Dec. 7	Payroll Taxes Expense	3,150	
		Social Security Tax Payable		2,400
		Medicare Tax Payable		750

PROBLEM 11-2

		Employee FICA Withholding		Employer's Taxes				
Employee	Annual Earnings	Social Security Tax	Medicare Tax	Social Security Tax	Medicare Tax	State Unemploy-ment	Federal Unemploy-ment	Total
Avery	$ 12,000	$ 720	$ 180	$ 720	$ 180	$ 378	$ 56	$ 1,334
Johnson	5,000	300	75	300	75	270	40	685
Jones	59,000	3,540	885	3,540	885	378	56	4,859
Smith	73,000	4,380	1,095	4,380	1,095	378	56	5,909
Wilson	141,000	6,000	2,115	6,000	2,115	378	56	8,549
Total	$290,000	$14,940	$4,350	$14,940	$4,350	$1,782	$264	$21,336

PROBLEM 11-3

		Debit	Credit
(1)	Accounts Payable—Mayday Co.	2,000	
	Notes Payable		2,000
(2)	Notes Payable	2,000	
	Interest Expense	60	
	Cash		2,060
(3)	Cash	8,000	
	Notes Payable		8,000
(4)	Notes Payable	8,000	
	Interest Expense	220	
	Notes Payable		8,220
(5)	Cash	5,910	
	Interest Expense	90	
	Notes Payable		6,000
(6)	Notes Payable	6,000	
	Cash		6,000

CHAPTER 12

MATCHING

1. H
2. B
3. E
4. A
5. F
6. G
7. C
8. D

FILL IN THE BLANK—PART A

1. proprietorship
2. limited liability company
3. mutual agency
4. equally
5. salary allowance
6. $60,000
7. current market values
8. $4,000 ($20,000 – $16,000)
9. Owens
10. capital balances
11. $9,000
12. loss; income-sharing ratio

FILL IN THE BLANK—PART B

1. proprietorship; limited liability company; partnership
2. partnership agreement
3. unlimited liability
4. statement of members' equity
5. interest
6. $150,000
7. gain; loss
8. $18,000 ($50,000 – $32,000
9. Long
10. realized
11. deficiency
12. $30,000

MULTIPLE CHOICE

1. a. Incorrect.
   b. ***Correct.*** If the partnership agreement is silent, then income and loss are divided equally.
   c. Incorrect.
   d. Incorrect.
2. a. Incorrect. Access to more capital *is* an advantage of a partnership.
   b. Incorrect. Partner income taxes may be less than with other forms of organization since partnerships are not taxed as separate entities.
   c. Incorrect. Access to more managerial skill *is* an advantage of a partnership.
   d. ***Correct.*** Partners have unlimited liability, thus, this is an incorrect statement.
3. a. Incorrect. Both are incorrect for a LLC.
   b. Incorrect. A limited life is not an advantage.
   c. ***Correct.*** A limited liability company has the limited liability feature and the nontaxable (flow-through) features of a partnership.
   d. Incorrect. LLCs are not taxed as separate entities.
4. a. Incorrect.
   b. Incorrect.
   c. Incorrect.
   d. ***Correct.*** When a new partner is admitted by the contribution of assets, the assets of the partnership would increase, as would the total partner capital. This would be necessary to keep the accounting equation in balance. All other answers would violate the accounting equation.
5. a. Incorrect.
   b. ***Correct.*** $40,000 – [($25,000 + $35,000 + $40,000) × 30%]
   c. Incorrect.
   d. Incorrect.
6. a. Incorrect. This would be Columbo's share.
   b. Incorrect. This would be equal sharing and would be correct only in the absence of a partnership agreement.
   c. ***Correct.*** 2/5 × $80,000
   d. Incorrect. This would be correct only if the total income were $100,000.

7. a. Incorrect. The revaluation is reflected in the capital accounts so that the newly admitted partner's relative portion of the capital equitably reflects current market values.
   b. Incorrect. This would be Haley's capital account impact.
   c. ***Correct.*** ($90,000 – $75,000) × 3/5; the capital account is debited for the loss in market value.
   d. Incorrect. Multiplying the loss of $15,000 by 3/2 is incorrect.

8. a. Incorrect. It is incorrect to calculate the loss as $60,000 × 1/6 since Patterson cannot be allocated deficiency.
   b. ***Correct.*** $60,000 × 1/3
   c. Incorrect. There is an income-sharing ratio, thus equal sharing of the deficiency cannot be assumed.
   d. Incorrect. This is Hill's allocation ($60,000 × 2/3).

9. a. Incorrect.
   b. Incorrect. Only the final distribution should be allocated on the basis of the current balances of the capital accounts.
   c. ***Correct.*** All gains and losses should be allocated on the basis of the income-sharing ratio.
   d. Incorrect. This is correct only when the partnership agreement is silent as to the income-sharing ratio.

10. a. Incorrect. The Statement of Owner's Equity reports changes in the owner's capital for a proprietorship.
    b. Incorrect. The Statement of Cash Flows reports changes in cash for a period of time.
    c. ***Correct***. The Statement of Partnership Equity reports changes in partner capital accounts for a period of time for a partnership.
    d. Incorrect. The Statement of Members' Equity reports changes in member capital accounts for a period of time for a limited liability company.

TRUE/FALSE

1. F Partners are owners in a partnership, and their capital contributions are not loans to the partnership (even though they may receive credit for interest on their capital balance). Neither are partners considered employees (even though they may receive a salary allowance).
2. T
3. T
4. F Any property contributed to the partnership by a partner becomes the property of the partnership.
5. F The claim against the net assets of a partnership is measured by a partner's *current* capital balance.
6. T
7. T
8. T
9. F A partnership is a nontaxable (flow-through) entity.
10. T
11. F All of the partners must agree.
12. F No partner's interest can be disposed of without all partners in agreement, thus dissolving the partnership.
13. F The purchase price only affects the accounts of the individual partners, not the partnership.
14. T
15. T
16. T
17. F Cash from the sale of assets must first go to satisfying the claims of creditors (liabilities).
18. T
19. T
20. F The most common error that occurs in liquidating a partnership is making an improper distribution of cash to the partners.

EXERCISE 12-1

Account	Debit	Credit
Cash	100,000	
Merchandise Inventory	80,000	
Cutco, Capital		180,000
Cash	10,000	
Land	115,000	
Equipment	45,000	
Merchandise Inventory	5,000	
Robbs, Capital		175,000

EXERCISE 12-2

	Date	Account	Debit	Credit
(1)	June 30	Hartly, Capital	20,000	
		Smetz, Capital	11,000	
		Grasso, Capital	7,000	
		Schafer, Capital		38,000
(2)	July 1	Cash	50,000	
		Hartly, Capital	7,000	
		Smetz, Capital	7,000	
		Grasso, Capital	7,000	
		Masko, Capital		71,000

EXERCISE 12-3

	Account	Debit	Credit
(1)	Inventory	12,750	
	Arway, Capital		4,250
	Batts, Capital		4,250
	Carlone, Capital		4,250
	Carlone, Capital	44,250	
	Arway, Capital		44,250
(2)	Inventory	6,000	
	Arway, Capital		2,000
	Batts, Capital		2,000
	Carlone, Capital		2,000
	Carlone, Capital	42,000	
	Cash		42,000

PROBLEM 12-1

(1)	Bulley's share	$100,000
	Scram's share	100,000
	Total	$200,000
(2)	Bulley's share	$ 80,000
	Scram's share	120,000
	Total	$200,000
(3)	Bulley's share	$ 60,000
	Scram's share	140,000
	Total	$200,000

(4)

Division of Net Income	Bulley	Scram	Total
Salary allowance	$30,000	$ 50,000	$ 80,000
Remaining income	60,000	60,000	120,000
Net income	$90,000	$110,000	$200,000

(5)

Division of Net Income	Bulley	Scram	Total
Interest allowance	$15,000	$ 35,000	$ 50,000
Remaining income	75,000	75,000	150,000
Net income	$90,000	$110,000	$200,000

(6)

Division of Net Income	Bulley	Scram	Total
Salary allowance	$15,000	$ 25,000	$ 40,000
Interest allowance	15,000	35,000	50,000
Remaining income	55,000	55,000	110,000
Net income	$85,000	$115,000	$200,000

(7)

Division of Net Income	Bulley	Scram	Total
Salary allowance	$80,000	$ 78,000	$158,000
Interest allowance	15,000	35,000	50,000
Total	$95,000	$113,000	$208,000
Excess of allowances over income	4,000	4,000	8,000
Net income	$91,000	$109,000	$200,000

PROBLEM 12-2

(1)

Processing Equipment	20,000	
Baskin, member equity		15,000
Robbins, member equity		5,000

Baskin: $20,000 × 3/4 Robbins: $20,000 × 1/4

(2) (a)

Cash	100,000	
Baskin, member equity	30,000	
Robbins, member equity	10,000	
Dreyer, member equity		140,000

Supporting calculations:

Equity of Baskin (after revaluation)	$400,000
Equity of Robbins (after revaluation)	200,000
Contribution by Dreyer	100,000
Total equity after admitting Dreyer	$700,000
Dreyer's equity interest after admission	20%
Dreyer's equity after admission	$140,000
Contribution by Dreyer	100,000
Bonus paid to Dreyer	$ 40,000

Baskin: $40,000 × 3/4 Robbins: $40,000 × 1/4

(b)	Cash	180,000	
	Baskin, member equity		47,250
	Robbins, member equity		15,750
	Dreyer, member equity		117,000

Supporting calculations:

Equity of Baskin (after revaluation)	$400,000
Equity of Robbins (after revaluation)	200,000
Contribution by Dreyer	180,000
Total equity after admitting Dreyer	$780,000
Dreyer's equity interest after admission	15%
Dreyer's equity after admission	$117,000

Contribution by Dreyer	$180,000
Dreyer's equity after admission	117,000
Bonus paid to Baskin and Robbins	$ 63,000

Baskin: $63,000 × 3/4   Robbins: $63,000 × 1/4

PROBLEM 12-3

(1)

	Cash +	Noncash Assets =	Liabilities +	Capital Triste (30%) +	Capital Sandpipe (50%) +	Capital Hinkle (20%)
Balances before realization	$100,000	$300,000	$120,000	$ 90,000	$ 60,000	$130,000
Sale of noncash assets and division of gain	+400,000	–300,000		+ 30,000	+ 50,000	+ 20,000
Balances after realization	$500,000	–0–	$120,000	$120,000	$110,000	$150,000
Payment of liabilities	–120,000		–120,000			
Balances after payment of liabilities	$380,000	–0–	–0–	$120,000	$110,000	$150,000
Distribution of cash to partners	–380,000			–120,000	–110,000	–150,000
Final balances	–0–	0	–0–	–0–	–0–	–0–

(2)

	Cash	+	Noncash Assets	=	Liabilities	+	Capital: Triste (30%)	+	Capital: Sandpipe (50%)	+	Capital: Hinkle (20%)
Balances before realization	$100,000		$300,000		$120,000		$90,000		$60,000		$130,000
Sale of noncash assets and division of loss	+130,000		–300,000				–51,000		–85,000		– 34,000
Balances after realization	$230,000		–0–		$120,000		$39,000		$25,000 Dr.		$ 96,000
Payment of liabilities	–120,000				–120,000						
Balances after payment of liabilities	$110,000		–0–		–0–		$39,000		$25,000 Dr.		$ 96,000
Receipt of deficiency	+ 25,000								25,000		
Balances	$135,000						$39,000		–0–		$ 96,000
Distribution of cash to partners	–135,000						–39,000		–0–		–96,000
Final balances	–0–		–0–		–0–		–0–		–0–		–0–

(3)

	Debit	Credit
Cash	130,000	
Loss and Gain on Realization	170,000	
Noncash Assets		300,000
Triste, Capital	51,000	
Sandpipe, Capital	85,000	
Hinkle, Capital	34,000	
Loss and Gain on Realization		170,000
Liabilities	120,000	
Cash		120,000
Cash	25,000	
Sandpipe, Capital		25,000
Triste, Capital	39,000	
Hinkle, Capital	96,000	
Cash		135,000

CHAPTER 13

MATCHING

1. M
2. P
3. F
4. K
5. B
6. G
7. H
8. I
9. C
10. A
11. N
12. Q
13. L
14. O
15. E

FILL IN THE BLANK—PART A

1. stock
2. stockholders' equity
3. retained earnings
4. $995,000
5. outstanding
6. common
7. preferred
8. $0
9. premium
10. $160,000
11. treasury
12. none
13. dividend
14. $32,500
15. retained earnings

FILL IN THE BLANK—PART B

1. stockholders
2. paid-in
3. deficit
4. stated
5. preferred
6. organizational expenses
7. $35,000
8. discount
9. $32,500 decrease
10. $895,000
11. stock split
12. $36
13. stock dividend
14. par
15. dividend yield

MULTIPLE CHOICE

1. a. Incorrect. Ownership represented by shares of stock is a characteristic of the corporate form of organization.
b. Incorrect. Separate legal existence is a characteristic of the corporate form of organization.
c. ***Correct.*** Unlimited liability of stockholders is not a characteristic of the corporate form of organization. Rather, stockholders of a corporation have limited liability that limits the liability to the amount invested.
d. Incorrect. Earnings subject to the federal income tax is a characteristic of the corporate form of organization.

2. a. Incorrect. The stated value is the amount the board of directors assigns to no-par stock.
b. Incorrect. The premium is the amount by which the issue price of a stock exceeds its par.
c. Incorrect. The discount is the amount by which the par value of a stock exceeds its issue price.
d. ***Correct.*** The amount printed on a stock certificate is known as par value.

3. a. Incorrect.
b. Incorrect.
c. Incorrect.
d. ***Correct.*** The amount of preferred dividends that must be declared in the current year before a dividend can be declared on common stock is $30,000, computed as [(5,000 shares × $6) × 5 years].

4. a. Incorrect.
b. ***Correct.*** When a corporation purchases its own stock, Treasury Stock is debited for the cost of the stock.
c. Incorrect.
d. Incorrect.

5. a. Incorrect. Retained Earnings is credited for the income of a period, not for the excess of proceeds from selling treasury stock over its cost.
b. Incorrect. Premium on Capital Stock is credited for the issuance of new stock at a price exceeding the par or stated value of the stock.
c. Incorrect. A corporation cannot have gains and losses from trading its stock.
d. ***Correct.*** The excess of the proceeds from selling treasury stock over its cost should be credited to Paid-In Capital from Sale of Treasury Stock.

6. a. Incorrect. The claims of preferred stockholders are satisfied after the claims of creditors upon liquidation of a corporation.
b. Incorrect.
c. Incorrect. The claims of common stockholders are satisfied last upon liquidation of a corporation
d. ***Correct.*** The claims of the creditors must first be satisfied upon liquidation of a corporation.

7. a. ***Correct.*** The amount transferred from the retained earnings account to paid-in capital accounts as a result of the stock dividend is $36,000, computed as [(12,000 shares × 5%) × $60].
b. Incorrect.
c. Incorrect. The amount transferred from the retained earnings account to paid-in capital accounts as a result of the stock dividend is based upon the market price of the stock, not the par value.
d. Incorrect.

8. a. Incorrect. 5,000 is the number of shares reacquired.
b. ***Correct.*** The number of shares outstanding is 55,000 shares, determined as the 60,000 shares issued minus the 5,000 shares reacquired.
c. Incorrect. 60,000 is the number of shares issued.
d. Incorrect. 100,000 is the number of shares authorized.

9. a. Incorrect. Donated Capital is credited for the fair value of assets donated to a corporation as an incentive to locate or remain in a community.
b. Incorrect. Retained Earnings is credited for the income of the period.
c. Incorrect. Treasury Stock is credited when reacquired shares are sold.
d. ***Correct.*** The entry to record the issuance of common stock at a price above par would include a credit to Paid-In Capital in Excess of Par—Common Stock.

10. a. Incorrect. The total stockholders' equity will decrease, not increase.
b. Incorrect. The total stockholders' equity will decrease, not increase.
c. Incorrect. The decrease is based upon the cost of the reacquired stock, not its par value.
d. ***Correct.*** The effect on total stockholders' equity of purchasing 10,000 shares of its own $20 par common stock for $35 per share is a decrease of $350,000 (10,000 shares × $35).

TRUE/FALSE

1. F The stockholders of a corporation have limited liability. In other words, the loss a stockholder may suffer is limited to the amount invested.
2. T
3. F The two main sources of stockholders' equity are paid-in capital and retained earnings, not long-term debt.
4. F The preferred stockholders have a greater chance of receiving regular dividends than do common stockholders, not vice versa.
5. T
6. T
7. T
8. T
9. F Sales of treasury stock result in a net increase, not decrease, in paid-in capital.
10. F Expenditures incurred in organizing a corporation, such as legal fees, taxes, fees paid to the state, and promotional costs, are charged to an expense account entitled Organization Expenses, not Goodwill.
11. F A commonly used method for accounting for the purchase and resale of treasury stock is the cost method, not the derivative method.
12. F A major objective of a stock split is to reduce the market price per share of the stock. A stock split does not affect the amount of total stockholders' equity.
13. T
14. F A liability for a dividend is normally recorded in the accounting records on the date of declaration, not the date of record.
15. T

EXERCISE 13-1

	Account	Debit	Credit
(1)	Cash	700,000	
	Common Stock		700,000
(2)	Cash	500,000	
	Common Stock		500,000
(3)	Cash	1,200,000	
	Common Stock		1,000,000
	Paid-In Capital in Excess of Par—Common Stock		200,000
(4)	Equipment	145,000	
	Common Stock		100,000
	Paid-In Capital in Excess of Par—Common Stock		45,000
(5)	Cash	300,000	
	Preferred Stock		250,000
	Paid-In Capital in Excess of Par—Preferred Stock		50,000

EXERCISE 13-2

	Date	Account	Debit	Credit
(1)	Feb. 20	Cash Dividends	60,000	
		Cash Dividends Payable		60,000
(2)	Mar. 22	Cash Dividends Payable	60,000	
		Cash		60,000
(3)	Dec. 15	Stock Dividends	200,000	
		Stock Dividends Distributable		160,000
		Paid-In Capital in Excess of Par—Common Stock		40,000
(4)	Jan. 14	Stock Dividends Distributable	160,000	
		Common Stock		160,000
(5)	Feb. 20	None		

EXERCISE 13-3

	Date	Account	Debit	Credit
(1)	Oct. 1	Treasury Stock	150,000	
		Cash		150,000
(2)	Oct. 31	Cash	65,600	
		Treasury Stock		60,000
		Paid-In Capital from Sale of Treasury Stock		5,600
(3)	Nov. 20	Cash	7,000	
		Paid-In Capital from Sale of Treasury Stock	500	
		Treasury Stock		7,500

PROBLEM 13-1

Year	Total Dividends	Preferred Dividends		Common Dividends	
		Total	Per Share	Total	Per Share
1	$ 7,000	$7,000	$7	–0–	–0–
2	9,000	9,000	9	–0–	–0–
3	28,000	8,000	8	20,000	5.00
4	48,000	8,000	8	40,000	10.00

PROBLEM 13-2

	(1)	(2)	(3)
	Column A	**Column B**	**Column C**
	Before Any Dividend	After Cash Dividend	After Stock Dividend
a. Total number of shares outstanding..........	100,000	100,000	105,000
b. Total par value of shares outstanding	$2,500,000	$2,500,000	$2,625,000
c. Total additional paid-in capital..................	$1,500,000	$1,500,000	$1,525,000
d. Total retained earnings............................	$6,440,000	$6,290,000	$6,290,000
e. Total stockholders' equity........................	$10,440,000	$10,290,000	$10,440,000
f. Amount required to pay a $1.50 per share cash dividend next year..................	$150,000	$150,000	$157,500
g. Percentage of total stock owned by Rafael..	1%	1%	1%
h. Total number of shares owned by Rafael .	1,000	1,000	1,050
i. Total par value of Rafael's shares............	$25,000	$25,000	$26,250
j. Total equity of Rafael's shares.................	$104,400	$102,900	$104,400

PROBLEM 13-3

Paid-in capital:		
Preferred $10 stock, $100 par (10,000 shares authorized; 7,500 issued)..	$ 750,000	
Excess over par	375,000	$1,125,000
Common stock, $25 par (150,000 shares authorized; 100,000 issued)...	$2,500,000	
Excess over par	500,000	3,000,000
From sale of treasury stock		4,000
Total paid-in capital		$4,129,000
Retained earnings		1,000,000
Total		$5,129,000
Deduct treasury common stock (1,000 shares at cost)		50,000
Total stockholders' equity		$5,079,000

CHAPTER 14

MATCHING

1. A	4. B	7. M	10. J
2. G	5. D	8. C	11. K
3. N	6. E	9. I	12. L

FILL IN THE BLANK—PART A

1. bond indenture (or trust indenture)
2. preferred
3. callable
4. debenture bonds
5. contract (or coupon)
6. premium
7. straight-line
8. effective interest rate
9. carrying amount
10. $388,000 ($400,000 – $12,000)
11. $2,030,000
12. Interest Expense
13. Cash
14. $2,000 (loss)
15. 12.6 [(29,000,000 + 2,500,000) / 2,500,000]

FILL IN THE BLANK—PART B

1. $2.20 [($120,000 – $10,000) ÷ 50,000 shares]
2. term
3. convertible
4. their face value
5. discount
6. increases
7. decreases
8. $10,000 (gain)
9. $5,045,000
10. $240,000 ($4,000,000 × .12 × 6/12)
11. $28,000 ($280,000 / 10 periods)
12. $120,000 ($4,000,000 × .12 × 3/12)
13. remains the same
14. installment
15. 1.5 [($250,000 + $500,000) ÷ $500,000]

MULTIPLE CHOICE

1. a. Incorrect.
   b. Incorrect.
   c. ***Correct.*** The earnings per share ratio measures the income earned by each share of common stock. It is computed by dividing net income less any preferred dividends by the number of common shares outstanding.
   d. Incorrect.

2. a. ***Correct.*** A bond that gives the bondholder a right to exchange the bond for other securities under certain conditions is called a convertible bond.
   b. Incorrect. A bond sinking fund is a special fund in which amounts are set aside for the payment of a bond issue at its maturity date.
   c. Incorrect. Term bonds refers to bonds of an issue that all mature at the same time.
   d. Incorrect. Bonds issued on the basis of the general credit of the corporation are called debenture bonds.

3. a. Incorrect. Callable bonds may be redeemed by the issuing corporation.
   b. Incorrect. Convertible bonds may be exchanged for other securities such as common stock.
   c. ***Correct.*** Debenture bonds are issued on the basis of the general credit of the corporation.
   d. Incorrect. Term bonds are bonds that all mature at the same time.

4. a. Incorrect. Bonds will sell at a discount if the market rate of interest is more than the coupon rate.
b. Incorrect. Bonds will sell for their face value if the market rate of interest equals the coupon rate.
c. Incorrect. The maturity value is the amount due when the bonds mature, which is equal to the face value of the bonds.
d. ***Correct.*** Bonds will sell at a premium if the market rate of interest is less than the coupon rate.

5. a. Incorrect.
b. ***Correct.*** The entry to record the amortization of a discount on bonds payable is a debit to Interest Expense and a credit to Discount on Bonds Payable.
c. Incorrect.
d. Incorrect.

6. a. Incorrect.
b. Incorrect.
c. ***Correct.*** Under the straight-line method of bond discount amortization, as a bond payable approaches maturity, the total yearly amount of interest expense will remain the same.
d. Incorrect.

7. a. Incorrect.
b. ***Correct.*** The carrying amount of the bonds is the balance of Bonds Payable (the face value) minus the balance of the Discount on Bonds Payable (the unamortized discount) or $855,000 ($900,000 – $45,000).
c. Incorrect.
d. Incorrect.

8. a. Incorrect.
b. Incorrect.
c. ***Correct.*** The entry to record the amortization of a premium on bonds payable debits Premium on Bonds Payable and credits Interest Expense.
d. Incorrect.

9. a. Incorrect.
b. Incorrect.
c. Incorrect.
d. ***Correct.*** The $40,000 gain on the redemption of the bonds is the difference between the carrying value of the bonds of $830,000 ($800,000 + $30,000) and the redemption price of $790,000.

10. a. ***Correct.*** The interest expense on an installment note decreases from the first payment to the last payment. This is because the principal is decreased with each payment.
b. Incorrect.
c. Incorrect.
d. Incorrect.

TRUE/FALSE

1. F The interest rate specified on the bond indenture is called the contract rate. It is not called the effective rate, which is sometimes called the market rate.

2. F If the market rate is lower than the contract rate, the bonds will sell at a premium, not a discount.

3. F The amortization of a premium on bonds payable decreases interest expense rather than increasing interest expense.

4. T

5. T

6. F Bonds that may be exchanged for other securities under certain conditions are called convertible bonds, not callable bonds. Callable bonds are bonds that a corporation reserves the right to redeem before their maturity.

7. T
8. T
9. T
10. F An installment note secured by a pledge of the borrower's assets is called a mortgage note.

EXERCISE 14-1

				Debit	Credit
(1)	June	1	Cash	500,000	
			Bonds Payable		500,000
	Dec.	1	Interest Expense	30,000	
			Cash		30,000
(2)	Apr.	1	Cash	942,645	
			Discount on Bonds Payable	57,355	
			Bonds Payable		1,000,000
	Oct.	1	Interest Expense	57,868	
			Discount on Bonds Payable ($57,355 / 20)		2,868
			Cash		55,000
(3)	Mar.	1	Cash	743,625	
			Premium on Bonds Payable		43,625
			Bonds Payable		700,000
	Sept.	1	Interest Expense	36,319	
			Premium on Bonds Payable ($43,625 / 20)	2,181	
			Cash		38,500

EXERCISE 14-2

		Debit	Credit
(1)	Bonds Payable	5,000,000	
	Loss on Redemption of Bonds Payable	50,000	
	Cash		5,050,000
(2)	Bonds Payable	5,000,000	
	Cash		4,900,000
	Gain on Redemption of Bonds Payable		100,000

EXERCISE 14-3

			Debit	Credit
(1)	(a)	Cash	60,000	
		Notes Payable		60,000
	(b)	Interest Expense	3,000	
		Notes Payable	6,283	
		Cash		9,283

(2) Interest expense, $3,000

PROBLEM 14-1

(1)	Dec. 31	Cash	531,161	
		Bonds Payable		500,000
		Premium on Bonds Payable		31,161
(2)	June 30	Interest Expense ($27,500 – $1,558)	25,942	
		Premium on Bonds Payable ($31,161 / 20)	1,558	
		Cash		27,500
(3)	Dec. 31	Interest Expense ($27,500 – $1,558)	25,942	
		Premium on Bonds Payable ($31,161 / 20)	1,558	
		Cash		27,500
(4)	Dec. 31	Bonds Payable	250,000	
		Premium on Bonds Payable [($31,161 – $1,558 – $1,558) / 2]	14,023	
		Gain on Redemption of Bonds		6,523
		Cash		257,500

PROBLEM 14-2

(1)	Jan. 1	Cash	885,295	
		Discount on Bonds Payable	114,705	
		Bonds Payable		1,000,000
(2)	June 30	Interest Expense ($50,000 + $5,735)	55,735	
		Discount on Bonds Payable ($114,705 / 20)		5,735
		Cash		50,000
(3)	Dec. 31	Interest Expense ($50,000 + $5,735)	55,735	
		Discount on Bonds Payable ($114,705 / 20)		5,735
		Cash		50,000
(4)	Dec. 31	Bonds Payable	500,000	
		Loss on Redemption of Bonds	41,618	
		Discount on Bonds Payable [($114,705 – $5,735 – $5,735) / 2]		51,618
		Cash		490,000

PROBLEM 14-3

APPENDIX 1

(1) (a)

Present value of \$1 at compound interest of 5½% in 20 semiannual periods	0.3427	
Face amount of bonds	× \$2,000,000	\$ 685,400
Present value of annuity of \$1 for 20 periods at 5½%	11.9504	
Semiannual interest payments	× \$ 110,000	1,314,544
Proceeds of bonds (present value)		\$1,999,944

Note: The difference of \$56 between the face value of the bonds and the present value is due to rounding.

(b) There is no premium or discount on the bond issuance.

(2) (a)

Present value of \$1 at compound interest of 6% in 20 semiannual periods	0.3118	
Face amount of bonds	× \$2,000,000	\$ 623,600
Present value of annuity of \$1 for 20 periods at 6%	11.4699	
Semiannual interest payments	× \$ 110,000	1,261,689
Proceeds of bonds (present value)		\$1,885,289

(b) The discount is \$114,711 on the bond issuance.

(3) (a)

Present value of \$1 at compound interest of 5% in 20 semiannual periods	0.3769	
Face amount of bonds	× \$2,000,000	\$ 753,800
Present value of annuity of \$1 for 20 periods at 5%	12.4622	
Semiannual interest payments	× \$ 110,000	1,370,842
Proceeds of bonds (present value)		\$2,124,642

(b) The premium is \$124,642 on the bond issuance.

PROBLEM 14-4

APPENDIX 2

(1)

First semiannual interest payment	\$2,250,000
6.5% of carrying amount of \$32,156,768	2,090,190
Premium amortized	\$ 159,810

(2)

Second semiannual interest payment	\$2,250,000
6.5% of carrying amount of \$31,996,958*	2,079,802
Premium amortized	\$ 170,198

* \$32,156,768 – \$159,810

(3)

Annual interest paid	\$4,500,000
Less premium amortized	330,008*
Interest expense for first year	\$4,169,992

* \$159,810 + \$170,198

Problem 14-5

Appendix 2

(1)	7% of carrying amount of $17,892,938	$1,252,506
	First semiannual interest payment	1,100,000
	Discount amortized	$ 152,506
(2)	7% of carrying amount of $18,045,444*	$1,263,181
	Second semiannual interest payment	1,100,000
	Discount amortized	$ 163,181
	* $17,892,938 + $152,506	
(3)	Annual interest paid	$2,200,000
	Less premium amortized	315,687*
	Interest expense for first year	$2,515,687
	* $152,506 + $163,181	

CHAPTER 15

Matching

1. E	5. J	9. O	13. H
2. G	6. D	10. P	14. R
3. K	7. N	11. C	15. I
4. L	8. B	12. Q	16. A

Fill in the Blank—Part A

1. current operations
2. integration
3. interest receivable
4. no control
5. cost
6. dividend revenue
7. gain
8. Other gain (loss)
9. investment
10. Other income
11. subsidiary
12. Valuation Allowance
13. income statement
14. Held-to-maturity
15. amortized cost
16. stockholders' equity
17. Valuation Allowance
18. current

Fill in the Blank—Part B

1. interest
2. interest revenue
3. gain
4. significant influence
5. equity
6. investment
7. loss
8. investment
9. $49,000 ($140,000 × 35%)
10. parent
11. consolidated
12. Valuation Allowance
13. Other income (loss)
14. interest revenue
15. Available-for-sale investments
16. balance sheet
17. Unrealized loss
18. fair value

Multiple Choice

1. a. Incorrect. Expansion of operations is a strategic purpose of a long-term investment in another company's common stock.
   b. Incorrect. Integration is a strategic purpose of a long-term investment in another company's common stock.
   c. ***Correct.*** Interest revenue is not a strategic purpose of a long-term investment in another company's common stock.
   d. Incorrect. Reduction of costs is a strategic purpose of a long-term investment in another company's common stock.

2. a. Incorrect. Since the proceeds exceed the book value, a gain, not a loss, of $6,300 is recorded.
b. ***Correct.*** A gain of $6,300 is recorded on the sale of the bond investments.
c. Incorrect. This is the book value of the bond investments.
d. Incorrect. This is the proceeds from the sale of the bond investments.

3. a. Incorrect. With less than 20% of the outstanding stock of the investee, it is assumed that the investor has no control.
b. ***Correct.*** With between 20% and 50% of the outstanding stock of the investee, it is assumed that the investor has significant control.
c. Incorrect. With greater than 50% of the outstanding stock of the investee, it is assumed that the investor has control.
d. Incorrect. With greater than 50% of the outstanding stock of the investee, it is assumed that the investor has control.

4. a. Incorrect. The cost method is used when the investor owns less than 20% of the outstanding common stock of the investee.
b. ***Correct.*** The equity method is used when the investor owns between 20% and 50% of the outstanding common stock of the investee.
c. Incorrect.
d. Incorrect.

5. a. Incorrect. This entry records the receipt of the dividends of Nichols Inc. by Charmayne Corp.
b. Incorrect. This entry incorrectly credits Dividend Revenue instead of Income of Nichols Inc.
c. ***Correct.*** The entry to record Charmayne Corp.'s share of Nichols Inc.'s net income of $300,000 debits Investment in Nichols Inc.'s, $120,000, and credits Income of Nichols Inc., $120,000.
d. Incorrect. This entry records all of Nichols Inc.'s income instead of just Charmayne Corp.'s 40% share of the net income of Nichols Inc.

6. a. Incorrect.
b. Incorrect.
c. ***Correct.*** Bond securities is not a classification for valuing debt and equity securities. The three classifications are available-for-sale securities, held-to-maturity securities, and trading securities. Depending upon the intent of management, bond securities may be classified into any of three classes.
d. Incorrect.

7. a. Incorrect.
b. Incorrect.
c. Incorrect.
d. ***Correct.*** Debt and equity securities that are purchased and sold to earn short-term profits from changes in their market prices are called trading securities. Debt securities that a company intends to hold until their maturity date are called held-to-maturity securities. Debt or equity securities that are not trading or held-to-maturity securities are classified as available-for-sale securities.

8. a. Incorrect.
b. Incorrect.
c. Incorrect. Realized gains or losses are not recognized until the trading securities are sold.
d. ***Correct.*** Changes in fair value of trading securities are recognized as unrealized gains or losses.

9. a. ***Correct.*** The balance of the valuation allowance for trading investments is reported in the financial statements as an addition to or a deduction from the balance of the investments in trading securities in the current asset section of the balance sheet.
b. Incorrect. The balance of the valuation allowance for trading investments is reported as an addition to or a deduction from the balance of the investments in trading securities in the current asset section of the balance sheet rather than the noncurrent section.
c. Incorrect.
d. Incorrect.

10. a. Incorrect.
b. Incorrect.
c. Incorrect. The valuation allowance for available-for-sale securities is reported on the balance sheet as an addition to or a deduction from investments. The unrealized gains or losses are reported in the stockholders' equity section of the balance sheet as an addition to or a deduction from stockholders' equity.
d. ***Correct.*** Unrealized gains or losses for available-for-sale securities are reported on the balance sheet as an addition to or a deduction from stockholders' equity.

TRUE/FALSE

1. F To have the degree of control of significant influence, the investor corporation must own between 20% and 50% of the outstanding stock of the investee corporation.
2. T
3. T
4. F The investor's share of net income of the investee corporation is debited to the investment account and credited to an income from investee account.
5. T
6. F Trading securities also include debt securities in addition to equity securities.
7. T
8. T
9. F An unrealized gain or loss on available-for-sale investments is reported as an addition to or a deduction from stockholders' equity on the balance sheet.
10. T

EXERCISE 15-1

		Debit	Credit
(a)	Bond Investment–Hart Industries Bonds	270,000	
	Interest Receivable	3,150	
	Cash		273,150
(b)	Cash	9,450*	
	Interest Receivable		3,150
	Interest Revenue		6,300
	* $270,000 × 7% × ½		
(c)	Cash	185,850*	
	Interest Revenue		2,250
	Gain on Sale of Investments		3,600
	Bond Investments–Hart Industries Bonds		180,000

*Sale proceeds ($180,000 × 102%)	$183,600
Accrued interest	2,250
Total proceeds from sale	$185,850

EXERCISE 15-2

		Debit	Credit
Feb. 20	Investments–Rhymer Co.	255,250	
	Cash		255,250
	(5,000 shares × $51 per share)		
Sept. 10	Cash	5,500	
	Dividend Revenue		5,500
	$1.10 per share × 5,000 shares		

Oct. 5	Cash	89,900*	
	Loss on Sale of Investments	12,200	
	Investments–Collins Co.		102,100**
	*(2,000 shares × $45) – $100		
	**2,000 shares × ($255,250 / 5,000 shares)		

EXERCISE 15-3

Jan. 9	Investment in Tolley Company Stock	130,000	
	Cash		130,000
Dec. 31	Investment in Tolley Company Stock	24,000	
	Income of Tolley Company		24,000
	Record share of Tolley Co. net income, 40% × $60,000		
Dec. 31	Cash	8,000	
	Investment in Tolley Company Stock		8,000
	40% × $20,000		

EXERCISE 15-4

Dec. 31, 2010	Valuation Allowance for Trading Investments	4,800*	
	Unrealized Gain on Trading Investments		4,800
	To record increase in fair value of trading investments.		

Valuation Allowance for Trading Investments, Jan. 1, 2010		$1,000 Cr.
Trading investments at cost, Dec. 31, 2010	$26,200	
Trading investments at fair value, Dec. 31, 2010	30,000	
Valuation Allowance for Trading Investments, Dec. 31, 2010		3,800 Dr.
*Adjustment		$4,800 Dr.

EXERCISE 15-5

Dec. 31, 2010	Unrealized Gain (Loss) on Available-for-Sale Investments	1,500	
	Valuation Allowance for Available-for-Sale Investments		1,500*
	To record decrease in fair value of available-for-sale securities.		

Valuation Allowance for Available-for-Sale Investments, Jan. 1, 2010		$4,000 Dr.
Available-for-sale investments at cost, Dec. 31, 2010	$90,000	
Available-for-sale at fair value, Dec. 31, 2010	92,500	
Valuation Allowance for Available-for-Sale Investments, Dec. 31, 2010		2,500 Dr.
*Adjustment		$1,500 Dr.

PROBLEM 15-1

Date	Account	Debit	Credit
Jan. 23	Available-for-Sale Investments–Smith Company	55,440*	
	Cash		55,440
	*(2,400 shares × $23 per share) + $240		
Feb. 6	Investments–U.S. Treasury Bonds	20,000	
	Interest Receivable	160*	
	Cash		20,160
	*$20,000 × 8% × (36 days / 360 days)		
Mar. 10	Trading Investments–Jones Company	182,704*	
	Cash		182,704
	*(3,800 shares × $48 per share) + $304		
May 31	Investment in Hill Company	3,704,000*	
	Cash		3,704,000
	*(100,000 shares × $37 per share) + $4,000		
July 1	Cash	800*	
	Interest Receivable		160
	Interest Revenue		640
	*$20,000 × 8% × ½		
Aug. 9	Cash	146,220*	
	Trading Investments–Jones Company		115,392**
	Gain on Sale of Investments		30,828
	*$20,000 × 8% × (36 days / 360 days)		
	** 2,400 shares × ($182,704 / 3,800 shares)		
Oct. 5	Cash	1,920	
	Dividend Revenue		1,920
	2,400 shares × $0.80 per share		
Nov. 11	Cash	110,000	
	Investment in Hill Company Stock		110,000
	100,000 shares × $1.10 per share		
Dec. 31	Interest Receivable	800	
	Interest Revenue		800
	Accrue interest, $20,000 × 8% × ½		
31	Investment in Hill Company Stock	236,500	
	Income of Hill Company		236,500
	To record equity income, $946,000 × (100,000 shares / 400,000 shares)		
31	Unrealized Loss on Trading Investments	7,112	
	Valuation Allowance for Trading Investments		7,112
	To record decrease in fair value of trading investments, $67,312 – $60,200		

Name	Number of Shares	Total Cost	Total Fair Value
Jones Company	1,400	$67,312	$60,200[1]

[1] 1,400 shares × $43 per share

Note: Hill Company is accounted for using the equity method, thus the fair value is not used on December 31 for valuing Hill Company stock.

31	Valuation Allowance for Available-for-Sale Investments....	16,560	
	Unrealized Gain (Loss) on Available-for-Sale Investments		16,560
	To record increase in fair value of available-for-sale investments, $72,000 – $55,440		

Name	Number of Shares	Total Cost	Total Fair Value
Smith Company	2,400	$55,440	$72,000[1]

[1] 2,400 shares × $30 per share

CHAPTER 16

MATCHING

1. A
2. B
3. G
4. D
5. C
6. F
7. E

FILL IN THE BLANK—PART A

1. statement of cash flows
2. direct; indirect
3. operating
4. investing
5. investing
6. financing
7. investing
8. increased
9. decreased
10. decreased
11. $34,250
12. $102,000
13. $195,000
14. $60,000
15. $49,500
16. $1,040,000
17. $330,000
18. financing
19. $60,000
20. cash flow per share

FILL IN THE BLANK—PART B

1. indirect
2. operating
3. direct
4. financing
5. financing
6. operating
7. financing
8. investing
9. noncash
10. deducted from
11. added to
12. $330,000
13. $746,250
14. $3,125,000
15. $46,000
16. $20,000
17. retained earnings
18. $51,000
19. operating
20. free cash flow

MULTIPLE CHOICE

1. a. Incorrect. The cash flows from financing activities is a major section of the statement of cash flows.
   b. ***Correct.*** The cash flows from selling activities is not a major section of the statement of cash flows.
   c. incorrect. The cash flows from operating activities is a major section of the statement of cash flows.
   d. Incorrect. The cash flows from investing activities is a major section of the statement of cash flows.

2. a. Incorrect. Noncash investing and financing activities are not reported within the statement of cash flows because cash is not affected by these transactions.
   b. ***Correct.*** Although noncash investing and financing activities do not affect cash, these transactions are disclosed in a separate schedule that accompanies the statement of cash flows. This helps users interpret major investing and financing transactions that involve stock swaps, asset swaps, and other noncash events.
   c. Incorrect. Noncash investing and financing activities are not reported within the statement of retained earnings because this statement shows the events that influence retained earnings, such as net income and dividends.
   d. Incorrect. Noncash investing and financing activities are not reported in the footnotes to the balance sheet.

3. a. Incorrect. Depreciation is added to net income in deriving cash flows from operating activities under the indirect method.
   b. Incorrect. Decreases in current assets are added to net income in deriving cash flows from operating activities under the indirect method.
   c. ***Correct.*** Decreases in current liabilities are subtracted from net income in deriving cash flows from operating activities under the indirect method. This is because expenses have been accrued but not paid. Thus, the expenses overstate the amount of cash that has been spent on operating activities.
   d. Incorrect. A loss on sale of equipment is added to net income in deriving cash flows from operating activities under the indirect method.

4. a. Incorrect.
   b. Incorrect.
   c. Incorrect.
   d. ***Correct.*** The cash paid for dividends is \$40,000 declared plus the difference between the beginning and ending dividend payable (\$12,000 – \$10,000), or \$40,000 + \$12,000 – \$10,000.

5. a. Incorrect. The increase in accrued expenses is deducted from operating expenses under the direct method.
   b. Incorrect. The decrease in prepaid expenses is deducted from operating expenses under the direct method.
   c. Incorrect. The increase in income taxes payable is deducted from operating expenses under the direct method.
   d. ***Correct.*** The increase in prepaid expenses is added to operating expenses under the direct method. The increase in a prepaid expense causes cash to be paid before the expense is recorded; hence, the increase must be added to the expense to reflect the cash outflow.

6. a. Incorrect. The receipt of cash from the sale of land is a cash flow from an investing activity.
   b. Incorrect. The receipt of cash from the collection of accounts receivable is a cash flow from operating activities.
   c. ***Correct.*** The payment of cash for the acquisition of treasury stock is a cash flow from a financing activity.
   d. Incorrect. The payment of cash for new machinery is a cash flow from an investing activity.

7. a. Incorrect. The retained earnings do not appear on the statement of cash flows.
   b. ***Correct.*** Cash received from customers is the first line when preparing the statement of cash flows under the direct method.
   c. Incorrect. The net income appears first when preparing the statement of cash flows under the indirect method.
   d. Incorrect. Depreciation is added to net income in the statement of cash flows under the indirect method, but it does not even appear under the direct method.

8. a. ***Correct.*** The withdrawal of cash by the owner of a business is a financing activity, similar to a dividend.
   b. Incorrect. The issuance of common stock to retire long-term debt is a transaction that exchanges long-term debt for capital stock, so it is a noncash investing and financing activity.
   c. Incorrect. The acquisition of a manufacturing plant by issuing bonds exchanges a fixed asset for long-term debt, so it is a noncash investing and financing activity.
   d. Incorrect. The issuance of common stock in exchange for convertible preferred stock exchanges two types of capital stock, so it is a noncash investing and financing activity.

9. a. ***Correct.*** The increase in inventories uses more cash than is shown by the cost of goods sold; thus, the increase in inventories must be added to cost of goods sold to reflect the payment of cash for merchandise.
b. Incorrect. The increase in accounts payable uses less cash than is shown by the cost of goods sold; thus, the increase in accounts payable must be deducted from cost of goods sold to reflect the payment of cash for merchandise.
c. Incorrect. The decrease in inventories uses less cash than is shown by the cost of goods sold; thus, the decrease in inventories must be deducted from cost of goods sold to reflect the payment of cash for merchandise.
d. Incorrect. The decrease in accounts receivable does not impact the cash paid for merchandise, but it impacts the cash received from customers.

10. a. Incorrect.
b. Incorrect.
c. ***Correct.*** The cash paid for income taxes is part of the cash flow from operating activities under the direct method.
d. Incorrect.

11. a. Incorrect. The loss should not be added to the book value of the land.
b. Incorrect. The loss should not be deducted from net income on the statement of cash flows
c. ***Correct.*** The loss should be deducted from the book value of the land in determining the cash flow from investing activities.
d. Incorrect. The loss should not be deducted from net income on the statement of cash flows.

12. a. Incorrect.
b. Incorrect.
c. ***Correct.*** \$290,000 – \$60,000. Free cash flows are the cash flows after investments in property, plant, and equipment to maintain existing productive capacity.
d. Incorrect.

TRUE/FALSE

1. T
2. T
3. T
4. F Only cash receipts and payments from operations are evaluated under the direct method; thus, depreciation is not analyzed under the direct method.
5. F Increases in current liabilities are added to net income under the indirect method because expense accruals exceed cash payments when current liabilities increase.
6. T
7. T
8. T
9. F Both the direct and indirect methods report the same cash flows from operating activities; thus, neither method is more accurate than the other.
10. T

EXERCISE 16-1

Item	Cash Flows From: Operating Activities	Investing Activities	Financing Activities	Schedule of Noncash Investing and Financing Activities
1. Decrease in prepaid expenses	✓			
2. Retirement of bonds................................			✓	
3. Proceeds from sale of investments..........		✓		
4. Increase in inventories	✓			
5. Issuance of common stock			✓	
6. Purchase of equipment		✓		
7. Cash dividends paid................................			✓	
8. Acquisition of building in exchange for bonds				✓
9. Amortization of patents	✓			
10. Amortization of discount on bonds payable	✓			

EXERCISE 16-2

Cash flows from operating activities:		
Net income, per income statement..		$150,000
Adjustments to reconcile net income to net cash flow from operating activities:		
Depreciation...	$ 45,000	
Changes in current operating assets and liabilities:		
Increase in trade receivables...	(10,000)	
Increase in inventories..	(15,625)	
Decrease in prepaid expenses	2,625	
Increase in accounts payable	17,000	
Decrease in salaries payable	(3,000)	36,000
Net cash flow from operating activities..		$186,000

EXERCISE 16-3

Cash flows from operating activities:		
Cash received from customers...		$520,000
Deduct: Cash payments for merchandise	$128,625	
Cash payments for operating expenses	160,375	
Cash payments for income tax	45,000	334,000
Net cash flow from operating activities..		$186,000

Supporting calculations:

Sales (reported on income statement)	$530,000
Less increase in trade receivables	(10,000)
Cash received from customers	$520,000
Cost of merchandise sold	$130,000
Plus increase in inventories	15,625
Less increase in accounts payable	(17,000)
Cash payments for merchandise	$128,625
Operating expenses (other than depreciation)	$160,000
Less decrease in prepaid expenses	(2,625)
Plus decrease in salaries payable	3,000
Cash payments for operating expenses	$160,375

PROBLEM 16-1

Stellar Inc.
Statement of Cash Flows
For Year Ended December 31, 2010

Cash flows from operating activities:			
Net income, per income statement		$114,000	
Adjustments to reconcile net income to net cash flow from operating activities:			
Depreciation	$ 48,000		
Gain on sale of land	(18,000)		
Changes in current operating assets and liabilities:			
Increase in trade receivables	(12,000)		
Decrease in inventories	6,000		
Decrease in prepaid expenses	2,400		
Increase in accounts payable	7,200	33,600	
Net cash flow from operating activities			$147,600
Cash flows from investing activities:			
Cash received from land sold		$ 54,000	
Less: Cash paid for purchase of equipment		96,000	
Net cash flow used for investing activities			(42,000)
Cash flows from financing activities:			
Less: Cash used to retire bonds payable		$ 60,000	
Cash paid for dividends		27,600*	
Net cash flow used for financing activities			(87,600)
Increase in cash			$ 18,000
Cash, January 1, 2010			66,000
Cash, December 31, 2010			$ 84,000

*30,000 + 21,600 – 24,000

Schedule of Noncash Investing and Financing Activities:

Acquisition of land by issuance of common stock	$ 20,000

PROBLEM 16-2

Stellar Inc.
Statement of Cash Flows
For Year Ended December 31, 2010

Cash flows from operating activities:			
Cash received from customers		$563,000	
Deduct: Cash payments for merchandise	$211,800		
Cash payments for operating expenses	169,600		
Cash payments for income tax	34,000	415,400	
Net cash flow from operating activities			$147,600
Cash flows from investing activities:			
Cash received from land sold		$ 54,000	
Less cash paid for purchase of equipment		96,000	
Net cash flow used for investing activities			(42,000)
Cash flows from financing activities:			
Less: Cash used to retire bonds payable		$ 60,000	
Cash paid for dividends		27,600*	
Net cash flow used for financing activities			(87,600)
Increase in cash			$ 18,000
Cash, January 1, 2010			66,000
Cash, December 31, 2010			$ 84,000

*30,000 + 21,600 – 24,000

Schedule of Noncash Investing and Financing Activities:

Acquisition of land by issuance of common stock	$ 20,000

Schedule Reconciling Net Income with Cash Flows from Operating Activities:

Cash flows from operating activities:			
Net income, per income statement		$114,000	
Adjustments to reconcile net income to net cash flow from operating activities:			
Depreciation	$48,000		
Gain on sale of land	(18,000)		
Changes in current operating assets and liabilities:			
Increase in trade receivables	(12,000)		
Decrease in inventories	6,000		
Decrease in prepaid expenses	2,400		
Increase in accounts payable	7,200	33,600	
Net cash flow from operating activities			$147,600

Supporting calculations:

Sales (reported on income statement)	$575,000
Less increase in trade receivables	(12,000)
Cash received	$563,000

Cost of merchandise sold	$225,000
Less decrease in inventories	(6,000)
Less increase in accounts payable	(7,200)
Cash payments for merchandise	$211,800

Operating expenses (other than depreciation)	$172,000
Less decrease in prepaid expenses	(2,400)
Cash payments for operating expenses	$169,600

CHAPTER 17

MATCHING

1. H
2. Q
3. L
4. X
5. M
6. A
7. J
8. C
9. T
10. O
11. U
12. G
13. B
14. Y
15. S
16. D
17. I
18. P
19. K

FILL IN THE BLANK—PART A

1. vertical analysis
2. profitability analysis
3. current position analysis
4. solvency
5. common-size
6. current
7. net sales to assets
8. quick
9. earnings per share on common stock
10. working capital
11. accounts receivable turnover
12. inventory turnover
13. liabilities to stockholders' equity
14. preferred dividends are earned
15. income from operations
16. stockholders' equity
17. dividends
18. independent audit
19. fixed assets to long-term liabilities
20. net sales

FILL IN THE BLANK—PART B

1. horizontal analysis
2. dividend yield
3. independent auditors'
4. number of days' sales in receivables
5. number of days' sales in inventory
6. interest charges earned
7. rate earned on total assets
8. rate earned on stockholders' equity
9. leverage
10. price-earnings
11. management discussion and analysis (MDA)
12. quick assets
13. common-size
14. solvency analysis
15. bankers'
16. number of days' sales in inventory
17. earnings per share (on common stock)
18. common-size
19. receivables
20. internal control

Multiple Choice

1. a. Incorrect.
b. Incorrect. Horizontal statements are one type of statement that uses both relative comparisons and dollar amounts.
c. Incorrect. Vertical statements are one type of statement that uses both relative comparisons and dollar amounts.
d. ***Correct.*** In common-size statements, all items are expressed in percentages.

2. a. Incorrect. The rate of return on total assets is a profitability ratio.
b. Incorrect. The price-earnings ratio is a profitability ratio.
c. ***Correct.*** The accounts receivable turnover is a measure of solvency (short-term).
d. Incorrect. The ratio of net sales to assets is a profitability ratio.

3. a. Incorrect.
b. Incorrect.
c. ***Correct.*** $4,000,000 / [$250,000 + $345,000) / 2]
d. Incorrect.

4. a. Incorrect.
b. ***Correct.*** $6,500,000 / [($175,000 + $297,000) / 2]
c. Incorrect.
d. Incorrect.

5. a. Incorrect. The independent auditor's report attests to the fairness of financial statements.
b. Incorrect. The footnotes provide additional descriptive details of the financial statements, but they rarely include forward-looking statements by management.
c. Incorrect. This is a new management assertion required by the Sarbanes-Oxley Act on the effectiveness of internal controls, but it does not include forward-looking statements about prospects and risks.
d. ***Correct.*** The management discussion and analysis provides an in-depth discussion of prior results and statements regarding future prospects and business risks.

6. a. Incorrect. The working capital ratio provides a measure of the short-term, debt-paying ability.
b. Incorrect. The quick ratio provides a measure of the short-term, debt-paying ability.
c. Incorrect. The receivables to inventory ratio is not an interpretable financial ratio.
d. ***Correct.*** The number of days' sales in receivables is a measure of the efficiency in collecting receivables.

7. a. Incorrect.
b. Incorrect.
c. ***Correct.*** ($510,000 + $30,000) / $30,000
d. Incorrect.

8. a. ***Correct.*** ($27,000 + $23,000 + $90,000) / $70,000
b. Incorrect.
c. Incorrect.
d. Incorrect.

9. a. Incorrect.
b. ***Correct.*** In a vertical analysis balance sheet, items are expressed as a percentage of total assets.
c. Incorrect.
d. Incorrect.

10. a. Incorrect.
b. Incorrect.
c. ***Correct.*** ($460,000 – $50,000) / 50,000 shares
d. Incorrect.

11. a. Incorrect. A high-dividend yield is usually associated with low P/E companies, since most of the shareholder return is in the form of predictable dividends, rather than share appreciation.
b. ***Correct.*** High P/E firms are usually associated with high-growth companies.
c. Incorrect. Debt position is not usually associated with the P/E ratio.
d. Incorrect. Current position is not usually associated with the P/E ratio.

12. a. Incorrect.
b. Incorrect.
c. Incorrect.
d. ***Correct.*** ($240,000 + $120,000) / $1,000,000

TRUE/FALSE

1. F This statement is true for a vertical analysis, not a horizontal analysis.
2. T
3. F The net sales to assets ratio is a profitability ratio that shows how effectively and efficiently assets are used to generate sales.
4. T
5. F The accounts receivable turnover is determined by dividing the net sales by the average accounts receivable outstanding during the period.
6. T
7. F The rate earned on total assets is determined by adding interest expense to net income, then dividing this sum by average total assets during the period.
8. T
9. T
10. F Working capital is the excess of current assets over current liabilities.

EXERCISE 17-1

	2010	Percent	2009	Percent
Revenues	$450,000	100%	$389,000	100%
Costs and expenses:				
Cost of sales	$200,000	44%	$176,000	45%
Selling and administrative expenses	100,000	23%	73,000	19%
Total costs and expenses	$300,000	67%	$249,000	64%
Earnings before income taxes	$150,000	33%	$140,000	36%
Income taxes	34,500	8%	32,200	8%
Net earnings	$115,500	25%	$107,800	28%

EXERCISE 17-2

	2010	2009	Increase (Decrease) Amount	Percent
Current assets	$250,000	$219,500	$ 30,500	14%
Fixed assets	435,000	401,600	33,400	8%
Intangible assets	43,700	46,000	(2,300)	–5%
Current liabilities	88,000	80,000	8,000	10%
Long-term liabilities	225,000	250,000	(25,000)	–10%
Common stock	214,000	167,600	46,400	28%
Retained earnings	200,000	170,000	30,000	18%

PROBLEM 17-1

Nordic Inc.
Comparative Income Statement
For Years Ended December 31, 2010 and 2009

	2010	2009	Increase (Decrease) Amount	Percent
Sales	$690,500	$585,000	$105,500	18.0%
Sales returns and allowances	25,500	23,000	2,500	10.9%
Net sales	$665,000	$562,000	$103,000	18.3%
Cost of goods sold	420,000	330,000	90,000	27.3%
Gross profit	$245,000	$232,000	$ 13,000	5.6%
Selling expenses	$ 43,000	$ 47,700	$ (4,700)	–9.9%
Administrative expenses	31,000	31,000	0	0.0%
Total operating expenses	$ 74,000	$ 78,700	$ (4,700)	–6.0%
Operating income	$171,000	$153,300	$ 17,700	11.5%
Other income	13,000	16,400	(3,400)	–20.7%
	$184,000	$169,700	$ 14,300	8.4%
Other expense	58,000	53,500	4,500	8.4%
Income before income taxes	$126,000	$116,200	$ 9,800	8.4%
Income taxes	34,000	32,400	1,600	4.9%
Net income	$ 92,000	$ 83,800	$ 8,200	9.8%

Nordic Inc.
Comparative Balance Sheet
December 31, 2010 and 2009

Assets	2010	2009	Increase (Decrease) Amount	Increase (Decrease) Percent
Cash	$ 76,000	$ 69,000	$ 7,000	10.1%
Marketable securities	98,900	130,000	(31,100)	–23.9%
Accounts receivable (net)	199,000	195,000	4,000	2.1%
Inventory	450,000	375,000	75,000	20.0%
Prepaid expenses	28,000	26,300	1,700	6.5%
Long-term investments	35,000	35,000	0	0.0%
Fixed assets (net)	871,000	835,000	36,000	4.3%
Intangible assets	18,000	22,800	(4,800)	–21.1%
Total assets	$1,775,900	$1,688,100	$ 87,800	5.2%
Liabilities				
Current liabilities	$ 129,000	$ 107,000	$ 22,000	20.6%
Long-term liabilities	420,000	440,000	(20,000)	–4.5%
Total liabilities	$ 549,000	$ 547,000	$ 2,000	0.4%
Stockholders' Equity				
Preferred 3% stock, $100 par	$ 102,000	$ 93,000	$ 9,000	9.7%
Common stock, $50 par	549,900	530,100	19,800	3.7%
Retained earnings	575,000	518,000	57,000	11.0%
Total stockholders' equity	$1,226,900	$1,141,100	$ 85,800	7.5%
Total liabilities and stockholders' equity	$1,775,900	$1,688,100	$ 87,800	5.2%

PROBLEM 17-2

Voyageur Inc.
Comparative Balance Sheet
December 31, 2010 and 2009

Assets	2010 Amount	2010 Percent	2009 Amount	2009 Percent
Cash	$ 500,000	5.3%	$ 425,000	5.4%
Marketable securities	200,000	2.1%	185,000	2.4%
Accounts receivable (net)	680,000	7.3%	575,000	7.3%
Inventory	860,000	9.2%	740,000	9.4%
Prepaid expenses	104,000	1.1%	95,000	1.2%
Long-term investments	450,000	4.8%	410,000	5.2%
Fixed assets (net)	6,556,000	70.1%	5,420,000	69.0%
Total assets	$9,350,000	100.0%	$7,850,000	100.0%
Liabilities				
Current liabilities	$1,090,000	11.7%	$1,050,000	13.4%
Long-term liabilities	2,150,000	23.0%	2,050,000	26.1%
Total liabilities	$3,240,000	34.7%	$3,100,000	39.5%
Stockholders' Equity				
Preferred 5% stock, $100 par	$ 350,000	3.7%	$ 350,000	4.5%
Common stock, $10 par	2,550,000	27.3%	2,550,000	32.5%
Retained earnings	3,210,000	34.3%	1,850,000	23.5%
Total stockholders' equity	$6,110,000	65.3%	$4,750,000	60.5%
Total liabilities and stockholders' equity	$9,350,000	100.0%	$7,850,000	100.0%

Voyageur Inc.
Income Statement
For Year Ended December 31, 2010

	Amount	Percent
Sales	$12,800,000	102.4%
Sales returns and allowances	300,000	2.4%
Net sales	$12,500,000	100.0%
Cost of goods sold	7,550,000	60.4%
Gross profit	$ 4,950,000	39.6%
Selling expenses	$ 1,550,000	12.4%
Administrative expenses	825,000	6.6%
Total operating expenses	$ 2,375,000	19.0%
Operating income	$ 2,575,000	20.6%
Other income	125,000	1.0%
	$ 2,700,000	21.6%
Other expense (interest)	150,000	1.2%
Income before income taxes	$ 2,550,000	20.4%
Income taxes	937,000	7.5%
Net income	$ 1,613,000	12.9%

PROBLEM 17-3

	Calculation	Final Result
a. Working capital	$2,344,000 – $1,090,000	1,254,000
b. Current ratio	$\frac{\$2,344,000}{\$1,090,000}$	2.2
c. Quick ratio	$\frac{\$1,380,000}{\$1,090,000}$	1.3
d. Accounts receivable turnover	$\frac{\$12,500,000}{\left(\frac{\$680,000+\$575,000}{2}\right)}$	19.9
e. Number of days' sales in receivables	$\frac{\$12,500,000}{365} = \$34,247$ $\frac{[(\$680,000+\$575,000)/2]}{\$34,247}$	18.3
f. Inventory turnover	$\frac{\$7,550,000}{\left(\frac{\$860,000+\$740,000}{2}\right)}$	9.4
g. Number of days' sales in inventory	$\frac{\$7,550,000}{365} = \$20,685$ $\frac{[(\$860,000+\$740,000)/2]}{\$20,685}$	38.7
h. Ratio of fixed assets to long-term liabilities	$\frac{\$6,556,000}{\$2,150,000}$	3.0
i. Ratio of liabilities to stockholders' equity	$\frac{\$3,240,000}{\$6,110,000}$	0.5
j. Number of times interest charges earned	$\frac{\$2,550,000+\$150,000}{\$150,000}$	18.0
k. Number of times preferred dividends earned	$\frac{\$1,613,000}{\$17,500}$	92.2
l. Ratio of net sales to assets	$\frac{\$12,500,000}{\left(\frac{\$8,900,000+\$7,440,000}{2}\right)}$	1.5
m. Rate earned on total assets	$\frac{\$1,613,000+\$150,000}{\left(\frac{\$9,350,000+\$7,850,000}{2}\right)}$	20.5%
n. Rate earned on stockholders' equity	$\frac{\$1,613,000}{\left(\frac{\$6,110,000+\$4,750,000}{2}\right)}$	29.7%

	Calculation	Final Result
o. Rate earned on common stockholders' equity	$\dfrac{\$1,613,000 - \$17,500}{\left(\dfrac{\$5,760,000 + \$4,400,000}{2}\right)}$	31.4%
p. Earnings per share on common stock	$\dfrac{\$1,613,000 - \$17,500}{255,000}$	$6.26
q. Price-earnings ratio	$\dfrac{\$29.75}{\$6.26}$	4.8
r. Dividends per share of common stock	$\dfrac{\$250,000}{255,000}$	$.98
s. Dividend yield	$\dfrac{\left(\dfrac{\$250,000}{255,000\text{ shares}}\right)}{\$29.75}$	3.3%